THE SWORD OF THE LORD

& THE REST OF THE LORD

THE
SWORD
OF THE
LORD

& THE REST OF THE LORD

KEVIN BASCONI

with

PAUL L. COX

The Sword of the Lord and the Rest of the Lord
Copyright © 2013 by Kevin Basconi

ISBN: 978-0-9833152-7-8

King of Glory Ministries International Publications 2013
King of Glory Ministries International
PO Box 903, Moravian Falls, NC 28654, 336-921-2825
www.kingofgloryministries.org

All rights reserved. No part of this book may be reproduced or transmitted in any form or by any means—electronic or mechanical, including photocopying, recording, or by any information storage and retrieval system—without written permission from the authors except as provided by the copyright laws of the United States of America. Unauthorized reproduction is a violation of federal as well as spiritual laws.

Unless otherwise noted, all scripture quotations are from the New King James Version of the Bible. Copyright © 1979, 1980, 1982 by Thomas Nelson, Inc., publishers. Used by permission.

Scripture quotations marked KJV are from the King James Version of the Bible.

Scripture quotations marked NIV are from The Holy Bible, New International Version®, NIV® Copyright © 1973, 1978, 1984, 2011 by Biblica, Inc.™ Used by permission. All rights reserved worldwide.

Scripture quotations marked NLT are from the Holy Bible, New Living Translation, copyright © 1996. Used by permission of Tyndale House Publishers, Inc., Wheaton, IL 60189. All rights reserved.

Greek definitions are derived from Strong's Greek Concordance.

Hebrew definitions are derived from Strong's Hebrew Concordance.

Art Director: Kevin Basconi
Cover Design & Layout: projectluz.com
Printed in the United States of America

This book Is dedicated to

God the Father, God the Son, and God the Holy Spirit

without You Guys none of this would have been possible!

Most discerning believers know we are in the last of the last days. Jesus said about these days that "people will be terrified at what they see coming upon the earth" (Luke 21:26-27, NLT). Jesus wants you to be in total peace *no matter what happens*. God calls this the "Sabbath rest." Kevin was given the revelation of this mystery in heaven. This is a *must* read revelation.

—SID ROTH
Host, It's Supernatural! Television

"*The rest of the Lord*." Hebrews 4 assures us that there ***is*** a rest for God's people. Kevin Basconi preached about this important subject at our church. As a result many people were set free, empowered, and healed! Now Kevin is making this revelation available to the Body of Christ in book form! Understanding the rest of the Lord is liberating. This book is a must read for the day and hour that we are living in. Understanding how you can enter into the different levels of the rest of the Lord can be life-changing!

—PASTOR ALAN KOCH
Christ Triumphant Church, Lee's Summit, Missouri

CONTENTS

INTRODUCTION
James Durham IX

CHAPTER 1
The Day of Atonement 2011 and the Storm 13

CHAPTER 2
The Sword of the Lord 19

CHAPTER 3
The Lord of Hosts! 25

CHAPTER 4
Both / And 31

CHAPTER 5
False Prophets, Foolish Prophets, and Prophets of Doom 43

CHAPTER 6
Salvation—Entering the Kingdom of Heaven 55

CHAPTER 7
Caves and Taters 63

CHAPTER 8
Good News in the Midst of the Storm! 75

CHAPTER 9
The Importance of Hearing God in the Middle of the Storm 81

CHAPTER 10
The Perfect Storm Is on the Horizon 87

CHAPTER 11
The Rock—Praise and Worship in the Midst of the Storm 93

CHAPTER 12
The Storms of Life and the Foolish Man 99

CHAPTER 13
Melchizedek and the Gift of Discernment by Paul L. Cox 107

CHAPTER 14
The Rest of the Lord and the Royal Priesthood of Melchizedek 113

CHAPTER 15
The Author and Finisher of Our Faith 123

CHAPTER 16
The Day of Atonement 2012—More Revelation Revealed 135

CHAPTER 17
Understanding the Sabbath Rest 147

CHAPTER 18
Understanding the Monthly Rest... 153

CHAPTER 19
Another Visitation of Jesus and Understanding That Jesus Honored the Feasts 161

CHAPTER 20
The Sabbath Rest and the Fullness of God's Rest 171

CHAPTER 21
The Heavenly Hosts—the Rest of God's Eternal Family 185

CHAPTER 22
Diligent Prayer and the Rest of the Lord 195

CHAPTER 23
Supernatural Transformation Transpires by Resting in the Glory   203

CHAPTER 24
The Hidden and Mysterious Treasures in the Kingdom of God 213

CHAPTER 25
Your Spiritual Senses and the Rest of the Lord 225

CHAPTER 26
Activating Your Spiritual Senses and 20/20 Spiritual Vision 235

CHAPTER 27
Conclusion: The Day of Atonement 2012 247

INTRODUCTION

James Durham

My wife, Gloria, and I had lunch with Kevin and Kathy Basconi in Moravian Falls, North Carolina, on the day after Yom Kippur in 2011. During lunch, Kevin shared the revelation he had received from the Lord. I could clearly see the profound impact this message from the Lord was having on Him. Over the next several months, we discussed many times the Lord's call to enter His rest as we both sought additional insight into the fullness of this revelation. During this time, I also received many messages about the storm and the call to enter His rest. The intensity and urgency of these messages has not subsided but has actually increased exponentially. The teaching in this book is a very important revelation from the Lord. I urge you to study it carefully. I urge you to seek the help of the Holy Spirit to give you wisdom, revelation, understanding, and counsel about the storm which is soon to manifest.

On Shabbat, November 3, 2012, I was lifted up into His presence where I entered into a very special time of rest, refreshing, renewing, and equipping. I saw many people who had assembled in this heavenly place. We were sitting quietly as angels ministered to us. Then, I heard the Lord say, "This is an important time to rest! Many things are about to happen which will change life as you now know it, and you need to be prepared to deal with them! Rest, eat, and be strengthened!"

I saw several people who were unwilling to sit down and rest. They also seemed resistant to receive what the Lord was giving and what He was saying. They began to turn away and move further from this place with the Lord. I remembered the words of 2 Thessalonians 2:3, *"Let no one deceive you by any means; for that Day will not come unless the falling away comes first."* I didn't hear it directly from the Lord, but I started to sense in the Spirit that the time of "the falling away" is at hand. This was a very uncomfortable feeling. I don't want to see the falling away, but the Word says it will happen. May you be among those who do not fall away! Amen!

The rest we were experiencing in heaven seemed to be steeped in purpose. It was not an ordinary Shabbat. It was about being rested and made ready for what will soon come. I am praying and seeking wisdom for properly responding to this word from the Lord. I pray that you will enter into this rest of the Lord and allow Him to refresh, renew, and equip you for this hour.

On Wednesday, November 7, 2012, the Lord gave me a vision of an early morning sky. As I looked at the horizon, I saw row after row of red and dark orange clouds across the sky as the sun started to rise. I remembered what Jesus said in Matthew 16:2-3, *"When it is evening you say, 'It will be fair weather, for the sky is red'; and in the morning, 'It will be foul weather today, for the sky is red and threatening.' Hypocrites! You know how to discern the face of the sky, but you cannot discern the signs of the times."*

As you spend time assimilating the visions Kevin is releasing, I pray that you will remain open to hearing the message. Many people want to avoid every unpleasant thing and prefer to ignore prophetic words about a coming storm. There will be a heavy price to pay for those who do not spend time preparing for the fulfillment of His promises. I believe the Lord released this word to Kevin in order to help you get ready for what is coming. May the Spirit of truth confirm for you this word from the Lord.

In the vision I received that Wednesday, it was clear that a storm is brewing on the horizon and will soon be upon us. What are we to do now? I heard the Lord say, "Intercessors arise! Watchmen arise! Gatekeepers arise! This is not a time to go into hiding! This is a time to come forth and take your stand! It is in the difficult times that the Kingdom is advanced! It is in times of hardship that the harvest is great!"

I remembered again what the Lord promised to Isaac in Genesis 26:1-3, *"There was a famine in the land, besides the first famine that was in the days of Abraham. And Isaac went to Abimelech king of the Philistines, in Gerar. Then the LORD appeared to him and said: 'Do not go down to Egypt; live in the land of which I shall tell you. Dwell in this land, and I will be with you and bless you.'"* Isaac trusted the Lord and stayed in the land of famine. The Lord blessed his obedience and fulfilled his promise to Isaac. In Genesis 26:12-14 we read, *"Then Isaac sowed in that land, and reaped in the same year a hundredfold; and the LORD blessed him. The man began to prosper, and continued prospering until he became very prosperous; for he had possessions of flocks and possessions of herds and a great number of servants."* Remember that obedience came first and was then followed by the blessing.

Isaac experienced another powerful outcome from the blessing and favor of the Lord. Genesis 26:14-16 tells us, *"So the Philistines envied him. Now the Philistines had stopped up all the wells which his father's servants had dug in the days of Abraham his father, and they had filled them with earth. And Abimelech said to Isaac, 'Go away from us, for you are much mightier than we.'"* This is a time for the Lord to make the enemies see you as "much mightier than" they. This is a time for Kingdom logic and Kingdom wisdom. Notice that the Philistines kept stopping up the wells during the time of famine. Their foolish choices made their situation worse and worse. This is not a season to stop up wells. This is a season to dig new wells and open once more those stopped up by the enemy. This is a season to receive blessing and favor in abundance from the Lord. This is a season to release a new flow of living water.

As you spend time studying the messages from the Lord in this book, I pray that the Holy Spirit will make it clear to you that a storm is coming. It is time to be alert, watching and ready. May this teaching which Kevin is releasing help you to enter the rest of the Lord during the time of preparation! May it help you to enter and remain in the Lord's rest during the storm! May it also assist you in being ready to enter that rest He is offering in His Eternal Kingdom! Amen!

Pastor James Durham served almost 30 years as an active duty army Chaplain reaching the rank of Major. He also has served as pastor and church planter for more than eight years. In 2010, James and his wife, Gloria, moved to Columbia, South Carolina, and transitioned from full-time service as a pastor in order to write books, teach seminars, lead revivals, and mentor many spiritual sons and daughters around the world. James is currently the pastor of Higher Calling Ministries, which he established in July, 2009. He is the author of two books: *A Warrior's Guide to the Seven Spirits of God: Part 1 and Part 2*. His current book writing projects include *Beyond an Ancient Door: A Guidebook for Third Heaven Visitation* and *100 Days in Heaven with Jesus.* James is a graduate of Oklahoma State University with a bachelor's degree in psychology; and Perkins School of Theology, Southern Methodist University, Dallas, Texas, with a master's degree in theology.

CHAPTER 1

The Day of Atonement 2011 and the Storm

Over the past few years, I have asked God to speak to me on the Day of Atonement. In 2011 Yom Kippur fell upon Friday, October 7, and Saturday, October 8. As I waited upon the Lord at this time, He began to speak to me through scriptures and a series of short visions.

On a beautiful, sunny, autumn evening, I entered into my prayer room. As I positioned myself in prayer, the Lord immediately began to speak to me in the authoritative voice of the Holy Spirit. He said, "A storm is coming." When I heard these words, I began to ponder them in my heart. I continued to wait on the Lord, asking Him to give me understanding of the words He had spoken to me.

After some time I was released into a vision in which I saw a tremendous storm full of black clouds moving across the horizon. This storm was massive and ominous. Gray swirls of dark and dirty dust filled the land as far as I could see. The storm was approaching from a great distance. I sensed a wicked presence and hordes of evil intent within the storm. I could see the storm bearing down, but I was not alarmed. In fact, a great peace filled my spirit.

I had the sensation of being lifted up. In an instant, it seemed as if my spirit was accelerating up through the ceiling of my prayer room. I could still see the storm as it slowly advanced. I could also see our log cabin where we live in the mountains, Moravian Falls, and the beautiful, pristine Carolina blue sky around me. As I continued to rise, I could see the curvature of the earth below, and I was amazed to see that this dark storm seemed to cover the entire horizon.

As I watched the storm approach, I saw whirlwinds and lightening flashes above and within this massive dark storm. I heard thunder; the whole earth seemed to tremble and shake (see Hebrews 12:26). The wind howled, and the deep darkness moved forward steadily in my direction. As I continued to rise in the spirit, I could make out more details of the storm. From my new vantage point, I could also see masses of humanity.

It appeared to me that these multitudes of human beings were mesmerized by the storm. I could hear fearful moans and what may have been the gnashing of teeth (see Matthew 8:12). From time to time my vision greatly increased, and I began to see their individual faces clearly. They were consumed with fear, and they seemed to have lost all hope. Many wept uncontrollably. These people were alive, yet they also seemed to be dead. The advancing darkness and associated fear was palpable, literally tangible.

It seemed as if the majority of the people were focused on this dark storm. I watched how the people reacted with great fear and anxiety. As the storm grew closer, the scriptures from Philippians 4:6-7 came to mind: *"Be anxious for nothing, but in everything by prayer and supplication, with thanksgiving, let your requests be made known to God; and the peace of God, which surpasses all understanding, will guard your hearts and minds through Christ Jesus."*

It was apparent to me that most of the people in the mass of humanity below did not know Jesus Christ. Therefore, it was impossible for them to know the peace of God in this situation. Of course, the peace of God *is* Christ Jesus, the Prince of Peace.

As I continued to watch the approaching storm, I observed the reactions of the masses of people below. I saw people who were clutching crosses and rosaries in their hands. Many of these people were crying out to God. However, they were also consumed with fear just like the people who did not know the Lord. This perplexed me, so I asked the Holy Spirit about it.

The Holy Spirit responded to me, "Although many people know about Me, they do not know Me. Therefore, when the storms of life and the tribulations of this present world come upon them, they too will quake in fear." (See John 16:33.) "Many have never developed their trust in God, nor have they matured their faith in the Son of God. They are as little children with immature and imperfect faith. But it is the Father's will for them to trust Him and to walk in perfect faith in the midst of the storm." (See Luke 12:28-32; 2 Corinthians 5:7.)

I continued to watch as this vision unfolded. It seemed that as the storm drew closer, a greater degree of fear came upon the people. As this massive, dark storm came near, the front edge began to envelope the masses of people. Instantly the scriptures from Isaiah birthed within my spirit.

> *Arise, shine; For your light has come! And the glory of the LORD is risen upon you. For behold, the darkness shall cover the earth, And deep darkness the people; But the LORD will arise over you, And His glory will be seen upon you (Isaiah 60:1-2).*

Perhaps what I was witnessing was the darkness that will certainly cover the earth and the deep darkness that will cover the people. In my heart I knew that as the deep darkness covers the people, those who really do not know the Lord will be consumed and even paralyzed by the spirit of fear. With these scriptures came the understanding that we are beginning to enter into those times spoken of in Isaiah. Perhaps what I was seeing was a precursor to the times of pre-tribulation. Only God Almighty knows for sure. Kathy once had a vision in which she was paralyzed by this type of gross darkness.

It is imperative that we truly know the Lord Jesus Christ at this hour (see Matthew 7:23). Even Christians who are lukewarm in their faith may find themselves consumed by fear and anxiety as this dark storm grows in intensity. It is a season to draw close to God while He may be found. We must cleanse our hearts and hands (see James 4:8). We must repent for our lukewarm relationship with the Messiah. Within my vision came the understanding that there is still time. There is still a season to seek God while He may be found (see Isaiah 55:6). Theologians have a term for this: repentance. It means turning 180 degrees away from sin and walking in a new direction and into a new life. Of course, it also means receiving Jesus Christ as Lord and Savior, Yeshua HaMashiach!

From my vantage point in the vision, I could see that the people who were near the leading edge of the storm were beginning to be overwhelmed with ungodly fear and terror. They were allowing yokes of darkness; demonic spirits of fear, anxiety, and worry; and all manner of other demonic spirits to oppress them. They had lost all hope. It was apparent to me that many of them would die.

For a moment the Lord opened my spiritual eyes so I could see into the spiritual realm. As the dark storm grew closer to the people, I saw hundreds of demonic beings begin to scamper and creep out from under the cover of the gross darkness at the leading edge of this evil storm. Most of these demons were hideous in appearance and were literally feeding on the fear and anxiety of the people. The demonic spirits would attach themselves to the people by clinging to their backs. Some had the look of serpents while others looked like deformed monkeys or other small animals. Occasionally I saw larger demonic beings emerge from the darkness to whip and torment the smaller demons that were working to place yokes of darkness upon the people. For the most part the people were totally ignorant of this evil and shadowy deception happening around them.

The demons continuously whispered lies into their ears. They jabbed and tormented their bodies. A few of the demons were not ugly, such as the one that I understood to be vanity; yet even this demon placed a heavy burden and yoke of darkness upon people. This demon worked especially hard to encumber and ensnare handsome men and beautiful women. I was astonished at the diversity and sheer numbers of the demonic hordes that crept out from the darkness to place yokes and evil burdens upon the unaware people.

The masses were paralyzed by fear as these heavy yokes of darkness caused them to react with terror to the approaching storm. They were totally given over to the gross darkness. The people began to turn upon one another, and this turmoil served to increase the level of the darkness and empower the demonic spirits that were feeding upon it. The fear that was birthed within the people helped to perpetuate an evil cycle of fear, anxiety, mistrust, and violence upon the earth. This is the height of deception and is truly the great lie.

After a time the storm came closer still. I could actually smell the stench of fear and feel the gross darkness. I could literally smell the horrific, disgusting odor of the demonic hordes. It was nauseating. The winds of terror began to ripple my hair. Yet, in the midst of the storm, I was at peace. Below me I could hear the agonizing screams as people cried out with fear and terror. I heard a beautiful young woman cry out in agony, "Someone save me!" All were in sheer horror. They were weighted down by yokes of darkness and were ensnared by the weight of sin (see Hebrews 12:1). I began to earnestly pray in the spirit, asking the Lord for mercy and not judgment.

I witnessed this scene unfold for quite a long time. As the storm grew closer, I was astonished at the height of the deception; how easily the deceit of the enemy overcame the people below me. I watched time and again as individuals unwittingly succumbed to the hosts of demons that crept out of the darkness and into their sphere of influence. I saw how the demons leaped from one individual to another. I was repulsed by the demonic laughter and the glee they displayed as they sought to torment the people. However, I also had supernatural understanding and revelatory knowledge that judgment for these demonic beings is close at hand.

After a long time, I realized that the darkness and the deception had begun to work on my heart and upon my mind. I purposed in my heart to gird up the loins of my mind, and I began to rebuke the demons from my place in the heavenly realms. Scriptures from Peter percolated up from within my spirit man:

> *Therefore gird up the loins of your mind, be sober, and rest your hope fully upon the grace that is to be brought to you at the revelation of Jesus Christ; as obedient children, not conforming yourselves to the former lusts, as in your ignorance; but as He*

who called you is holy, you also be holy in all your conduct, because it is written, "Be holy, for I am holy" (1 Peter 1:13-16).

As I watched this scenario unfold, the hopelessness and the gross darkness that were coming upon the people were beginning to affect me too. Fear and doubt began to cling to me like a cheap perfume. In my heart I cried out in prayer, *Lord, these people need help! I need your help! Lord Jesus, help us!*

CHAPTER 2

The Sword of the Lord

I was startled from my heartfelt prayer by the sound of a shofar. It was the loudest sound I had ever heard. It was a glorious sound. It was a triumphant sound. As I turned 180 degrees, I saw a splendorous sunset. I was so focused on the storm that I had not noticed it before. This sunset was stunningly beautiful to behold; it was breathtaking. The evening sky was filled with supernatural, seemingly phosphorescent colors.

At that instant the glory of God manifested and the sky split open. The brilliance and intensity of the light that radiated as the heavens opened was as an explosion of an atomic bomb. For a moment I was unable to see because of the radiance that accompanied the explosion that served to rend open the heavens and the sky above. Tears began to stream from my eyes as I tried to look at this magnificent sight. I began to squint, seeking to gaze upon the glory that was emanating from the supernatural rip in the horizon. I was astonished to see the radiant colors of the sunset multiply. These supernatural colors seemed to be living!

The tangible glory of God was being poured out upon the earth like the waters that cover the seas (see Habakkuk 2:14). Rivers of living light exploded across the horizon. It was amazing, and I was awestruck by the outpouring of glory. The glory of God enveloped me, washing away all remnants of fear or anxiety of the approaching storm.

Rays of golden light inundated me from the place where the sky had been ripped open, and a reverential fear of the Lord became real within my spirit. As I sought to focus, tears continued to pour from my eyes. I forgot about the storm and the masses of people who were huddled below me gripped by terror, fear, and yokes of deep darkness. The fear that gripped *me* was a holy reverential fear of God. I strained to look at the supernatural opening.

Slowly, I began to gaze into the glory. The sounds of the trumpet that I had heard blasted once more. As the reverberations from the blast filled my ears and my spirit, revelation begin to bubble up from somewhere deep within me. I saw a multitude of heavenly beings begin moving swiftly from the rip in the atmosphere. The glory of God grew more intense and approached me in the same way that the gross darkness was approaching the masses. However, the storm of God's glory seemed to advance much more quickly.

High and Lifted Up

By now I could see more clearly and great hopefulness began to spring up within me. For the first time I saw the Lord, and He was high and lifted up. He was growing closer to me. Jesus was riding a magnificent white charger. The Lord was arrayed for battle, and in His mighty right hand I could see a powerful sword. The winds of heaven began to swirl around me as Jesus grew near, and the sounds of trumpets and worship filled the air.

The Lord's pure white steed was mighty and magnificent to behold. He was about fifteen or sixteen hands high. His bridle was adorned with twelve types of beautiful jewels that glistened in the glory of God.

Jesus came very near, and I could see His hands in great detail. Rays of lightening seemed to flash from them (see Habakkuk 3:4). His left hand held the reigns of the white charger and had a signet ring upon the ring finger. Jesus took His right hand and again unsheathed His sword as the charger quickly covered the last few paces between us. A great clap of thunder exploded as Jesus drew it from its resting place.

This heavenly sword was created of the finest craftsmanship. It was constructed of both brilliant gold and stunning silver. There were intricate patterns inscribed upon the blade, and the handle was powerful and strong. Embedded within the sword was a magnificent ruby that could be seen just below Christ's hand. Lightening shot from the tip of Messiah's sword as He drew near. The sword emanated power and authority.

By now I could smell frankincense and myrrh. I could see the muscles of the Lord's mighty charger rippling as he galloped the last few paces to draw near. I was overcome by the awe and majesty of Jesus. I fell to my knees in the presence of the King. When I looked up Jesus was right beside me. I could see these words written upon His immaculate white robe: "*KING OF KINGS AND LORD OF LORDS*" (Revelation 19:16). His robe emanated the perpetual glory of God and seemed to be made of a luminescent, phosphorescent material that billowed majestically in the wind. His countenance and visage were amazing and all-powerful. I was overcome by the majesty and stateliness of the Lord. As He drew to a full stop, the Messiah's mighty charger exhaled with great power as lightning flew from the tip of the sword in Christ's right hand once again. Thunder roared in my ears and my eyes were drawn to the sword of the Lord.

At that moment I saw the words "The Rest of the Lord" written upon the shaft of the Lord's sword in beautiful filigree lettering. Christ looked intently into my eyes. His eyes burned with passion and power. He smiled at me and said, "Come up here." As He said this, Jesus extended His left hand out to me, and I could see the nail scar embedded there. I reached out with my left hand, and in one sweeping motion the Lord took my hand and effortlessly lifted me up. I swung me around behind Him to sit upon His mighty white charger.

The Lord cried out something in a language I could not understand; and with a fluid sweeping motion of His right hand, He pointed to the dark storm with His sword. Instantly Christ's charger reared up on his hind legs and vaulted forward as sounds of shofars once more rang in my ears. I clung to the Lord tightly with my hands wrapped around His waist. A mighty shout rose from the multitude of angelic hosts that were accompanying the Lord. The sound of their simultaneous call was deafening. I looked below to see if the huddled masses heard the heavenly shout. However, it seemed that only a few did. This surprised me greatly.

I looked over my right shoulder to see an innumerable multitude of angels riding on chargers. Each one had his sword raised like Christ, and there was triumph in the air. As the Messiah led the way, I watched as thousands upon thousands of the Lord's angelic host poured through the rip in the heavens (see Matthew 25:31). I was mesmerized by what I was seeing and experiencing. I could feel the might of the Lord's charger as it moved below me while I held firmly onto Jesus' waist. His long hair fluttered in the breeze as it billowed from beneath His golden crown. At times His flowing hair tickled the left side of my face sending electricity coursing through my spirit, soul, and body. It was exhilarating. Christ's glorious crown was inlaid with intricate designs and topped with twelve large jeweled stones. The crown seemed to rotate in a supernatural fashion upon His head displaying one of the twelve jewels each instant (see Revelation 19:12).

Jesus charged forward in the direction of the storm. As we advanced and I began to grow a bit more comfortable with my surroundings, I began to look around. I could still see the dark storm approaching. We were several meters above the terrified people as they panicked in fear below. The majority of them did not see the Lord Jesus Christ and His angelic host as we passed over their heads. I was amazed by this because of the vibrancy of the glory and the intensity of the sounds of the shofars that continued to sound the call to war.

After a time I witnessed a few people turn from gazing at the storm. They looked up to see the Lord of Hosts. Their eyes were opened to see and their ears were opened to hear God. When this would happen, they would turn to the Lord. An angel mounted on a steed would stop near them and reach out a hand for them. (Perhaps this was symbolic of turning to the Lord in repentance.) At times the person would grasp the helping hand of the angelic being and would be lifted up above the storm. However, there were also times when a person would refuse the hand of the Lord's angelic hosts and return to being steeped in fear and anxiety. This also amazed me.

I understood that God is releasing His angelic hosts to help people at this hour. I have written extensively about this in the trilogy of books, *The Reality of Angelic Ministry Today.* The Book of Hebrews teaches us that God's angelic hosts are *"ministering spirits sent forth to minister for those who will inherit salvation"* (1:14). As I pondered this in my heart, the Lord moved quickly and vaulted up higher to a strategic heavenly position. What happened next continued to amaze me!

CHAPTER 3

The Lord of Hosts!

I watched as the Lord rose high above the storm and the glory of God was seen by the masses. Yet, in spite of the appearance of the Lord, most people chose to remain cloaked in darkness and yoked to the spirits of fear. It occurred to me that they were comfortable in their deception and unwilling to change. Once we had risen well above the storm, Jesus began to command His angelic hosts to encircle the storm and the evil therein. I watched in amazement as powerful angelic leaders or archangels came up to the Lord to receive battle instructions one by one.

These angelic beings were powerful and emanated the very glory of God. I witnessed numbers of angelic leaders, what we might refer to as archangels, approach Christ the King and receive battle instructions. Each one of these angelic leaders was flanked by several other angels who seemed to be under their immediate command. The glory that these angels emanated was incredible, and I was hesitant to look upon their faces. Each angel was robed in immaculate shining white garments. Each mighty heavenly being was fully equipped for battle with various weapons, including swords, bucklers, horns, and other paraphernalia that I was not familiar with.

As these angelic beings approached the Messiah, the Lord Jesus would speak to each group of powerful angels in a language I did not comprehend. However, I did understand that the Lord was giving each angelic leader detailed plans and instructions for his role in the coming battle. Each angel appeared to have hundreds of legions of angelic hosts under their command. From time to time I would sneak a peek at one of the archangels; but the glory that was shining from their faces was too great, and I could not perceive the appearance of their facial features.

Once as I stole a quick look, I saw one of the attendant angels looking at me in amazement. Our eyes locked for a brief moment. His expression was one of astonishment, and it occurred to me that this angel was very surprised that I was in this place. His robe was impeccably white, and upon his waist was a golden belt that held a sword and buckler. In his right hand was a shiny golden shield that was inlaid with intricate filigree and designs. He peered at me over the top edge of his scalloped golden shield.

His eyes were extremely handsome and his shoulder length, blond hair flowed over his broad shoulders. His hair glistened in the glory of God and reflected the magnificent colors of the sunset. In an instant it appeared that he understood why I was allowed to be present in this place. As this happened a slight smile ceased his face, and I saw his perfect and impeccable white teeth for a moment. However, in my heart I was also wondering why I was being allowed to be at this place.

I was looking into his eyes when the Lord completed His instructions to this angelic warrior's leader. As they spun upon their steeds to leave, for an instant the angel acknowledged me and nodded his head slightly. He smiled once more and departed in formation. Another company of angelic leaders soon took this group's place, and the Lord once again gave concise and critical marching orders to the leader. I observed this time and time again. Conservatively, I would estimate that I witnessed hundreds of legions of God's angels pass by in formation one by one. (See 2 Kings 6:16-17; Romans 8:31.)

Each time the Lord would communicate clearly to the angel present; and then, pointing with His mighty sword, He would indicate a direction and specific tactical location for the angel to lead his legions of accompanying angelic hosts. I was certain that these legions of warrior or guardian angels were being assigned over many cities and nations. Although I was not able to understand the language that the Lord was speaking to these angelic leaders, I understood that the Lord was giving each archangel specific orders and plans for the imminent battle. These angels were beautiful and magnificent to behold. I watched as drove after drove of angels approached the Lord and received their battle orders in this way.

After a very long time, there was a lull in the procession of the angelic leaders. The Lord turned upon His charger and looked deeply into my eyes. A great smile creased His face. He said: "Do you understand?" I was frozen by His proximity and could not articulate any words. It seemed that I was paralyzed by the glory of God. With His right hand Jesus drew His sword once again from its sheath. It gleamed in the manifest glory of God. He held it up to allow me to see the words "The Rest of the Lord" once more. Christ's sword was very close to my face. Then, pointing to the multitude of angelic hosts that were maneuvering around us, Jesus said, "Be diligent to enter into My rest" (Hebrews 4:11).

At that moment I understood that the angelic host also consisted of the great cloud of witnesses, or those who had preceded me into the heavenly realms. Jesus considered these heavenly residents to be the "rest of the Lord." Jesus was speaking to me in a parable. I was lost in my thoughts for a moment as I gazed upon the words "The Rest of the Lord" inscribed upon the Lord's sword. As the glory vaulted through the atmosphere from the rip in the sky, the Lord's sword seemed to be alive with luminescent colors dancing upon the blade. The pirouetting of these supernatural colors was mesmerizing. I became lost in my thoughts for a moment. I gazed upon Christ's living sword for several moments as time itself seemed to be supernaturally suspended. I looked at every detail of the sword of the Lord, and I became lost in the spirit and within my own thoughts. The words "The Rest of the Lord" became supernaturally etched upon my mind like they were engraved into the heavenly metal of the Lord's mighty sword.

After a very long time of observing the sword of the Lord, these words sprang up from within my spirit: "Lord, I thought that the rest of the Lord was a scripture from Hebrews chapter 4." I looked up to see Jesus smile. His eyes were blazing with love and compassion as He said, "Yes, but My rest is much more than that. The rest of the Lord is the Kingdom of Heaven. When you learn to enter into the rest of the Lord, you can enter into the rest of the Lord." In an instant I understood that there is another aspect or realm of Christ's Kingdom that constitutes the "rest of the Lord." There are secrets and hidden mysteries of God that very few are able to unlock or discover on this side of eternity.

Those supernatural treasures constitute and comprise the "rest of the Lord" in the heavenly realms. These are secret places and special treasures of God. The Father has hidden treasures and secrets to give to His friends. And I recall thinking, *"It is your Father's good pleasure to give us the kingdom"* (Luke 12:32). When I thought this the Lord laughed and a shofar blast sounded nearby as if to punctuate this Kingdom principle. I looked once more into the eyes of the Messiah, and His eyes continued to burn with the fire of passion and love (see Revelation 19:12). For a mere instant I was able to perceive just a tiny portion of the unconditional love and passion that Jesus has for the lost and the huddled masses that were being tormented below.

At that time many in the masses below were being totally overcome with the gross darkness of the approaching storm. Within my spirit, knowledge flowed forth that the key to overcoming the darkness of this approaching storm was to understand the rest of the Lord and actually learn how to enter into it. My senses were on overload, and Christ was smiling at me with great pleasure as we sat together in heavenly places far above the storm below. I was overawed, stunned even by the way His eyes blazed with compassion for the precious ones below.

"Lord," I said, "help me to understand all of this." He said, *"This is surely the season to be diligent to enter into My rest, lest anyone fall according to disobedience"* (Hebrews 4:11). At that moment the Lord glanced at the people below us who were engulfed in the darkness and midst of the storm. He said, "Remember, My word *is living and powerful, and sharper than any two-edged sword, piercing even to the division of soul and spirit, and of joints and marrow, and is a discerner of the thoughts and intents of the heart. And there is no creature hidden from My sight, but all things are naked and open to the eyes of Him to whom all of these must give an account*" (vv. 12-13).

With that the Lord pointed His mighty sword into the approaching darkness below and an incredibly powerful lightning bolt shot from its tip. Thunder rang out, and in that same instant a hideous scream emanated from within the darkness below. For the first time I noticed that my clothing was covered with sweat. With Christ's help, I dismounted from the right side of His magnificent white charger. It was apparent that my time with Jesus this day was almost over. The Lord held up His sword to allow me to look up at it once more. Yet again the words "The Rest of the Lord" danced in the heavenly light show. Jesus smiled at me and said, "Now go and learn what this means."

A shofar sounded and the Lord's mighty white charger reared up on his hind legs and then bolted up higher. Winds swirled around me and the fragrance of frankincense lingered upon my palate. I watched as a multitude of angelic hosts mounted upon fine steeds filled in the ranks and followed the Lord higher still. Suddenly the astoundingly loud sound of a shofar exploded once more, possibly for the seventh time, and I found myself back in my prayer room. I could still hear worship, and it seemed as if the sound of hoofs pounded across the roof of our cabin. I lay there as a bead of sweat trickled across my forehead rolling into my right eye. My eyes still burned slightly from gazing at the glory of God. I luxuriated in the presence of the Lord for several hours pondering within my heart and contemplating the things that I had seen and heard in the vision. Exactly one year later on the Day of Atonement 2012, I was given a vision expanding this experience.

As I began to write many of the words that you have just read, the Lord continued to speak to me and to minister to me. The Holy Spirit also spoke to me in a very clear and concise manner for the remainder of the Day of Atonement in 2011. The Lord spoke to me about the storm that I had witnessed. The Lord also highlighted numerous scriptures for me to meditate upon and to study in reference to the things that I had just seen and heard. I share those scriptures and revelations with you in subsequent chapters.

CHAPTER 4

Both / And

As I have pondered these amazing events in my heart over the last year, the Lord has revealed five levels or types of the rest of the Lord.

1. The rest of the Lord, the fullness of God's rest and the mantle of Melchizedek
2. The rest of the Lord, the Sabbath rest
3. The rest of the Lord, the heavenly hosts, the rest of God's family
4. The rest of the Lord, resting in His glory and allowing Him to work on our behalf
5. The rest of the Lord, the hidden and mysterious treasures in the Kingdom of God

I will share the understanding that the Lord has given to me about these five levels of the rest of the Lord later in this book. However, on the Day of Atonement in 2011, the Lord continued to speak to me from scriptures and through a series of visions. I want to share these with you in chronological order. One thing that I have discovered over the past year on this journey into the miraculous is that Jehovah is a chronological God. So, as a way of honoring Him, I will share the material in this book in linear segments.

I pray that as you read these chapters, you will draw closer to the Lord and will receive revelation concerning how you can personally enter into the rest of the Lord in your own life and circumstances. I believe that understanding the rest of the Lord and entering into God's rest is imperative at this hour. In fact, the Lord instructed me to tell you that and to write this book about this subject. It is important for us to know these things.

The Lord has been faithful to help me to understand more revelation concerning the rest of the Lord in the year that passed between the Day of Atonement 2011 and the Day of Atonement 2012. Once again, on the Day of Atonement 2012, the Lord visited me and revealed some wonderful insights about His role in helping each of His children to enter into the rest of the Lord. Jesus appeared to me as the royal Priest according to the order of Melchizedek. During this experience the Lord spoke to me prophetically about the importance of the rest of the Lord and why we must understand this important aspect of God's Kingdom at this hour. I will share those insights with you later in this book. However, I also believe that the things that the Lord showed me in 2011 should be shared first. So here is the culmination of the events from the Day of Atonement 2011.

The Culmination of the Day of Atonement 2011

It was obvious to me that the Lord was seeking to emphasize the importance of understanding the rest of the Lord. Hebrews 4:11 establishes this principle: *"Let us therefore be diligent to enter that rest, lest anyone fall according to the same example of disobedience."* Over the last twelve months I have been continually amazed and astounded at the complexity, depth, height, width, length, and importance of this subject. God is a multidimensional Spirit!

As important as this is, it is apparent that many of God's people have failed to enter into the rest of the Lord. Scripture provides us with numerous keys that can help us to understand how we can be diligent to enter into the rest of the Lord. Scripture also gives us numerous examples of hindrances to entering into the rest of the Lord.

We will look at these keys and hindrances in depth in the subsequent chapters. However, it is clear that disobedience and unbelief are the two main obstacles to a person entering into the promise of the rest of the Lord. Idolatry is another obstacle that we must overcome to enter into the rest of the Lord. Yet, I am also certain that it is the Lord's heart for all of His people to cross the threshold and experience His rest firsthand.

In the afternoon of the Day of Atonement 2011, I began to ask the Lord for wisdom to understand the things that I had both seen and heard as I witnessed the dark and evil storm approaching. I understood that the experience or vision was parabolic in nature. However, I also know that it carries a very significant and important message for us today. I reminded the Lord of His promise from James 1:5: *"If any of you lacks wisdom, let him ask of God, who gives to all liberally and without reproach, and it will be given to him."* I placed a demand upon heaven by asking the Lord for wisdom concerning the things that I had just seen and heard.

The storm that I had witnessed was both parabolic and real. Perhaps this experience was both/and. In other words, there will be *both* spiritual *and* natural events that will parallel and correspond to the dark and evil storm that I have described in the coming year(s). I understood that this storm was allowed by God. The Lord had created it and had allowed it to exist. Scripture spells this out clearly in Colossians 1:16: *"For by Him all things were created that are in heaven and that are on earth, visible and invisible, whether thrones or dominions or principalities or powers. All things were created through Him and for Him."* The Lord had created and allowed this storm much like He had created Nebuchadnezzar and Pharaoh to serve His purposes.

When I asked the Lord about this as Yom Kippur 2011 progressed, He directed me to Matthew 7. In fact the Lord had spoken to me from these passages of scripture on the Day of Atonement previously, so I was not surprised. Sometimes in God's Kingdom it is just both/and.

Once again, Matthew 7 is a very timely passage of scripture for us in the coming season. I suggest that you take some time to meditate upon it. These are the words of the Messiah; let's study these scriptures as they can help us to discover several important keys that can empower us to be diligent to enter into the rest of the Lord. This passage has very clear and timely principles for this season and beyond. Therefore, I want to look at these scriptures line upon line.

On July 9, 2011, I had a powerful encounter with the Holy Spirit. This supernatural encounter opened the door for a small book that I have written entitled *God's Prophetic Warning for America: Pray for the Peace of Jerusalem Now!* An important theme of that book is that we are entering into a season of reaping the seeds that we have sown as individuals, states, and nations. Reaping is one of many themes of that little book, and the concepts within it will continue to have relevance in the coming season(s). Matthew 7:12 also highlights this Kingdom dynamic of sowing and reaping. *"Therefore, whatever you want men to do to you, do also to them, for this is the Law and the Prophets."*

This passage speaks of reaping from our own actions because this is the law of the prophets. Some theologians call this the "law of love," and it is illustrated in Galatians 5:14: *"For all the law is fulfilled in one word, even in this: 'You shall love your neighbor as yourself.'"* Of course, this also refers to the Mosaic Law, so it too can be both/and.

The Law and the Prophets

We are entering into a season when we shall truly reap what we have sown. What have you been sowing over the last decade? What have you sown recently? Have you sown in love or have you sown with hidden or selfish agendas? Have you sown in unity or in discord? Perhaps it would be wise for each of us to ask ourselves what has been the true motivation for our actions. We should remember that anything we do in our lives and ministries that is not motivated by the love of God will have far-reaching consequences.

So, whatever you have sown, you can expect to begin reaping those same things in this season. I believe that we may each wish to consider this; and if we need to repent concerning the things that we have sown, repent quickly. We should ask the Lord for grace and mercy. It is a good idea to ask the Holy Spirit to assist us in this process. This is an extremely important dynamic because of where we are on the Lord's calendar at this hour. God is a chronological God, and at times He will call us to repent and make atonement for our transgressions. We are in such an hour today. It is a time for us the repent and ask the God of the universe for mercy and not judgment (see James 2:13).

What I am outlining is the scriptural principle of Galatians 6:7-8: *"Do not be deceived, God is not mocked; for whatever a man sows, that he will also reap. For he who sows to his flesh will of the flesh reap corruption, but he who sows to the Spirit will of the Spirit reap everlasting life."* We will begin to reap the seeds that we have sown in the past.

The Narrow Gate

Narrow is the gate and difficult is the way which leads to life, and there are few who find it.

Another thing that God is honoring and taking into account in this season is found in Matthew 7:13-14: *"Enter by the narrow gate; for wide is the gate and broad is the way that leads to destruction, and there are many who go in by it. Because narrow is the gate and difficult is the way which leads to life, and there are few who find it."* It is important to remember that these are the words of Jesus. The narrow gate in this passage of scripture can also refer to a spiritual gate.

At times the Lord will give us "gates of breakthrough"; and by God's grace and help, we can break through into the rest of the Lord through such spiritual gates. Gates like these are very real in Christ's Kingdom. Spiritual gates are an aspect of the rest of the Lord, and they are a part of the hidden and mysterious things concealed in the Kingdom of God. At times the gates are narrow or hard to find because they are spiritually discerned. They are another part and another level of the rest of the Lord. Again, we will look at this aspect of the hidden and mysterious things of Christ's Kingdom within the rest of the Lord a bit later.

King David experienced this Kingdom dynamic at Baal Perazim. When we live in obedience to the Lord and live a lifestyle of holiness, the Lord will fight our battles for us and we can declare of the Lord like King David did in 2 Samuel 5:20: *"'The LORD has broken through my enemies before me, like a breakthrough of water.' Therefore he called the name of that place Baal Perazim."* Gates of breakthrough are aspects or keys that can help us to enter into the rest of the Lord.

King David achieved this breakthrough by hearing God very clearly and then being obedient to follow God's instructions. He did a specific prophetic act at a specific geographical location at a specific God-ordained moment of time. This series of obedient acts, lined up in the correct order, allowed God to release a supernatural breakthrough, giving David a tremendous victory over his enemies. The favor and grace of Elohim then exploded into David's life and sphere of influence. God wants to do similar things in our lives as we learn to enter into the rest of the Lord. Let me encourage you to read and meditate upon 2 Samuel, chapter 5, at this season. There are some very important lessons found in these scriptures that we can learn about being diligent to enter into the rest of the Lord.

Getting back to the narrow gate, I believe that Matthew 7:13-14 also refers to holiness and obedience. As we seek the Lord and live our lives in this way, the Lord will begin to open spiritual gates for us and give us breakthroughs. These supernatural breakthroughs are another aspect of entering into the rest of the Lord. The narrow gate is a lifestyle of holiness. We need to seek to live our lives in holiness and obedience at this hour. King David experienced this kind of supernatural lifestyle and entered into the rest of the Lord. Jesus also demonstrated this kind of supernatural lifestyle, and they both accomplished it by entering into the rest of the Lord. Holiness and obedience are both essential keys that will help us to enter into the rest of the Lord. Why?

The answer is found in Hebrews 12:14-15: *"Pursue peace with all people, and holiness, without which no one will see the Lord: looking carefully lest anyone fall short of the grace of God; lest any root of bitterness springing up cause trouble, and by this many become defiled."*

(See also Psalm 24:4; Matthew 5:8.) God's Word demands holiness; there is no compromise and nothing less expected from us. Holiness is an important part of diligently seeking to enter into the rest of the Lord. If we desire to rise above the approaching storm, we must walk in obedience to the Holy Spirit and in holiness unto the Lord (see Exodus 28:36). This is a key to entering into the rest of the Lord.

If we do not walk in holiness, we cannot see the Lord. In the vision of the dark storm, the reason that the people were consumed with anxiety and fear was because they could not see the Lord. Why not? Because they were not walking according to God's will. They were not living a life of holiness. They were not living a life in obedience to the Lord, and they were not trusting in the Lord to wholly keep them. Therefore, in my vision of the dark storm, the people could not see God and His glory even though Jesus was close enough to reach out and touch. Remember, the Lord Jesus taught that the Kingdom of Heaven is at hand (Matthew 3:2).

The people in the vision of the dark and evil storm were walking upon the broad path or the broad way of destruction of Matthew 7:13. They had tolerated evil in their lives, and the darkness had the legal right to blind their minds to the Gospel. They could not see, hear, or discern God. The god of this world or of this present age had blinded their minds. The dynamic of this deception is currently unfolding upon the earth. It is outlined clearly in the following scripture:

> *Therefore, since we have this ministry, as we have received mercy, we do not lose heart. But we have renounced the hidden things of shame, not walking in craftiness nor handling the word of God deceitfully, but by manifestation of the truth commending ourselves to every man's conscience in the sight of God. But even if our gospel is veiled, it is veiled to those who are perishing, whose minds the god of this age has blinded, who do not believe, lest the light of the gospel of the glory of Christ, who is the image of God, should shine on them (2 Corinthians 4:1-4).*

Remember, this spiritual blindness affects many people within the world, even those many call Christians. The salvation of the Lord was as near as their hand, but they could not see Him. They were spiritually deaf and spiritually blind. This condition will cause the masses to be enamored by the darkness of the storm. They will have no hope because of their inability to see and hear God.

Isaiah 6:9-10 describes people like this as well: *"Go, and tell this people: 'Keep on hearing, but do not understand; Keep on seeing, but do not perceive.' Make the heart of this people dull, And their ears heavy, And shut their eyes; Lest they see with their eyes, And hear with their ears, And understand with their heart, And return and be healed."* We need to understand that this portion of scripture can apply to anyone—Jew, Gentile, saved, or unsaved alike.

But those who know the Lord can be empowered by the Holy Spirit to walk in both obedience and holiness. And just as Jesus encouraged me in the vision, we can be diligent to enter into the rest of the Lord. I will write in more detail about how you can enter into the Lord's rest later in this book. The rest of the Lord is simply having faith in God to keep you wholly, exclusively, and totally in safety. It means trusting Him to be your ever-present help and ultimate covering in times of trouble or dark storms (see Psalm 46:1).

One of the most important and basic keys to entering into the rest of the Lord is developing your personal ability to hear the Spirit of God clearly. That is why the ruler of darkness works so hard to keep the people of the world in spiritual deafness, dumbness, and blindness. By the way, this is also true for people in the church. We must overcome this kind of spiritual oppression to enter into the rest of the Lord. A key to this is overcoming a religious spirit that perpetuates the ungodly mindset that you must hear God through the spiritual leader, whether it is a pastor, prophet, guru, or shaman.

Again, as we look at Matthew 7 we are discovering keys that can help us be diligent to enter into the rest of the Lord, which is absolutely imperative. We are discovering obstacles that work to hinder us from entering into God's sovereign rest. We need to understand how to be diligent to enter into Christ's rest so we can be empowered to rise above the approaching darkness. We need to learn to recognize these obstacles and learn how to overcome them as individuals. In the rest of the Lord is peace and safety. In the rest of the Lord is everything that we need, desire, and require. In the rest of the Lord is victory!

Yes, it is a season to seek to walk in obedience and holiness so that we can see the Lord. It is a season to return to the Lord with our whole heart. It is a season to hear God clearly. It is a kairos moment of time to learn to trust God completely. It is a time to repent and ask the Lord to create within us clean hands and a pure heart. We must turn away from the world and turn to God. Holiness is the narrow gate, and at times the key to open this gate is repentance. (See Psalm 5:10-14.) Remember, the narrow gate can also be a spiritual gate of supernatural breakthrough.

We need to turn around 180 degrees, turn away from the dark storm and gaze upon the glory of God. That is Jesus! The Lord has been repeatedly reminding me of His promise from Isaiah 26:3: "*You [God] will keep him in perfect peace, Whose mind is stayed on You, Because he trusts in You.*" This scripture can be a prophetic promise for you in this season. You can make the conscious choice to keep your eyes and your gaze focused upon the Lord. As the gross darkness of this imminent storm approaches, we must stay focused upon Jesus Christ and His Kingdom like a laser. We must! Keeping focused upon the Christ and His Kingdom is a crucial key to entering into the rest of the Lord.

This promise in Isaiah 26:3 of God's perfect, double peace reigning in our lives hinges on our decision. It is very similar to the promise from Psalm 91:1-2: "*He who dwells in the secret place of the Most High Shall abide under the shadow of the Almighty. I will say of the LORD, 'He is my refuge and my fortress; My God, in Him I will trust.'*" There are two aspects to entering into the secret place of hiddenness and protection of Psalm 91. First, you must make a conscious choice to abide under the shadow of the Lord. That means drawing close to God. Second, you must decree and speak this out over your life. In the midst of the storm, we will need to prophesy, decree, and declare that we *will* trust in the Lord. Trust in the Lord (Psalm 115:11) no matter what the circumstances may look like in the natural.

Psalm 91 is a wonderful portrait of the rest of the Lord. It is a wonderful passage of scripture that we can study and be conscientious to meditate upon. As we read this prophetic Psalm, it can help us to understand several spiritual dynamics of the diligence needed to enter into the rest of the Lord. Briefly, to enter into the rest of the Lord as outlined in Psalm 91, we must make a conscious decision to make God our resting place as described in verse 2: *"I will say of the LORD, 'He is my refuge and my fortress; My God, in Him I will trust.'"* To enter into God's rest, we must make the choice to place our total trust in Him.

One of the things the Lord has been burning into my spirit over the last several years is the need for God's people to hear from the Spirit of God for themselves. Many in the church have developed an unhealthy dependence upon prophets and prophetic ministry. I will discuss this in much more detail later in this book when I write about perfect spiritual vision or 20/20 spiritual vision. However, on the Day of Atonement the Lord spoke to me from the scriptures about false prophets. He indicated that many have allowed the prophetic ministry and prophets to become idols in their lives and in their hearts. This was a continuation of the things that the Lord taught me in 2007. I have written in detail about these unholy mindsets in book 1 of the trilogy, *The Reality of Angelic Ministry Today, Dancing with Angels 1: How to Work with the Angels in Your Life.*

It is imperative for each of us to develop our personal ability to hear the Spirit of God on a one-on-one basis. There is a real need for us to judge prophetic words at this hour. Many people who place their trust and confidence in prophetic words and in prophetic ministry are at times being deceived and are allowing a spirit of fear to dominate their lives and actions. At times we might allow trust in God's prophets to replace and supersede our trust in God. We allow the man to replace the Messiah in our relationship with God. This can escalate into idol worship. This kind of ungodly reliance on prophets and prophecies can rob us of our ability to trust the Lord fully. Ungodly reliance on prophets and prophecies can disqualify us from entering into the rest of the Lord.

Fear is the opposite of faith and trust. When we allow prophetic words to instill fear in our spirits and then we base our actions on the fear spawned by prophecies, we cannot enter into the rest of the Lord at all. Fear then replaces our faith in God. As a result, we invest our time fighting battles that Christ has already won for us on the Cross of Calvary. We bring the finished work of Jesus to no effect and move from grace and faith to works and fear. This is religion and will not bear godly fruit. In the next few chapters, I will share the things that the Lord placed in my heart about having an unhealthy or ungodly dependence on prophecy and the prophetic ministry. In fact, these things can be sinful and idolatrous in the eyes of God Almighty.

Again, the narrow gate referred to in Matthew 7:13-14 can also refer to spiritual gates. Remember, at times the Lord will give us "gates of breakthrough." The Lord will help to position us to break through these spiritual gates or "Baal Perazim," which can be termed our personal valleys of breakthrough. These kinds of spiritual gates can also be called "Mahanaim." Jacob experienced such a spiritual gate in a specific geographic location where he saw the angels of God ascending and descending into his sphere of influence. It tells about it in Genesis 32:2: *"When Jacob saw them* [God's angels], *he said, 'This is God's camp.' And he called the name of that place Mahanaim."* There are still gates of breakthrough like this in God's Kingdom today. And when we become diligent to enter into the rest of the Lord, we *can* find these spiritual gates, even though Jesus taught us: *"Narrow* [difficult to discover, discern, or find] *is the gate and difficult is the way which leads to life, and there are few who find it"* (Matthew 7:14).

When we learn to move into God's ordained position by chronological and geographical obedience, we will come to places like this where spiritual gates will be available for us to step through. As we do, we will be given grace to enter into the rest of the Lord. To say it another way, when we are led by God's Spirit to be in the right place at the right time, God releases supernatural favor into our lives and into our personal spheres of influence in amazing ways. At these narrow gates or spiritual gates, God releases Kingdom blessing into our lives. At such times and places through God's grace, favor, and help, we can break through into the rest of the Lord. In the next chapter I will share more about the importance of hearing the Lord correctly and rightly judging prophetic words.

CHAPTER 5

False Prophets, Foolish Prophets, and Prophets of Doom

Beware of false prophets.

Beware of false prophets, who come to you in sheep's clothing, but inwardly they are ravenous wolves. You will know them by their fruits. Do men gather grapes from thornbushes or figs from thistles? Even so, every good tree bears good fruit, but a bad tree bears bad fruit. A good tree cannot bear bad fruit, nor can a bad tree bear good fruit. Every tree that does not bear good fruit is cut down and thrown into the fire. Therefore by their fruits you will know them. Not everyone who says to Me "Lord, Lord," shall enter the kingdom of heaven, but he who does the will of My Father in heaven (Matthew 7:15-20).

Jesus had a way of sharing the Good News. The Messiah was anointed. He was a prophet of hope. The Father sent Jesus into the world that through Him the world might be totally saved. That is very good news. The Messiah came that we might have life and have it in great abundance (see John 10:10). Jesus came to take away our fear and suffering; and through His finished work of Calvary, He accomplished His mission totally—100 percent. It is truly finished! And as a result, we can live in peace, prosperity, and health. We need not suffer.

To walk in God's Kingdom, we must know what the Kingdom consists of and how to appropriate everything that is ours in Christ's Kingdom. We will study more on this in subsequent chapters. But, we *can* make a conscious decision to live in victory based upon Christ's work. However, we do have to choose how we will live our lives. We can choose to live in light and victory. We can choose to live in the secret place of the Most High God. We can choose to be diligent to enter into the rest of the Lord. On the other hand, we can also choose to live yoked to fear and darkness. We need to make a conscious decision to discover the benefits of Christ's inheritance for each of us. You can make that conscious decision right now. Pray this*:*

> *Lord, I choose today to discover my inheritance in Christ and I choose to be diligent to seek to enter into the rest of the Lord. Father, I am Your child and a joint heir of Christ; I am Your child, a child of light. Amen.*

We are living in a time that is notable because of the incredible explosion of prophecy and prophetic ministries. The internet has opened the floodgates for the prophetic movement and allowed copious amounts of prophecies to be proliferated with little or no apostolic oversight. Although the internet has been a great blessing to many, it can also be the source of curses and false prophecy.

It is important at this time that we judge prophecy. Much harm is being done to God's people and to the unsaved world in the name of the Lord. We must judge prophecy. Not every prophetic word that is coming down the electronic pike is of the Lord. Many well-meaning people are prophesying from their own flesh. You may wish to invest some time studying Ezekiel, chapters 13 and 14, to learn more on this issue of the heart.

Prophecy can be misused. Clearly, there are men who have operated in a prophetic gifting who have historically prophesied from out of their soul or flesh. Let's look at what the Lord says to Ezekiel about this subject:

> *Son of man, prophesy against the prophets of Israel who prophesy, and say to those who prophesy out of their own heart, "Hear the word of the LORD!" Thus says the Lord GOD: "Woe to the foolish prophets, who follow their own spirit and have seen nothing!" (Ezekiel 13:2-3).*

Prophets and prophetic individuals do not always prophesy through the unction of God's Spirit. Many times we prophesy from a mixture of our personalities, emotions, soul, and God's Spirit. This character flaw has been inherent in prophetic people throughout history. God spoke to the seer prophet Ezekiel about this snare of the enemy. Prophets have been giving incorrect prophetic words for millennia, and that will certainly continue in this hour. In fact, we are seeing a dramatic increase of errant prophecies today. The spirit of Balaam and the error of Balaam are loose in the world and rampant in the church today (see Jude 1:11). There are a lot of prophets on the internet and television that have absolutely nothing to do with the church, Christianity, or God.

These are secular prophets who also fall into the category of false prophets. You will find these secular prophets in all sorts of occult and new age programming on the internet and cable and network television programming. The world is hungry for the supernatural, and the enemy is well aware of this. He is working overtime to deceive humanity with these types of false prophets and false prophecies. Just last May it was prophesied all over the earth that the world would end. This prophecy led to much anxiety while we were ministering in Jamaica. But, praise God, He used it to draw dozens to salvation in our meetings.

The Messiah warned us about this misuse of the prophetic gift: *"But I have a few things against you, because you have there those who hold the doctrine of Balaam, who taught Balak to put a stumbling block before the children of Israel, to eat things sacrificed to idols, and to commit sexual immorality"* (Revelation 2:14).

When we prophesy for profit or when we use a gift of the Holy Spirit to enrich ourselves or our ministries, we also move in the error of Balaam. Jesus will hold this against us, and this will also hinder us from entering into the rest of the Lord. We should evaluate this issue within our hearts at this hour. After all, whose kingdom are we trying to build, anyway?

We need to guard our hearts against allowing the idols of adoration and worship of prophets and prophecy from being established in our spirits and lives. The following passage outlines this kind of unholy use of the prophetic gifting:

> *And the word of the LORD came to me, saying, "Son of man, these men have set up their idols in their hearts, and put before them that which causes them to stumble into iniquity. Should I let Myself be inquired of at all by them? Therefore speak to them, and say to them, 'Thus says the Lord GOD:* **"Everyone** *of the house of Israel* **who sets up his idols in his heart, and puts before him what causes him to stumble into iniquity, and then comes to the prophet, I the LORD will answer him who comes, according to the multitude of his idols**, *that I may seize the house of Israel by their heart, because they are all estranged from Me by their idols'" (Ezekiel 14:2-5, emphasis added).*

The Lord is after our hearts. The Messiah desires to capture and captivate our hearts completely with His love and grace. There should be no room for anything but Him. Anything that takes the place of Christ in our hearts is an idol.

God really despises idolatry. When we allow idolatry to become resident in our heart, which is really our soul, it greatly grieves the Lord. This passage illustrates very clearly that the Lord will speak a false or errant prophecy to people like this. These are people who worship the prophets and prophecy. They are afflicted with idols that have been set up within their hearts. The prophets will speak prophetically what they hear from the Lord, but the prophetic word they will receive will be one that will be incorrect, inaccurate, and tainted by their worship of idols. These idol worshipers will hear exactly what they want to hear. The prophet's prophetic words will not be the truth and will not convey what God would truly wish to speak or to say to them. God wants for His people to hear the truth. Accurate prophetic words bring deliverance and freedom. They would bring God's healing and prophecies of hope and wisdom into their heart and spirits. God's prophetic words will always lead to repentance and restoration in the Lord.

At times this idol worship can be worship of man in the form of a prophet or prophetic ministry. This dynamic is still true today. When we choose elevate prophetic ministry or the prophetic word above the Word of God or hearing the Lord for ourselves, God will speak to us according to the multitude of idols within our own hearts. In other words, we will hear incorrect or errant prophetic words. This scenario is now playing out time and time again in this hour. A lot of false prophetic words are floating around cyberspace and beyond. Be careful what you read and allow to flow into your eye gates and hearts. We need to guard our hearts. We need to ask the Lord to search our hearts and help us to identify idols that may be hidden within our soul (see Psalm 51:10-12). We need to ask the Lord to reveal any hidden agendas that we may be unwittingly harboring within the recesses of our hearts.

Judging Prophetic Words

In the writings of the prophet Jeremiah, the Lord speaks of how He will deal with an individual according to the issues within his heart. You can see this in Jeremiah 17:10: *"I, the LORD, search the heart, I test the mind, Even to give every man according to his ways, According to the fruit of his doings."* If we have allowed the gift of prophecy to become more to us than a relationship with the Lord, then we are guilty of having idols within our hearts. In fact, if we esteem or love anything in the world more than the Lord, we are guilty idolatry.

We can at times allow the gift of prophecy and God's prophets to become idols in our hearts. I, for one, have been guilty of this. As a result, the Lord will surely answer us according to the multitude of the idols that we hallow, knowingly or even unwittingly. God also uses the ministry of the Holy Spirit to reveal His heart to each of us and to give us time to repent. We are in a season to repent and ask the Lord to search our hearts and minds so that we can repent. (See Ezekiel 4:14.) It is certain that the dynamics that are outlined in these scriptures apply to our generation and to the hour in which we are living. Perhaps we may wish to pray about how this biblical dynamic affects us as individuals. This deception is what Jude called the error of Balaam in chapter 1, verse 11. This error will surely hinder an individual from entering into the rest of the Lord. The error of Balaam will also open the door for us to be deceived and focused upon the dark and evil storm instead of being focused upon the salvation and redemption of Christ.

It is vital that we learn to hear the voice of the Lord clearly for ourselves at this hour. We must study the Word of God to show ourselves approved so that we may rightly divide the word of truth and correctly judge prophecies (2 Timothy 2:15). We need to have a healthy and scripturally-based mindset in reference to prophecy and prophetic ministry. This will help us to discern between the spirit of truth and the spirit of error. Many scriptures give us clear guidelines in terms of judging prophetic words. At times the Lord will use prophetic words to judge our hearts. Moses spoke of this scriptural principal in Deuteronomy:

> *If there arises among you a prophet or a dreamer of dreams, and he gives you a sign or a wonder, and the sign or the wonder comes to pass, of which he spoke to you, saying, 'Let us go after other gods'—which you have not known—'and let us serve them,' you shall not listen to the words of that prophet or that dreamer of dreams, for the LORD your **God is testing you** to know whether you love the LORD your God with all your heart and with all your soul. You shall walk after the LORD your God and fear Him, and keep His commandments and obey His voice, and you shall serve Him and hold fast to Him (Deuteronomy 13:1-4, emphasis added).*

This passage is clearly showing us that if the prophetic word is contrary to the laws of God—or in our case as the New Testament church and the canon of Scripture—we must not believe or receive the prophecy. We need to judge all prophetic words through the lens of the more sure word of prophecy, the Bible. Prophecy should only serve to confirm what the Lord has already spoken to us Spirit to spirit.

We need to be diligent and hold fast to God at this hour. The Apostle John warned about false prophets in the first century, and his warning is still relevant today. We also need to understand that not all false prophets are intentionally seeking to mislead people. Although some prophetic individuals are purposely deceptive, both secular and religious, many are actually well-intentioned but still deceived. We need to guard our hearts from these people. At the same time we should be praying for these prophets to be healed and set free from deception and the error of Balaam.

> *Beloved, do not believe every spirit, but test the spirits, whether they are of God; because many false prophets have gone out into the world (1 John 4:1).*

We are encouraged to test the spirit of prophecy and the prophets. I believe that the Lord still uses His friends the prophets. However, we should test all prophecy and hold on to those prophetic words that are true. Recognize the prophetic words that line up with Scripture. There are blessings that come from listening to God's anointed prophets and believing their words. I want to encourage you to listen to God's prophets, but listen in a healthy and holy manner. Test all prophecy for yourself.

> *Believe in the LORD your God, and you shall be established; believe His prophets, and you shall prosper (2 Chronicles 20:20).*

The issue today is that in some circles there is a very unhealthy emphasis on the office of the prophet. Some denominations elevate the prophets and the prophetic word above the Word of God. Some people often depend upon the prophets to hear God on their behalf. This is very dangerous, and it can evolve into a form of idolatry in the church (see Ezekiel 14:4). We need to guard our hearts against this and judge prophecy and prophetic words for ourselves as individuals. Even the Lord Jesus warned us about this phenomenon. Again, it is imperative that we begin to cultivate our own ability to hear the voice of the Lord clearly on an individual basis.

Sure, there can be misuse of any anointing or spiritual gifting. This has been a common occurrence throughout church history and with God's people over the millennia. We need to have a healthy balance of the spiritual gifts. We need all of the gifts of the Holy Spirit (see 1 Corinthians 12:6-10). What I am speaking of is being able to grow into the very image of Jesus Christ. We should all be developing into mature sons and daughters of God. In fact, the whole earth is eagerly waiting for the revealing of the true sons of God (Romans 8:19).

The Lord operated in all of the gifts of the Holy Spirit's in His ministry, and He always acted with maturity and wisdom. My prayer for each of us is that we would learn to walk like Christ in both nobility (kingly authority) and humility (a Christlike attitude). I pray that we would learn to have a healthy balance of the Spirit and the Word and understand how to operate in the gifts of the Holy Spirit in a balanced and healthy manner, just like Christ. After all, Jesus was our role model, and He operated in the gifts of the Spirit in a healthy and holy way. We can too.

That was His example for us, and that should be our goal. We must all seek to *"come to the unity of the faith and of the knowledge of the Son of God, to a perfect man, to the measure of the stature of the fullness of Christ; that we should no longer be children, tossed to and fro and carried about with every wind of doctrine* [errant prophetic words], *by the trickery of men, in the cunning craftiness of deceitful plotting, but, speaking the truth in love, may grow up in all things into Him who is the head—Christ"* (Ephesians 4:13-15).

Remember, the Lord Jesus warned us about this phenomenon of false prophets. Christ's warning needs to ring clearly in our spirits at this hour. Look at what He said in Mark 13:22-23: *"For false christs and false prophets will rise and show signs and wonders to deceive, if possible, even the elect. But take heed; see, I have told you all things beforehand."*

The Apostle Peter also warned us to be on guard concerning the abuse and misuse of the prophetic office and prophetic words. We are certainly living with those same issues at this hour. We are warned against believing destructive heresies, also known as lies. Peter ensures us that God will judge false prophets. Again, pray for mercy, grace, and healing.

> *But there were also false prophets among the people, even as there will be false teachers among you, who will secretly bring in destructive heresies, even denying the Lord who bought them, and bring on themselves swift destruction. And many will follow their destructive ways, because of whom the way of truth will be blasphemed. By covetousness they will exploit you with deceptive words; for a long time their judgment has not been idle, and their destruction does not slumber. For if God did not spare the angels who sinned, but cast them down to hell and delivered them into chains of darkness, to be reserved for judgment; and did not spare the ancient world, but saved Noah, one of eight people, a preacher of righteousness, bringing in the flood on the world of the ungodly...then the Lord knows how to deliver the godly out of temptations and to reserve the unjust under punishment for the day of judgment (2 Peter 2:1-5, 9).*

Again, I want to reiterate that we should believe in the prophets and listen to them carefully. Amos 3:7 tells us this important fact: *"Surely the Lord GOD does nothing, Unless He reveals His secret to His servants the prophets."* There is no question that God is still speaking to His people through His servants and friends the prophets.

However, I also want to remind you that the Lord gave us a very strong warning about false prophets. We have only looked at those warnings briefly here; but I want to encourage you to scour the Scriptures for yourself, asking the Holy Spirit to guide and lead you. Ask the Lord to reveal to you any areas where you may have unhealthy or ungodly beliefs within your soul or heart. As the Lord reveals these to you, the precious Holy Spirit will help you to repent. Then the Lord will heal you if need be. He will create within you a clean heart and an upright spirit. This will surely enable you to hear the voice of the Lord much more clearly, and that will enable you to be led by His Spirit every day.

That is being diligent to enter into the rest of the Lord. And that, my friend, can be truly life changing! Therefore, I want to encourage you that this is a season to the test prophets and prophecies. Not every prophetic word that is published on the internet, television, or anywhere else is correct. We all miss it from time to time. So be diligent to judge prophetic ministry at this hour. Ask the Lord to search your heart and soul. Remember, some false prophets appear every weekday during daytime network television programming. They also are seen regularly during the evening newscasts around the earth as well. Not all false prophets are in the church.

False prophecies and prophets will hinder your ability to enter into the rest of the Lord. If we are deceived by these, we will allow the enemy to rob our peace and keep us from walking in an intimate and personal relationship with the Lord. Our ears will become dull of hearing and our hearts will be hardened to the truth of the glorious Gospel. We must begin to learn to cultivate our own personal ability to hear God's voice and to be led by His Spirit for ourselves at this hour. The Lord illustrated this dynamic in Matthew 13:15, saying, *"For the hearts of this people have grown dull. Their ears are hard of hearing, And their eyes they have closed, Lest they should see with their eyes and hear with their ears, Lest they should understand with their hearts and turn, So that I should heal them."*

In this passage of scripture, Jesus was quoting Isaiah 6:10. We have studied this passage previously. The Lord was confirming what Isaiah prophesied about spiritual blindness. But God's heart for His people is that we would see with our eyes, hear with our ears, and understand with our heart. Why? So that we would return and be healed. There is no question about this. Hearing and seeing the Lord clearly are absolutely mandatory to truly entering into the rest of the Lord. We need to turn fully to the Lord and allow the precious Holy Spirit to help us to have our spiritual eyes and ears healed. We need to allow the Lord to heal our spirits or the eyes of our hearts. Only by allowing this refining work and fire of the Holy Spirit to burn out these issues from our hearts can we be fully healed. And only when we are healed can we see and hear God clearly and thereby be prepared to truly enter into the rest of the Lord.

Lord, help us to turn with our hearts and repent. Help us to judge prophecies and hear from heaven for ourselves. Lord, help us to learn how to be led by Your Spirit in all aspects of our lives. Open the eyes of our heart, Lord Jesus, and send the Holy Spirit to guide, heal, and help lead us today. Amen.

That is what true salvation is all about—learning to enter into the fullness of God's rest, understanding with our hearts, and turning to God to be truly saved or born from above. In this chapter I have pointed out how imperative it is to hear God's voice clearly for ourselves as individuals at this hour. Hearing God is an important key to entering into God's rest. In the next chapter we look at this dynamic of entering into the rest of the Lord in more detail.

CHAPTER 6

Salvation—
Entering the Kingdom of Heaven

Not everyone...shall enter the kingdom of heaven.

Not everyone who says to Me, "Lord, Lord," shall enter the kingdom of heaven, but he who does the will of My Father in heaven. Many will say to Me in that day, "Lord, Lord, have we not prophesied in Your name, cast out demons in Your name, and done many wonders in Your name?" And then I will declare to them, "I never knew you; depart from Me, you who practice lawlessness!" (Matthew 7:21-23).

One of the principles that Jesus outlines in Matthew 7 is that some who believe that they know Christ as Savior do not. They *do not* know Him. They are lost. Some people estimate that as many as 85 percent of people who say they are Christians are not actually saved or born again. If this is true (and I pray it is not) many professing Christianity will miss it. In fact, they may miss heaven and hit hell. They will be like the ones in verses 21-23 above. They will stand before the Lord on Judgment Day and recount the works they did for God.

"Lord, I prophesied. Lord, I had a powerful deliverance ministry and cast out a lot of demons and helped to set the captive free. Lord, I preached the Bible. Lord, I helped feed the poor and provided them with water and shelter. Lord, I attended church and I paid my tithes. Lord, I taught Sunday school." There are many other things along this line they might say, and yet Matthew 7:23 tells us that Jesus will say to them, *"I never knew you; depart from Me, you who practice lawlessness!"*

On the Day of Atonement the Lord convicted me about this. *"The day of the Lord will come as a thief in the night"* (2 Peter 3:10; 1 Thessalonians 5:2). Many in the Body of Christ are unprepared. Many of us are like the ten foolish virgins (see Matthew 25:1-3). Yes, many who have done great works for the Kingdom of God will stand before the Lord and Jesus will have no knowledge of them. Why? Because they did not enter into the rest of the Lord. They did not learn to develop an intimate relationship with the person of Jesus. They did not allow the Holy Spirit to help them, to guide them, and to lead them. It is a time to make sure that your election and calling are sure. It is a time to make sure that your faith is founded upon Christ and not upon religion and religious activities. Your church cannot save you from hell. Your denomination cannot save you from hell. Your good deeds and good works cannot get you into heaven.

We need to develop an intimate and personal relationship with God the Father, God the Son, and God the Holy Spirit. Be diligent to confirm that your salvation is established upon the Rock. The salvation of Jesus Christ is the only way into heaven. *"There is no other name under heaven given among men by which we must be saved"* (Acts 4:12). Jesus said, *"I am the way, the truth, and the life. No one comes to the Father except through Me"* (John 14:6). There is only *"one God and only one Mediator between God and men, the Man Christ Jesus, who gave Himself a ransom for all"* (1 Timothy 2:5-6). This Jesus, the Son of the living God, is the only way for you to receive salvation and remission of your sins. If you are not sure that you are born from above or "born again," perhaps you may wish to pray the prayer of salvation at the end of this book now.

In the vision of the storm, I saw many Christians quaking in fear and trembling. They did not know who Christ was, and they were hopelessly filled with horror and anxiety. Although they had a form of godliness, they did not know God. As a result, they were just as lost as the rest of the world. They were in subjugation to fear and every other demonic oppression and yoke of darkness. They did not know the truth or the Gospel; and as a result, they were not able to use the Word of God as a weapon of warfare in the midst of the darkness of the storm. We need to learn the Word of God and begin to hide it within our hearts and souls.

Fear and Trembling

The Apostle Paul understood that even though many people had made conscious decisions to become Christians, they were still immature in their faith. He referred to these kinds of believers as carnal (see 1 Corinthians 3). This same dynamic is still prevalent among the Lord's people at this hour. In fact, it is a ploy of the enemy to keep believers in a state of immaturity and carnality and ignorant of the power of God's Word. Actually, that is what the enemy wants to do; he wants to keep you in ignorance. If you do not know what your inheritance is, you can never step into it and enjoy the benefits of it. That is defeat. Through ignorance you can allow the enemy to kill, steal, and destroy you and yours (see John 10:10). Enforce your boundaries! The enemy wants to keep you in bondage to religion.

Hosea 4:6 outlines this type of spiritual bankruptcy: *"My people are destroyed for lack of knowledge."* The enemy of your soul wants you to be kept in ignorance and darkness in order that he may steal, kill, and destroy you. We must be diligent to search out and uncover the inheritance that Christ purchased for each of us. We must comprehend with our entire spirit, soul, and body the magnitude and finality of the triumph of Christ accomplished for each of us in our individual circumstances. Ignorance is not bliss; it is the playground of demons who seek to rob you from your rightful place in God's Kingdom.

You must fully understand the magnitude of what Jesus purchased for you when He died upon the Cross of Calvary. We need to comprehend the power that was released to each of us when the Father raised Jesus Christ from the dead. Otherwise the enemy can keep you from achieving God's perfect plan and purpose in your life. The enemy will have the ability to oppress you and subject you to his kingdom of darkness. The god of this age will have succeeded in blinding your mind to the glorious light and revelations of Christ (2 Corinthians 4:4). The truth is that Jesus died to make you an overcomer and to give the authority to rule and reign in this life *now* (see Revelation 5:9-10).

Philippians 2:12-13 encourages us: *"Therefore, my beloved, as you have always obeyed, not as in my presence only, but now much more in my absence, work out your own salvation with fear and trembling; for it is God who works in you both to will and to do for His good pleasure."* The God of the universe desires to work within you! That is amazing to think about isn't it? The God of the universe seeks to empower you through His Holy Spirit (see Ephesians 3:14-21). But the devil seeks to keep you in bondage to a religious spirit and idol worship.

Every believer must seek to work out their own salvation at this hour. This is yet another way that we can be diligent to enter into the rest of the Lord. The question that is being asked at this hour is this: Who are you going to serve? You can serve the Lord, or you can serve the kingdom of darkness and all the fleeting pleasures that seem to be available to you in that darkness. We need to make sure that our relationship with the Lord is strong and true.

God versus Mammon

Jesus gave some very pertinent advice along these lines. Look at what He told us in Matthew 6:24-25: *"No one can serve two masters; for either he will hate the one and love the other, or else he will be loyal to the one and despise the other. You cannot serve God and mammon. Therefore I say to you, do not worry about your life, what you will eat or what you will drink; nor about your body, what you will put on. Is not life more than food and the body more than clothing?"*

In the passage above the Lord illustrates the pull that the kingdom of darkness has upon humans. The word *mammon* is of Chaldean origin. Mammon is actually wealth or wealth personified. In other words, mammon is an idol in some people's hearts. In our society we have surely made an idol out of riches and the glamour of wealth. We worship mammon, and the worship of mammon or wealth is a form of idol worship in America and beyond. This worship of mammon is loosed in the church too. Our priorities are turned all around and perverted for the most part. The god of this age is working overtime to blind our eyes, and he has succeeded in keeping many of us in abject ignorance. Ignorance is not bliss; it is a demonic yoke of darkness.

Again, we see the devil's strategy outlined in 2 Corinthians 4:3-4: *"If the gospel is veiled, it is veiled to those who are perishing, whose minds the god of this age has blinded, who do not believe, lest the light of the gospel of the glory of Christ, who is the image of God, should shine on them."* Don't be deceived by the devil's strategy.

Praise God! The Lord has given us precious and wonderful promises in His Word. God has given us His strategies for victory. John underlines this in 1 John 5:4: *"For whatever is born of God overcomes the world. And this is the victory that has overcome the world—our faith."* The Gospel has the power to help us overcome the world, but we need to get it firmly implanted within our spirits, souls, and bodies.

We need to earnestly seek to renew our minds. We need to get our mindsets changed, rehabilitated, and transformed according to Romans 12:2: *"Do not be conformed to this world, but be transformed by the renewing of your mind, that you may prove what is that good and acceptable and perfect will of God."* Renewing our mindsets can also help us to enter into the rest of the Lord.

Money is not evil in itself; it is the love of wealth and mammon that can lead to wickedness and sin (see 1 Timothy 6:10). So, how should we use the monies that the Lord is giving into our hands to steward? We need to use them in a holy and righteous way. We need to seek to hear the Lord, we need to listen to the precious Holy Spirit, and we need to seek His perfect will and plan for our monies and wealth. We should seek the direction that is found in the scriptures and invest our monies in the Kingdom of God and in His purposes. We need to learn to be led by the Spirit of the Lord in this area of our lives and ministries. Tithing is great, but we also need to learn how to freely give alms. It is a wonderful experience to enter the rest of the Lord with your finances. Giving God your money is liberating!

We have a tendency to forget the poor and the widow and use the money that the Lord gives us to promote our own agendas. Instead of doing the things the Lord would have us to do, we build larger edifices and develop larger programs. We allow mammon to control our lives and ministries, and this is a form of idol worship in the church. We tend to build ministry machines that are fueled by more and more mammon. This kind of religious growth robs us of our ability to trust in the Lord and the freedom to enter into the rest of the Lord.

In Matthew 6:24-25 the Lord addresses mammon, saying, *"You cannot serve God and mammon. Therefore I say to you, do not worry about your life, what you will eat or what you will drink; nor about your body, what you will put on. Is not life more than food and the body more than clothing?"*

Yes, our lives are truly more than eating, drinking, and caring for our other natural needs. Don't work for money; rather allow money to work for you. "Begin to earn a giving instead of earning a living," as my friend Pastor James Durham says. Life is a spiritual journey and the Lord will make sure that our spirit is safe and secure within His Kingdom. Yet, the message of the world is totally opposite: "Horde food, save money, save for a rainy day, get the latest fashion." The world tells us to pamper our soul and flesh and tells us: "Forget about your spirit, it is not real." That is a lie of the god of this age, and it is foolishness to believe it.

Jesus said that we should be more concerned with our spirit. Look at how eloquently Jesus sums this up:

> *Look at the birds of the air, for they neither sow nor reap nor gather into barns; yet your heavenly Father feeds them. Are you not of more value than they? Which of you by worrying can add one cubit to his stature? So why do you worry about clothing? Consider the lilies of the field, how they grow: they*

neither toil nor spin; and yet I say to you that even Solomon in all his glory was not arrayed like one of these. Now if God so clothes the grass of the field, which today is, and tomorrow is thrown into the oven, will He not much more clothe you, O you of little faith? Therefore do not worry, saying, "What shall we eat?" or "What shall we drink?" or "What shall we wear?" For after all these things the Gentiles seek. For your heavenly Father knows that you need all these things. But seek first the kingdom of God and His righteousness, and all these things shall be added to you. Therefore do not worry about tomorrow, for tomorrow will worry about its own things. Sufficient for the day is its own trouble (Matthew 6:26-34).

In this passage of scripture, Jesus is describing entering into the rest of the Lord in terms of our finances. He is saying that we need to rest in the Lord and trust God to meet our basic needs for food, clothing, and shelter.

We should truly seek first the Kingdom of God and His righteousness. This is another key that can help us to enter into the rest of the Lord. In other words, we need to make sure that our salvation is firm and sure. It's important that we confirm the "surety" and assurance of our spirit. Our heavenly Father will supply all of our soulish and carnal needs. The Father already knows every single thing that you need before we ask (Matthew 6:8).

In the vision of the storm, I saw these "Gentiles" or unbelievers. They were terrified and overcome by yokes of darkness because they were in danger of losing their stuff. The stuff had become mammon to them, it had become their idol. It had become the thing that they worshiped, and as such it had replaced God. This was also true for many Christians in the visions too. The approaching storm will blow away our idols of mammon and force us to deal with the reality of the Kingdom of God face to Face. The Lord was allowing the storm to bring people back to Him. The dark storm is the mercy of God. The approaching dark storms will surely blow away our mammon and idols. So, where is that going to leave us as individuals?

As I mentioned earlier, as these challenging times unfold upon the earth, we will need to develop our individual ability to hear the voice of God. As we learn to rest in the Lord, He will speak to us and give us direction. Some people never mature in this area of their walk with God. They remain immature; or as the Apostle Paul said, they remain *"babes in Christ"* (1 Corinthians 3:1). They allow the spiritual leaders in their lives to guide them and to hear God on their behalf. This is dangerous practice. Our lack of ability to hear God becomes a very serious liability when we become lazy and develop an unhealthy dependence on prophecy and prophetic ministry. When this happens, we allow the man (the prophet) to replace the Messiah. We can allow prophecy to replace our own need to study and learn God's Word and to wait and listen to God for ourselves. We become like the people in Isaiah 6:9-10 that Jesus spoke about:

> *Go, and tell this people: "Keep on hearing, but do not understand; Keep on seeing, but do not perceive." Make the heart of this people dull, And their ears heavy, And shut their eyes; Lest they see with their eyes, And hear with their ears, And understand with their heart, And return and be healed.*

It is imperative that we learn to hear the voice of the Lord at this hour. When we develop our ability to hear God and rest in His marvelous presence, then we will be healed. As this approaching darkness and evil storm manifests, it will become even more dangerous to be spiritually deaf and blind. I want to look at this unhealthy dynamic in the next chapter.

CHAPTER 7

Caves and Taters

In earlier chapters I was sharing about an unhealthy focus and single-mindedness concerning prophetic ministry and prophetic words. I want to touch on this issue again. There are some prophetic streams that are prophesying death, doom, and destruction. Yes, there is a storm coming, but we can rise above it. They are only focusing on the approaching darkness of the storm, and that is dangerous. They fail to place Christ and His resurrection power into their equations and prophetic words of doom and darkness.

There is hope. Keep your eyes focused upon Jesus, and learn to hear from heaven for yourself. The Lord will keep you in perfect peace in the midst of the storm when we seek His Kingdom first and when we learn to develop a personal relationship with the King, Jesus. God is more than able to keep you in perfect peace and safety. When we choose to make the secret place of the Most High God our resting place, He will protect us, as it is so articulately stated in Psalm 91. Again, I am speaking of resting in the Lord in the midst of the storms of life.

Some prophets and prophetic people are forgetting the power of the God who gave them their prophetic anointing or gifting. He is the one who is all-powerful and the one who has already overcome the world and the dark storms therein. He is Elohim, the Creator of the heavens and the earth. Elohim is the name used for God in Genesis 1: *"In the beginning God created the heavens and the earth"* (v. 1).

Christ was there as the earth was created; and therefore He has the ability, authority, and the sovereign power to overcome the earth and every dark storm therein. Jesus Christ already overcame the world, so we just need to learn how we can rest in His victory. (Remember, all prophetic words do not come from Christians; some come in the middle of your nightly newscast or during your favorite daytime television programs. Maybe you should consider a media fast.)

We need to remember that Jesus overcame the world for a purpose. Look at Christ's prophetic promise to you in John 16:33: "*These things I have spoken to you, that in Me you may have peace. In the world you will have tribulation; but be of good cheer, I have overcome the world.*" Yes, there will be some tribulation and storms, but the Lord has already won the victory for you. You don't have to live in defeat, you don't have to suffer and live in a cave or an apocalyptical paradigm. You don't need to live your life embracing a survivalist mentality of fear and foreboding.

You are a victor. You don't need to fight the war. You need to understand that you just need to be diligent to enter into the rest that the Lord has already provided for you. Learn to enforce your boundaries. Jesus *overcame* (past tense) the world for you. Sometimes we need declare, decree, and prophesy into the wind in the hearing of the enemy and remind him that he is defeated and disarmed. You are more than a conqueror when you are in Christ (see Romans 8:31-39). When you are resting in the secret place of the Most High God you rest in Christ's finished work.

Did Christ come into the world to give us hope or fear? There is no question that the Father sent His Son to give us total and complete salvation. We see what kind of salvation Jesus gave to each of us in Isaiah 53. Look closely at verses 4 and 5: "*Surely He has borne our **griefs** And carried our **sorrows**; Yet we esteemed Him stricken, Smitten by God, and afflicted. But He was wounded for our transgressions, He was bruised for our iniquities; The chastisement for our peace was upon Him, And by His stripes we are healed*" (emphasis added).

The word *griefs* in this passage is translated from the Hebrew word *choliy*. This can be translated as malady, anxiety, calamity, disease, grief, or sickness. Jesus took our sickness and all of our infirmities upon His body so that we need not suffer from them. Matthew 8:17 makes this aspect of the Lord's atonement for you very clear: "*He Himself took our infirmities And bore our sicknesses.*" Since Jesus took them, or purchased them, we do not have to carry that yoke or burden of darkness any longer. That is *unless* we choose to.

The word *sorrows* in Isaiah 53:4, translated from Hebrew *mak'ob*, can also be translated as anguish, affliction, pain, sorrow, or suffering. Jesus suffered for you and me once and for all. If we believe in the Messiah and diligently hold fast to His word, then we do not need to suffer. That is *unless* we choose to do so. Derek Prince taught that a Christian can have anything, (including physical sickness and emotional turmoil), that he wants to have. That is a very sad but true statement.

Hold Fast to Jesus and His Finished Work on Calvary

So, if you want to suffer, you can. If you choose to believe prophecies and sermons that declare over you and your sphere of influence that you are going to suffer, you can. If you choose to declare, prophesy, and speak over your life that you will suffer and live in a cave and survive on taters, that is your free will and choice. Woe unto you! Suffer all that you want. It is your choice to make. I will be praying for you. I will pray that your blinded mind will be enlightened to the truth. Jesus overcame the world. He suffered so that you don't have to.

As for me and my house, I choose to make a conscious decision to accept and hold fast to the Lord Jesus and His finished work on Calvary. Either God's Word is true or God is a liar. I choose to say that I will not suffer or lack any good thing (see Psalm 34:10; Proverbs 10:4). I will prosper and be in health (see 3 John 1:2). In fact, Jesus Himself bore my sins and sickness in His own body on the tree so that I, having died to sins, might live in righteousness, prosperity, and total freedom from darkness and emotional distress (see 1

Peter 2:24). I can live in perfect peace and perfect health because by Christ's stripes I *am* healed (present tense). In fact, my entire peace was upon Jesus upon the Cross of Calvary and yours was too. However, you need to choose to believe it and to receive it.

Speak this out loud over your life now:

> *I choose to make a conscious decision to accept and hold fast to the Lord Jesus and His finished work on Calvary. I will not suffer or lack any good thing. I will prosper and be in health. Jesus Himself bore my sins and sickness in His own body on the tree, that I, having died to sins, might live for righteousness, prosperity, and total freedom from darkness and in perfect peace and perfect health because by Christ's stripes I am healed. My entire peace was upon Jesus at Calvary, and I can live in the double peace of God from this day forward. I choose to believe it to receive it today. I will live in gladness and joy of heart because of the abundance of everything that the Lord will give to me.*

Isaiah 53:5 prophesies, "*The chastisement for your peace was upon Him* [Jesus Christ]." (Don't you love it when God prophesies over your life?) The word *peace* here comes from the Hebrew word *shalom*. It can be translated as to be safe, to be made well or happy, to have perfect welfare and health or prosperity, or to be totally saved and set free. This peace that the Messiah purchased for you is perfect peace. It is the same peace spoken of in Isaiah 26:3.

Sometimes we just need to feed upon the anointed prophecy in the Word of God until it takes root in our spirit and begins to bear fruit worthy of repentance. I trust the prophecies of the Scripture much more than the prophecies of man—especially those prophecies of man that are full of gloom, doom, and defeat. You can count on the prophecies within the Bible; the answer to them is always yes and amen.

Trusting In Him

I want to encourage you to guard your heart with diligence. Another way that we can enter into the rest of the Lord is by trusting Him. We need to stand upon God's Word and reject prophetic words and sermons that do not line up with the canon of Scripture. We need to reject messages and prophecies that speak death over our lives and not the victory that Jesus came and gave freely to you and me. Judge all prophecy. Proverbs 4:23 reminds us to protect our hearts and be careful of the things that we allow to enter into our spirits through our hearts (eyes and ears): *"Keep your heart with all diligence, For out of it spring the issues of life."* The issues of life refers to everything that we need to live as victorious overcomers with every one of our needs met fully and totally, with more than enough, with enough stuff to spare and to give to those who need a hand (peace, prosperity, health, and total wholeness).

We need to learn to be diligent to enter into the rest of the Lord. Again this means trusting the Lord no matter what the circumstances may look like. We need to trust in the Lord with all of our heart. We cannot depend upon our own intellect and carnal knowledge or understanding (see Proverbs 3:5).We need to trust the Lord to give each of us supernatural revelation, health, prosperity, favor, total peace, and well-being, just as the Lord promised and prophesied over you in Isaiah 53. Again, we must learn to develop our ability to hear from God, Spirit to spirit. We must feed upon the Word of God found in the Bible until it becomes a part of our spiritual DNA. In this way, we will be building ourselves up to overcome the storms of life.

God is seeking to prepare His Bride and to transform us into overcomers who will rise above the darkness of the storm. We are more than conquerors in Christ Jesus (see Romans 8:37). Our Christ is shown as the Conqueror in Revelation 6:2: *"I looked, and behold, a white horse. He who sat on it had a bow; and a crown was given to him, and he went out conquering and to conquer."* That is exactly how I saw the Lord Jesus Christ in the vision of the dark storm. He was mighty, victorious, and the ultimate Conqueror. He has prevailed upon your behalf. We are to be overcomers and conquerors right alongside of Jesus. God encourages us that as we prevail and are transformed into Christlike overcomers by the finished and refining work of the Holy Spirit, we will receive a supernatural inheritance that is laid up for us in the heavenly realms.

Look at the promise in Revelation 21:7: *"He who overcomes shall inherit all things, and I will be his God and he shall be My son."* You have a supernatural inheritance laid up for you. Romans 8:37 also illustrates what our Christlike nature should be in this life: *"Yet in all these things we are more than conquerors through Him who loved us."* We are to be more than conquerors; we are to be kings and priests (Revelation 1:6; 5:10). We are sons and daughters of the Most High God.

However, in some of the churches today we are taught that we must suffer and expect the worst. They speak and preach from the pulpits that we must just suffer through till we die, then we will have rest and peace; we need to get ready to live in caves and eat taters; we should plan, speak, and expect the worst possible case scenarios; if we just have some luck and a little of God's grace, if we can just be good enough, we might barely get by; we've got to just hang in there till the storm passes; just find a safe place and hunker down. It is possible that I am exaggerating just a smidge here, but I am seeking to make an important point. That's unbiblical nonsense! The way that some ministers and prophets talk, you would think there is no hope at all.

You need to know and to understand that the enemy wants you to listen to and believe that kind of prophetic teaching. That kind of defeatist doctrine and ungodly theology will lead to an ungodly belief system that does not recognize the victory of Christ in your life. The enemy does not want you to get the revelation of who you are in Christ, and he definitely does not want you to understand the power and victory that Jesus gave to you through the triumph of the Cross and the power of the Resurrection. The enemy does not want you to enter into God's rest. In fact, he is quite happy to have you drudging along tirelessly at dead religious works and fruitless pursuits.

It seems that some of our teachers, pastors, and prophets do not have faith in God's ability to keep us safe and secure in the midst of this approaching dark storm. They preach that we must suffer. They counsel from their carnality that we need to plan for the worst. It would seem that they have no revelation of the Cross and the power that Jesus released to you and me when He died for us and rose from the dead. Perhaps, if they do understand, they have forgotten what the Bible really says; or maybe the god of this age has succeeded in blinding their minds to the reality of the power of God in Christ Jesus. That is available to each of us through the power of the Holy Spirit. I say, "Wake up!"

Choose Wisely What You Speak into Existence

According to Isaiah 53, Jesus suffered for me so that I don't have to suffer. You can say that you are going to suffer; that is your choice. You can say that you and yours will be overcome in the midst of the approaching darkness; that is your choice too. I am sure that it is true for you because by your words you will be justified and by your words you will be condemned. That is not my idea. That is what Jesus said in Matthew 12:37: *"For by your words you will be justified, and by your words you will be condemned."* You choose what you allow to enter into your ears and into your spirit.

You choose what you speak into existence in your life and sphere of influence. Are you speaking and calling forth God's blessings or are you calling forth a curse upon your life, family, and friends? Let me encourage you to enforce your spiritual and natural boundaries. Protect your spirit. Be diligent about what you allow your eyes to see and what you allow your ears to hear. In this way you can be careful about what you allow to enter into your spirit. Learn to keep your spirit from being defiled.

At times words spoken into your spirit become prophecies of defeat for you unless you enforce your boundaries. Be careful who you allow to enter into your home to speak into your life and hearing. Be vigilant and conscientious about what you see and hear. Choose carefully about where you go. Kathy will not even enter into some stores because of the evil and ungodly merchandise that is sold there. Enforcing your boundaries is an important key to entering into the rest of the Lord.

Our word confessions need to be Christlike and scriptural. *"As for me and my house we will serve the LORD"* (Joshua 24:15). As for me and my house we will prosper and be in health even as our soul prospers (3 John 1:2). When ministers speak and preach that we must all suffer and endure loss as this dark storm approaches, they are bringing the Cross of Calvary and the power of God to no effect in their spheres of influence. They actually release word curses over people. Since we are created in God's image, we have the power to create our circumstances as we speak things into being. Job 22:28 illustrates this Kingdom principle: *"You will also declare a thing, And it will be established for you; So light will shine on your ways."* This is another important way and Kingdom key to entering into the rest of the Lord. We must learn to have positive word confessions and bridle our tongues (see James 1:26; 1 Peter 3:10).

God gives His children the privilege of speaking things into existence, both good and bad. As for me, my word declaration is this:

> *I am truly blessed and highly favored with great, great grace and divine intervention in my life today. I am a king's kid and a royal priest according to the order of Melchizedek; and I am walking in the FOG, the favor of God! That is who I am. I am more than an overcomer! I am more than a conqueror in Christ! I am going to prosper and be in health even as my soul prospers. Divine health is mine, divine favor is mine. I will grow in the favor with both God and man. I will lack no good thing! I choose to trust in God, and I will rest in the Lord. I will rest in the fact that God cares for me and the Lord shall withhold no good thing from me. He will keep me from evil; and everything that I set my hands to will prosper exponentially, every day, all the time. And I will be diligent to enter into the rest of the Lord every day. Amen!*

(Please feel free to appropriate this word confession and apply it liberally to your life and circumstances as needed. In fact, take two and call me in the morning.)

The way some people are talking and prophesying today, you would think that Jesus was defeated. You would think that He did not have any power at all. They err because they do not know the fullness of the truth, and perhaps they prophesy out of the multitude of the idols within their hearts. Some bring a word of hopelessness and despair. These remind me of the ones who I saw in the midst of the dark storm. They were horrified and under deep yokes of darkness and deception. They did not know who they were in Christ Jesus. They did not have any understanding of the power that the Lord had released to them to utilize and employ in the midst of the storm (see Hosea 4:6). They were deceived by the forces of darkness and under the influence of deceptive demonic spirits.

The god of this age has indeed blinded their eyes. Second Corinthians 4:3-4 makes this fact clear: *"Our gospel is veiled...to those who are perishing, whose minds the god of this age has blinded, who do not believe, lest the light of the gospel of the glory of Christ, who is the image of God, should shine on them."* This passage speaks of having your spiritual eyes and ears blinded so that you are unable to enter into the trust and rest of the Lord. When we understand the truth of the Gospel and the revelation of Christ's finished work, the glory of God shines upon us or rests upon us.

This is another important key to entering into the rest of the Lord. We need to understand and have the fullness of the revelation what the Word of God really means. Not what we think it is supposed to mean, not what we have been taught that the Scriptures are supposed to mean, but the truth of God's heart about the Gospel. We need to press into the glory of God, and we should seek to rest in the glory of God every day. Again, this is another key to entering into the rest of the Lord. I will share more about how to accomplish this later.

Honestly, to hear some of the prophetic words and sermons today you might just want to go ostrich. You might just want to stick your head in the sand and give up. Some people have resigned themselves to being overcome and enveloped by the darkness of the approaching storm. How about you? They are making plans to fortify themselves to withstand the onslaught of evil. Yep, they are going to become experts at growing crops and surviving off the land. Some are seeking to create enclaves and protected communities that they can retreat into for safety and security. That is great if that is what the Lord is truly calling you to do. But what about retreating into God? What about trusting in God? What about God? Did He lose His power to protect you? Is the Creator of the heavens and the earth no longer dependable and worthy of your trust? Is God Almighty's right arm shortened that He cannot save and protect you today? (See Isaiah 59:1.)

You would think that they are expecting the USA to become as bad as the society that is portrayed in the 1981 science fiction movie, *The Road Warrior*, starring Mel Gibson. Yes, you had better learn to reload your ammo and batten down the hatches. You would think that some people are planning to exist in caves and survive by eating potatoes and mushrooms.

Well, guess what? If that is what you are speaking forth with your words, you can expect it to happen. If that is what is hidden within your heart's desire, then God will let you have it (see Psalm 37:4). If that is your worst fear, then it is possible that you can expect it to come to pass. So perhaps you better prepare for it. If you believe that you are going to suffer, then you can. Remember, that is what Jesus said in Matthew 12:37: *"By your words you will be justified, and by your words you will be condemned."* Honestly, there are some prophetic people out there who are prophesying all gloom and doom and they leave Christ out of the equation. And there are a lot of people who just believe these prophetic words and doctrines without question. They seem to have such an adoration and worship of the prophets that they never consider judging prophetic words. Many times they don't even consider asking the Lord for confirmation of prophecies they hear. Fear replaces faith, and *"without faith it is impossible to please* [God]" (Hebrews 11:6).

They act impulsively without judging the prophetic words. Many times this kind of reckless behavior robs them of the rest of the Lord. It can disqualify them from entering into the fullness of God's rest because they are chasing false visions and errant prophetic words of another man or woman instead of hearing from God for themselves. They just eat up ill-conceived prophetic words hook, line, and sinker. They lap up the word curses spoken over their lives like a puppy laps up cold milk. They may invest decades working to bring an errant prophetic word to pass in their lives and ministries.

This, of course, delights the enemy because when they are chasing false hopes and false prophetic words, they cannot fulfill God's preordained destinies for their lives. They cannot enter into the rest of the Lord and the fullness of Christ's Kingdom. People like this remain, for the most part, powerless and defeated throughout life. They can at times be caught up in endless cycles of defeat, poverty, depression, helplessness, hopelessness, and look very much like the people that I saw gripped with fear and terror in the vision of the darkness of the approaching storm.

I don't want to sit under that kind of prophetic teaching. I don't want to submit to that kind of defeatist doctrine that devalues the finished work of Christ and the tree of Calvary. Do you? Praise God! I have some good news. Yes, it is true; there is a dark storm coming. And it is most likely that America will come under the curse of Zechariah 2:8 if we do not resolutely support and stand with Israel. Yes, there will be a downfall of mammon, and the financial stability of America and the world will continue to be shaken. The idol of mammon as we know it will certainly fall and perhaps collapse entirely. However, in all of these things we are more than conquerors in Christ Jesus.

Nevertheless, we need to understand that in the midst of these possible events we can rise above the storm as we choose to make the secret place of the Most High God our refuge. We can rise above the storm as we keep our gaze and minds focused upon the Messiah. We can be diligent and learn to enter into the rest of the Lord and rise above the darkness and evil of the storm. God is more than able to keep us in perfect peace and safety.

I want to conclude by saying, if the Lord is instructing you to learn to grow crops and develop a self-sufficient or survivalist lifestyle, then by all means please be obedient to the Lord in that. However, I would also recommend that you seek the Lord diligently and make sure that you are being motivated by the Holy Spirit and not by a spirit of fear. Learn to rest in the Lord in all things and hear His voice clearly.

We need to seek God's wisdom at this hour. We need to seek God's face at this hour. We need to begin to intercede and conscientiously pray to stop these doomsday prophetic words from coming to pass in our lives and within our nations. *"The LORD's hand is not shortened, That it cannot save; Nor His ear heavy, That it cannot hear"* (Isaiah 59:1). When we cry out in the mighty name of Jesus for mercy and not judgments, our heavenly Father hears our prayers. I know that the Lord is good, and His mercy is everlasting. His truth endures to all generations (see Psalm 100:5). We can change the destiny of our lives and of our nation on our knees, because the God of the universe is listening to our prayers and His eyes are upon our actions at this hour. God is seeking those who will be diligent to enter into His rest and change the world in their sphere of influence. A shaking is coming, but when we trust and rest in the Lord we can experience the most prosperous and productive times of our lives. There is good news on the way!

CHAPTER 8

Good News in the Midst of the Storm!

Let me encourage you that you do not need to live in a cave and eat taters. Not unless you want to. I remember when someone once asked Derek Prince if a Christian could have a demon. He told them that a Christian can have anything that he wants to have. There is a mouthful of wisdom in that statement. Do you want to suffer? You can. Do you want to be overcome by fear and yokes of darkness as the storm approaches? You can. Or do you want to walk in the spirit of a conqueror that Christ has for you? You can do that too!

How? We need to be diligent to enter into the rest of the Lord. The most important thing that you need to accomplish that goal is to hear the Lord's voice clearly. You need to learn to hear the voice of the Holy Spirit for yourself. You need to learn to hear the voice of God clearly and then be quick to obey what He tells you to do. That is obedience. As you learn to hear the Lord and to walk in obedience, you can rise above the dark storm and ride on a mighty white charger as an overcomer and conqueror.

Mice or Men—
Small Acts of Obedience Can Open Huge Doors

On the Day of Atonement 2011, the Lord reminded me of an experience that I had as a new believer. I had just had a supernatural visitation of the Lord Jesus, and He told me that He was calling me to be an artist, an author, and an evangelist. I was living in a little house at 121 Beech Street. It was a little run down, but I decided to fix up the basement and make a small art studio down there.

I painted the dirty walls and ceilings and set up a work station. However, there weren't enough electrical outlets to power the lights and the little space heater. So I ran an extension cord from the kitchen to the basement, which enabled me to see and to stay warm. After the first night in the little makeshift art studio, I was really happy that I was able to finish a miniature watercolor painting. I fell into my prayer room delighted to be doing a little something that the Lord had told me. I was trying to be obedient. It is amazing how seemingly small acts of obedience can open huge doors of Kingdom opportunities (see Isaiah 22:22).

The circumstances of my life were quite difficult at that time. So setting up an art studio and beginning the process of creating works of art was a real stretch for me. I did it with smoke and mirrors so to speak. But I did it because I thought this would be pleasing to Jesus. Right on queue the enemy sought to derail my efforts by seeking to initiate an atmosphere of fear within my mind. Some of the biggest and most important spiritual battles that we will fight take place right between our ears. Our minds are often the most important battleground. That is why we need to learn to hear God's voice clearly today.

The next evening when I went into the basement to work on a new painting, the extension cord had been chewed up and there were pieces of it everywhere. It was ruined. I put a new one in its place and worked that night. The next morning the new cord was also destroyed and chewed into a million pieces. A thought wormed its way into my mind: *There must be a very big rat down here to do that.* I hate rats; they make my skin crawl. I tried for several days to catch the rat without success. In the meantime I lost a few more extension cords to this monstrous rat invader. In my mind the rat had grown to the size of a leviathan.

When I prayed and asked the Lord for some wisdom, He instructed me to bring my old cat named Hobo over to spend the night in the basement. Again, I heard the Lord speak to me and I moved in obedience to His instructions. I must admit, I was skeptical that Hobo could handle a rat the size of the one that was eating up my extension cords. I was sure that this rat was immense. The behemoth was stealing my productivity and my peace of mind. By this time my mind had blown this rat up to be a giant; and Hobo and I were just grasshoppers in the beast's sight. I thought that this destructive invader must surely be at least the size of a groundhog. At that time I did not know about the importance of bringing my thoughts into captivity for Christ Jesus, as Paul tells us in 2 Corinthians 10:5.

Well, the very next day I put Hobo, the great mouser, in the basement and waited to hear a noisy and vicious confrontation. Hobo was a rare ridgeback Appalachian swamp cat with lineage going back to the swamp behind Gooseneck Road near Aiken, South Carolina. By the way, Hobo went on to be with the Lord on October 6, 2011. He was an amazing cat, and I am sure that he is in the heavenly realms by now. He is most likely laying around in the heather and flowers of the fields of Psalm 23 and chasing after the multicolored butterflies that linger on the gentle breezes there. But I digress.

After about three minutes, I heard Hobo scratching on the door. When I opened it He had a tiny mouse to display as a trophy to me. In fact he had two. *That was quick*, I thought. I could not keep from laughing at myself for allowing my vain imagination to run wild. I had turned a pair of tiny, relatively harmless mice into a leviathan and terrifying hobgoblin. I never lost another extension cord. Learning to hear God and obeying Him had paid off!

You see, what I had built up in my mind to be a monstrously large and deadly rat was merely a couple of tiny mice. I share this Hobo testimony to say this: The Lord spoke to me on the Day of Atonement and explained that this massive approaching dark storm is just like that monstrously large and deadly rat. It is an illusion. It is like a tiny mouse. The approaching darkness and storm is exactly like the principle of 1 Peter 5:8: *"Be sober, be vigilant; because your adversary the devil walks about like a roaring lion, seeking whom he may devour."*

Although the enemy may walk about *like* a roaring lion, he is *not*. In fact, Jesus totally defeated, disabled, and disarmed him on the Cross. What's more, the Lord Jesus Christ gave you and me all power and authority over the enemy when He rose from the dead after three days (see Luke 9:1; Matthew 10:1; Mark 6:7). But some of us are like I was at Beech Street. We think of the enemy as a monstrously large and terrifying hobgoblin capable of causing us great harm. In our vain imaginations and unregenerate minds, he may *seem* like a roaring lion, but he is not. The reason for this is that he has been permanently defeated. No, he is not a monstrously large and deadly rat; he is a tiny harmless mouse. The enemy is not the king of the jungle anymore; he is totally vanquished and subjugated by Christ. We need to get this revelation—the devil is defeated, dethroned, and powerless! That is unless we give him any power through the fear that he seeks to instill within our hearts, minds, and soul. Doubt and fear are two of the enemy's most successful deceptions. We need to remember that *"God has not given us a spirit of fear, but* [a spirit] *of power and of love and of a sound mind"* (2 Timothy 1:7).

Rising Above Your Enemy

In the second book of the trilogy, *The Reality of Angelic Ministry Today, Dancing with Angels 2: The Role of the Holy Spirit and Open Heavens in Activating Your Angelic Encounters*, I wrote about an experience in which I was allowed to ascend into the courtroom of heaven. There I saw the devil, and he was ranting and bringing all sort of railing accusations against me in the presence of the Lord. I mention this incident because during that experience I saw the enemy as he truly is, defeated, dethroned, and powerless.

In the presence of Almighty Father God, the enemy cowers and shakes with unquenchable fear. It is only through lies and deception that he has convinced mankind that he is powerful. Once the Body of Christ receives this revelation, they will walk in the victory and power that the Lord Jesus Christ purchased for each of us on the Cross of Calvary. Victory is ours! One of the most important keys to accessing our rightful place of dominance and victory is by understanding that we can enter into the rest of the Lord. In the vision of the dark storm, the people had the opportunity to rise above the circumstances, and you can too.

As I waited upon the Lord on the Day of Atonement, the Lord reminded me of this experience, and said, "This dark storm is a lot like that. People believe that it is going to be overpowering, but I have overcome the world [see John 16:33]. I have overcome the storm. Even though many of My people believe the lies of the enemy, he is defeated. Just like Hobo defeated those little mice quickly, so shall I quickly overcome and calm the approaching darkness and storm [see Mark 4:39]. However, it is imperative that My people keep their eyes focused upon Me in the midst of the storm. There are many people today who know about Me, but they do not know Me. Just like My disciples continued to cower in fear even after I came into the boat with them, so do these people cower in fear from the storm. Like My disciples, they do not know Me yet. Therefore, they must begin to learn My ways. My yoke is easy, and My burden is light [Matthew 11:30]."

Whoever is born of God will overcome the world. Friends of God will have the victory and overcome the world through faith in the Son of God (see 1 John 5:4). The ones who will overcome the storms of this world are those who believe that the Christ is the Son of God. They will seek to know Him and will be diligent to enter into the rest of the Lord. They will learn to develop a personal relationship with the Messiah. These sons and daughters of God will become well able to hear the slightest whisper of the Holy Spirit and respond in immediate obedience. These overcomers will enter easily into the rest of the Lord and be led by the Spirit of God in the midst of the storm. The world will see the glory of God arise upon them.

So shall it be with this approaching storm for those who truly know the Lord. God's friends will develop their ability to hear His voice and walk in obedience to Him. The approaching darkness will be of little consequence to them. It need not affect them to any great degree unless they choose to allow the approaching darkness to engulf them. We need to enforce our spiritual boundaries and learn the reality of who we actually are in Christ. The blood of Jesus has made us kings and priests who can enter into the rest of the Lord. In this hour be careful of doctrine and prophecies that bring the Cross of Christ and the victory of the Lord's atonement to little or no effect. Remember, you can have whatever you wish. You can walk in suffering and defeat, or you can walk in God's perfect peace and total victory. The choice is yours! You can have whatever you want!

As the Day of Atonement continued, the Lord continued to speak to me from Matthew 7. The Holy Spirit also reminded me about of the testimony of a man who lived in the prophetic community. He stood for God and His Christ and found victory. We can learn from his testimony. He was saved from a lot of aggravation and hard work by hearing God for himself. You see, He was given a prophetic word that a great winter storm was approaching. I share this story in the next chapter.

CHAPTER 9

The Importance of Hearing God in the Middle of the Storm

Whoever hears these sayings of Mine

Therefore whoever hears these sayings of Mine, and does them, I will liken him to a wise man who built his house on the rock: and the rain descended, the floods came, and the winds blew and beat on that house; and it did not fall, for it was founded on the rock (Matthew 7:24-25).

It is absolutely imperative that we each learn to hear the voice of Jesus at this hour. We need to learn to recognize the voice of God as the storms of life approach. The Lord encouraged us that the people who can hear His voice well are considered to be wise men who built their houses upon rock. Why? One reason is because if we hear the Lord clearly, we will recognize false prophets and errant prophetic words. You can know the truth and the truth can really set you free (John 8:32). Trust in the Lord and build your life according to His will and in obedience to His plans for your divine destiny. Build upon the whole Word of God, the more sure word of prophecy. Build your life upon the Rock!

The Prophet and the Snowstorm

I once knew a man who lived in a prophetic community. He had been praying according to the principle of Philippians 4:6-7, asking the Lord about firewood. The Lord spoke to this man and told him that the winter would be extremely mild and that he would not need a great deal of firewood. The Lord told him it would be unseasonably warm and it would not snow at all that winter. He heard the Holy Spirit clearly for himself. He trusted what he had been told by the Lord because he had been developing a personal relationship with the Lord. This development enabled him to hear the voice of God clearly and to be led by the Lord's Spirit. This is an excellent example of entering into the rest of the Lord.

That same fall a well-respected and well-known prophet of the Lord came to the area to minister. This prophet spoke a prophetic word about the weather for the coming winter. Basically his prophecy said that it was going to be one of the worst winters in decades and the people needed to stock up on food and prepare by arranging for alternative heat sources. The prophet said that there would be times when the people of the area would be stranded in their homes for up to six weeks without electricity because of the great amount of snow that was going to fall.

A neighbor who lived near the man came to his house and told him every detail about the prophet's prophetic word. The neighbor repeated the prophecy excitedly, saying that it was going to be one of the worst winters in decades and the people needed to stock up on food and prepare by arranging for alternative heat sources. The neighbor seemed to be anxious and quite concerned about the seasoned prophet's prophecy. The neighbor asked the man what he was going to do in preparation for the one of the worst winters in decades. "Nothing," responded the first man, "we are going to have an extremely mild winter and you don't need to be concerned about these things."

The neighbor became angry because the other man did not believe the prophetic word about it being one of the worst winters in decades. The neighbor became offended because the man did not agree with the seasoned prophet's prophetic word. The neighbor was upset because the man actually had the audacity to disagree with a prophetic word given by the seasoned prophet.

Many in the community began to make far-reaching and drastic arrangements in preparation for one of the worst winters in decades. Those preparations took a lot of money and hard work. For many folks these preparations were motivated by anxiety and not the peace of God. Some invested a lot of time and energy to get goods and new stoves and to stock up on wood, food, medical supplies, and other stuff. Many people were motivated by fear produced by the prophecy.

The man from the prophetic community rested in the Lord. He enjoyed the fall and relaxed as the seasons changed. He trusted that he had heard the Lord clearly. Fall slowly turned into winter. The community experienced a beautiful Indian summer. The weather was mild and warm. In fact, the man from the prophetic community did not have to use his fireplace until mid-November. December, January, and February passed without snow, and the temperatures were very nice, even unseasonably warm. March came and went with no snow. Finally spring came and winter ended. It did not snow all winter long; but three days into spring, a snowstorm came and snow covered the ground. When the sun came out the next day, the snow melted away quickly.

When this happened the man from the prophetic community rejoiced in the Lord. He was grateful that he had heard the voice of the Lord clearly. He was also a little sad for his neighbors. Was the well-respected prophet a false prophet? The answer is no. However, the well-respected prophet did give an errant prophetic word. The seasoned prophet missed it. The result was that many people just believed the prophetic word without seeking to hear the Lord for themselves. They did not even think about testing the prophecy. As a result, some of the people invested a lot of energy, time, and money in things that were not really necessary.

Anxious for Nothing

Many people grew anxious for nothing because they did not test the prophetic word. They did not pray for themselves according to the scriptural principle of Philippians 4:6-7: *"Be anxious for nothing, but in everything by prayer and supplication, with thanksgiving, let your requests be made known to God; and the peace of God, which surpasses all understanding, will guard your hearts and minds through Christ Jesus."* They did not seek the Lord, and perhaps it is possible that they did not trust the Lord to care for them and sought to protect themselves in their own might and strength.

These things were not sinful or actually wrong, just unnecessary. However, we need to judge prophecies. If we do, then we can avoid a lot of unnecessary anxiety and work. We need to be diligent to enter into the rest of the Lord. We need to trust the Lord and build our house on the rock. There may well come a time when we will need to take actions like the last testimony outlined. However, it is also very important that we seek to hear the voice of the Lord clearly for ourselves. That is the best course of action. Listen to the prophets, but judge each prophetic word individually. Allow Holy Spirit to guide you and lead you as you learn to be led by Him. This is a better way. Hear the Lord for yourself. If you listen to every prophetic word that comes along, you might find yourself "as dizzy as a termite in a yoyo," as one ole boy puts it. Trust me, that is not a good position to be in, especially in the midst and darkness of a storm!

I want to encourage you to keep your spirit, soul, body, and entire being focused upon the Lord. Feed upon His Word daily. Pray to Him often. Speak to Him as a man does with a friend. Talk to Him until you develop your ability to hear the voice of the precious Holy Spirit even when He speaks to you in the faintest whisper. This is the hour to draw close to the Lord. And as you draw close to Him, you will be learning how to enter into the rest of the Lord. You will be developing your spirit to be diligent to seek Him. When the storm approaches you will be hidden in the secret place of the Most High God (Psalm 91:1). You will be protected and the God of Peace will keep you in safety and health (vv. 2-16). He will supply all of your needs (Philippians 4:19). Jesus will keep you in perfect peace as you learn to keep your eyes focused upon Him (Isaiah 26:3).

By doing these simple things, you will initiate the process of being diligent to enter into the rest of the Lord. Most of the time you will discover the storms of life will swiftly and supernaturally pass you by. Even those that are predicted by seasoned prophetic individuals will pass away very quickly and have no lasting consequence in your life as you learn to trust in the Lord and enter into His rest. Just like the snowstorm predicted in the last testimony, when the sun came out the next day, the snow melted quickly and its impact was soon but a memory.

Having shared all of this, it *is* important to prepare for this approaching storm. A perfect storm is on the horizon. However, we can rise above the storms of life by resting in the Lord and seeking God's wisdom in every situation. We need to *"be anxious for nothing, but in everything by prayer and supplication, with thanksgiving, let your requests be made known to God; and the peace of God, which surpasses all understanding, will guard your hearts and minds through Christ Jesus"* (Philippians 4:6-7). Really, it is all about learning how to trust God and learning how to be diligent to enter into the rest of the Lord.

Perhaps now would be a good time for you to pray to the Lord and consider these things. Take a moment to speak to God as a man does to his friend. Perhaps, you may wish to do a little soul searching and ask the Holy Spirit to reveal any hidden dependence you have upon anything other than God that you have allowed to take root in your heart and spirit. It is possible that the precious Holy Spirit may reveal something to you. If you need to, take some time to speak to God about this now. We will look at more keys that will empower us to hear God clearly and to be led by the Spirit of God during the midst of the perfect storm in the next chapter.

CHAPTER 10

The Perfect Storm Is on the Horizon

In the vision, the approaching dark storm seemed to be irresistible. It was the proverbial "perfect storm." Is there actually such a thing as a perfect storm? In fact, there have been several perfect storms. Usually they are caused by a series of metrological phenomena that fall in a perfect order to create a once-in-a-lifetime weather event. These so-called perfect storms usually cause a great deal of damage in the natural realm.

The storm of gross darkness was also being birthed by a series of supernatural events that were perfectly aligned with the unfolding of history of the human race. In other words, these events unfolded exactly as the Lord had planned them to occur. Remember, our God is a chronological God. The perfect storm, this storm of gross darkness I saw in the vision, was actually a part of the Lord's perfect plan. Scriptures refer to how the Lord releases weather patterns and stormy attributes in the natural.

I have written in *The Reality of Angelic Ministry Today* trilogy how an increase in angelic visitations and activities will also affect the earthly weather patterns. I believe that the Lord is beginning to speak from His throne of mercy, grace, and judgment. As a result, there are meteorological phenomena that are manifesting upon the earth in a precise order. In the natural these can easily be labeled perfect storms. Actually they are supernatural signs and wonders released as Christ's Kingdom of Heaven invades and crashes into the earthly realms.

Nahum 1:3 gives a great example of this Kingdom dynamic: *"The Lord is slow to anger and great in power, And will not at all acquit the wicked. The Lord has His way In the whirlwind and in the storm, And the clouds are the dust of His feet."* As I pondered the vision of the dark storm on the Day of Atonement, this was one of the scriptures that the Holy Spirit dropped into my heart. Another passage that the Lord placed in my heart associated with the storm that I witnessed is found in Exodus 34:6-7: *"The Lord passed before him and proclaimed, 'The Lord, the Lord God, merciful and gracious, longsuffering, and abounding in goodness and truth, keeping mercy for thousands, forgiving iniquity and transgression and sin, by no means clearing the guilty, visiting the iniquity of the fathers upon the children and the children's children to the third and the fourth generation.'"*

We are living in that hour, and the Lord is accelerating both His mercy and His justice and judgments. Again, it is a season of reaping the seeds that we have sown. God is truly showing mercy, graciousness, and longsuffering; and He is abounding in goodness and truth. God is keeping mercy for thousands, forgiving iniquity and transgression and sin. It is a kairos or God-ordained moment of time to receive the forgiveness and remission of our sins through the finished work and cleansing blood of the Messiah.

On the other hand, the Lord is preparing to allow the release of this approaching darkness. This perfect storm is designed to draw the people to the Lord. He will forgive our iniquity, transgressions, and sin. However, at the same time, the Lord will by no means exonerate the guilty who do not repent. There will be an acceleration of the generational curses, as God will ascribe the iniquity of the fathers upon the children and the children's children to the third and the fourth generation. That is one reason why we see such an increase of debauchery, godlessness, and witchcraft in America and beyond.

This is a knowing that I received as I watched the darkness of the storm engulf the masses of terrified people below me while the vision unfolded. Occasionally an individual would recognize the Lord and turn to Him. They would be saved and then they would rise above their circumstances and the darkness of the storm. They would be saved, or born from above, or born again. The Lord would impute their iniquities and cover their sin. The Lord did this in my life when I was saved or born from above. My testimony mirrors this Kingdom dynamic. (An audio CD or digital Mp3 of Kevin's testimony is available for free in the King of Glory Ministries International Online Resource Center: www.kingofgloryministries.org/store.)

Psalm 32:1-2 demonstrates this attribute of God: *"Blessed is he whose transgression is forgiven, Whose sin is covered. Blessed is the man to whom the LORD does not impute iniquity."*

As the vision of the dark storm continued, I witnessed it cover the whole earth. As it did, the Lord spoke to me saying, "My eyes are turned towards America." On July 9, 2011, the Lord had shaken me to consciousness and said to me, "I am about to shake America because of the sins of pride and arrogance." (If you are interested in learning more about this experience, I have written a small book titled *America Pray for the Peace of Jerusalem NOW!*) Somehow I understood that the storm that I was seeing in this vision on the Day of Atonement in 2011 was directly related to that encounter with the Holy Spirit on July 9, 2011.

It is absolutely imperative that America, as a nation, begins to pray for our own salvation, for the peace of the Jerusalem, and for the nation of Israel. America's destiny is inexorably linked to Israel, and we must stand firm as a partner with Israel at this hour. If we fail to fully support Israel, I believe that there will be direct consequences for the USA. In fact, the storm that I was witnessing in the vision was correlated to how America as a nation responds to Israel at this hour.

I encourage you to please pray for the peace of Jerusalem.

When the eyes of the Lord turn to an individual or an entire people group, it is very important (see Psalm 14:2). The Lord will continue to test America. Second Chronicles 16:9 is a very relevant and timely scripture for America at this hour: *"For the eyes of the LORD run to and fro throughout the whole earth, to show Himself strong on behalf of those whose heart is loyal to Him. In this you have done foolishly; therefore from now on you shall have wars."*

In the church we often quote the first part of scripture. However, we seldom quote the second half. If the Lord sees foolish behavior, what could well be termed iniquity and sin, then there is a consequence: *"From now on you shall have wars."*

I encourage you to please pray for the peace of America at this hour too. We need to repent. Our nation must return to God Almighty, Elohim, the Creator of heaven and earth, while there is still an open window to repent and to return to the Lord. The darkness of the storm will begin to cover the great land of America unless we turn around 180 degrees and repent and turn back to God. Proverbs 15:3 describes how the Lord looks upon a land: *"The eyes of the* Lord *are in every place, Keeping watch on the evil and the good."* We also see how all-encompassing the vision of the Father is in Jeremiah 16:17: *"For My eyes are on all their ways; they are not hidden from My face, nor is their iniquity hidden from My eyes."*

The Lord is watching carefully and rewards us according to the fruit of our doings. We can see that dynamic in Jeremiah 32:19: *"You are great in counsel and mighty in work, for your eyes are open to all the ways of the sons of men, to give everyone according to his ways and according to the fruit of his doings."* That is the season that America as a nation is moving into at this hour. As I said earlier, it is a season for reaping the seeds that have been sown. We must take time to gaze inwardly into our hearts as individuals and as a nation. We must repent for any iniquities and sin that we are harboring secretly in our hearts. After all, the heart is wicked and we really do not know many of the secret issues and secret sins that are hidden within it (see Jeremiah 17:9). The good news is that God is very willing and can easily help us to overcome our iniquities and the hidden agendas that are hidden deep within our hearts.

In the vision, I was amazed and astounded by the sheer numbers of God's angels that rode in through the rip in the sky with the Messiah. I observed God's angels move and ride over the masses of people below them. These angels were also looking intently at the individuals below. The angels were just waiting for one to turn to the Lord and to repent. When an individual would take their eyes off of the storm and recognize Jesus and see the glory of God, an angelic rider would immediately reach out and pull that saint up above the darkness.

God's angels worked to help the people rise above the evil of the storm. This multitude of angelic beings also constituted the eyes of the Lord spoken of in Zechariah 4:10: *"For who has despised the day of small things? For these seven rejoice to see The plumb line in the hand of Zerubbabel. They are the eyes of the LORD, Which scan to and fro throughout the whole earth."* "These seven" represent the seven spirits of God, the Holy Spirit. However, the eyes of the Lord can also represent the Lord's angelic hosts. During this encounter on the Day of Atonement, I discovered that there are many different types of God's angels.

We are in an hour of evaluation that is being executed by the Lord and His hosts, angelic co-laborers. That is one reason for the vast increase of angelic activity in the earthly realms at this hour. The measuring line or plumb line is in the hand of the Lord. He is measuring our hearts as individuals, as congregations, as regions, as states, and even as nations. This surely includes the nation of America. There is a Kingdom dynamic of holy judgment and reaping that is unfolding in the earth at this hour.

That is one reason that the unrest in Europe, Africa, the Middle East, and beyond is coming to such a boiling point today. It is the work of God. It is the manifestation of nations and people groups reaping the collective seeds that they have sown over the last several decades, even centuries. America will not be immune to these dynamics, and we will begin to see much more turmoil and strife in our land. The riots and demonstrations that we are seeing in Europe and the Middle East will also occur in the USA unless we repent immediately. Darkness and storms will begin to cover the earth. We must remember to keep our eyes squarely focused upon the Lord and His Kingdom. Then we will be supernaturally lifted up above the storms as we are diligent to enter into the rest of the Lord.

We can find true rest and peace in God. We can change the destiny of America or any other nation on our knees. Please allow me to encourage you to pray for mercy and not judgment for the nation of America at this hour. God has placed a wonderful and mighty destiny on America and it is not too late for the people of America to rise up and to seize this God-ordained destiny! However, I believe that we must pray like never before! Pray for America. Pray for the peace of Jerusalem. Pray for America to support and to stand strong with Israel!

The form of these storms will be both spiritual and natural. As they approach, they will affect food supplies. There will surely be spiritual famines too; in fact, these are upon us now. There will be an increase in famine in diverse and unusual places. At times the weather will be too hot, and at others times it will be too cold, too wet, or too dry. We will see the weather patterns change and shift. The climate will shift over entire regions. This will not be the result of "global warming." These changes will be the result of the Lord speaking from His throne of grace, mercy, and, judgment. However, there is great hope for those who know their God.

But in the middle of all of this, the foolish man will build his house on the sand. He will put his faith and confidence in man's wisdom and worldly systems. He will trust in wealth and idol of mammon to protect and save him as the darkness and storms approach. The darkness and the storm shall appear and beat on his house, and it will fall. In fact, the fall of that man, people group, or nation will be spectacular and astonishing to the rest of the earth.

Even now we see nations falling. We see things unfolding that with our carnal minds we deemed impossible even months ago. The wisdom of this world is foolishness in the eyes of God, and the Lord catches the wise in their own craftiness and brings their well-laid plans to nothing (1 Corinthians 3:19). That is why we need the unmerited wisdom and grace of God. We need Christ and His Kingdom in our lives today like never before. We need to be diligent to enter into the rest of the Lord. We need to trust in Jesus Christ as our Rock of Salvation! Let's examine how we can be firmly established upon the Rock in the next chapter.

CHAPTER 11

The Rock—Praise and Worship in the Midst of the Storm

Founded on the rock

Therefore whoever hears these sayings of Mine, and does them, I will liken him to a wise man who built his house on the rock: and the rain descended, the floods came, and the winds blew and beat on that house; and it did not fall, for it was founded on the rock (Matthew 7:24-25).

We need to establish our lives upon the Rock of Christ. For upon Him alone can we stand in this hour. Yes, the darkness and the storm will come. The winds of change will blow, and the terror of the wicked and rain of evil may well descend. But when we are founded, rooted, and established in the Lord, we will stand. We will prevail. We will be more than conquerors in Christ Jesus. It is imperative that we know who we are in Christ and who Christ is in us. We need to be diligent to enter into the rest of the Lord. We need to be certain that our election and callings are sure at this hour (2 Peter 1:10).

In the vision of the storm, Jesus was adamant and told me that His people need to be diligent to enter into the rest of the Lord. We need to know the reality of Christ and the literal truth of His Kingdom like never before.

This is a season to make sure that we are building our faith and lives squarely upon the Rock, the Lord Jesus Christ. We can find several wonderful keys that can help us to do this in Psalm 18. Again, these keys are also useful in helping us to understand how we can enter into the rest of the Lord. I want to encourage you to study this Psalm at this hour. Let it sink down into your spirit. Ask the Holy Spirit to help you understand the surety of Christ as your personal Rock.

> *The LORD is my rock and my fortress and my deliverer; My God, my strength, in whom I will trust; My shield and the horn of my salvation, my stronghold. I will call upon the LORD, who is worthy to be praised; So shall I be saved from my enemies. The pangs of death surrounded me, And the floods of ungodliness made me afraid. The sorrows of Sheol surrounded me; The snares of death confronted me. In my distress I called upon the LORD, And cried out to my God; He heard my voice from His temple, And my cry came before Him, even to His ears. Then the earth shook and trembled; The foundations of the hills also quaked and were shaken, Because He was angry. Smoke went up from His nostrils, And devouring fire from His mouth; Coals were kindled by it (Psalm 18:2-8).*

We need to decree and declare that Jesus is our Rock and our strong tower. We need to call out to God. He is more than able to deliver us from the approaching storm because in the Lord we have a stronghold and place of total safety. At times it is absolutely necessary to begin to praise the Lord in the midst of the darkness and the storm. We need to be like Paul and Silas in Acts 16:25. Even though it may appear that all hell is coming against us, we will need to focus our minds upon God's goodness and praise Him for His loving-kindness. When we praise God He hears our prayers and worship and then He answers on our behalf quickly.

Praising and worshiping the Lord in the midst of the approaching storm will be one way that you can be diligent to enter into the

THE ROCK—PRAISE AND WORSHIP IN THE MIDST OF THE STORM

rest of the Lord. Trust the Lord to hear you, and believe that the Lord will answer. Trust and depend upon the Lord to protect you and to provide for all of your needs. Purpose within your spirit that you will trust in the Lord with all your heart no matter what the circumstances may look like (Proverbs 3:5-6). Remember that the glory of God will surely rise upon you as you turn to Him and seek His Kingdom first (Isaiah 60:1).

Don't get into the habit of depending upon your own wisdom, resources, and knowledge to solve problems. Don't base your actions solely upon prophetic words. Rather, in everything that you plan and do, acknowledge Christ and He shall direct your paths. He shall give you peace in the middle of the storm. He shall make a way where there seems to be none. He will give you peace in a way that you will not be able to comprehend with your carnal mind (Philippians 4:7-8). Keep your spirit and mind focused upon Jesus in the midst of the storm and He will be your true peace. Again, these are keys that can help you to be diligent to enter into the rest of the Lord.

> *He bowed the heavens also, and came down With darkness under His feet. And He rode upon a cherub, and flew; He flew upon the wings of the wind. He made darkness His secret place; His canopy around Him was dark waters And thick clouds of the skies (Psalm 18:9-11).*

Remember, the Lord is in the midst of the storm. You are not alone. Just turn your gaze upon Jesus and you will see the glory of God. In the midst of the darkness, the Lord has a secret place that you can enter and find solace and safety. You can mount up and ride with the Lord and His angelic hosts. You can be transformed into an overcomer in the midst of the storm. In the greatest darkness, the glory of God can be reflected from you in the most brilliant way. You can be a beacon of light. God can use you to pierce the curtain of darkness that has blinded your brothers' and sisters' searching eyes. The world will see Christ in you in the middle of the darkness and storm. Arise and shine!

> *From the brightness before Him, His thick clouds passed with hailstones and coals of fire. The* LORD *thundered from heaven, and the Most High uttered His voice, Hailstones and coals of fire. He sent out His arrows and scattered the foe, Lightnings in abundance, and He vanquished them (Psalm 18:12-14).*

Again it is very important to remember that the Lord is in the midst of the storm. You are not alone. God created the approaching darkness for His purposes. The Lord and the glory of God will be seen in the ultimate darkness and the Lord will orchestrate the angelic hosts of heaven to war on your behalf. The sword of the Lord is all-powerful. From the tip of Christ's sword, lightening will penetrate the gross darkness and cripple the evil therein.

The eyes of the Lord are in the midst of the storm. Jesus is able to see everything that seeks hiddenness in the darkness. But evil cannot hide from the burning eyes of Christ. He will execute judgment on the demonic realm and pierce them with His sword. That is why we need to be diligent to enter the rest of the Lord because He will fight on our behalf. When we cease from *our* works, He will begin to work for us (see Hebrews 4:10). This is true for all aspects of our lives. However, if we allow doubt and a hardened heart of unbelief to overwhelm us and if we permit our eyes to focus on the storm, we then fall into disobedience (see Mark 6:52; 8:17). Fear will replace faith, and if this occurs you will not have the liberty to enter into the rest of the Lord.

Therefore, we need to remember that the Word of God, the sword of the Lord, *"is living and powerful, and sharper than any two-edged sword, piercing even to the division of soul and spirit, and of joints and marrow, and is a discerner of the thoughts and intents of the heart"* (Hebrews 4:12). The Messiah has defeated and overcome the darkness of the storm on our behalf with His finished work of Calvary. The evil enemies of our Lord cannot hide from His sight because *"there is no creature hidden from His sight, but all things are naked and open to the eyes of Him to whom we must give account"* (v. 13). We are victorious in Christ our Rock! Let each individual therefore praise God and be diligent to enter into His rest. Be diligent to stand upon the Rock. Let us prophesy into the darkness of the storms of our lives: *Christ is my Rock and may He forever be exalted!* As I saw in my vision, it is no accident that the words "The Rest of the Lord" are inscribed upon the Lord's mighty sword.

> *The LORD lives! Blessed be my Rock! Let the God of my salvation be exalted. It is God who avenges me, And subdues the peoples under me; He delivers me from my enemies. You also lift me up above those who rise against me; You have delivered me from the violent man (Psalm 18:46-48).*

As we learn to exalt the Rock, Christ will deliver us from our enemies. Jesus will begin to fight for each of us and will subdue the darkness that seeks to oppress His saints. He will avenge each of us and will lift us up above the storm and the evil that seeks to come against us. God will deliver us from the storm and the violence therein as we learn to trust in Him and seek to diligently enter into His rest. We must allow the Lord to war on our behalf at times and cease from our own efforts.

> *Therefore I will give thanks to You, O LORD, among the Gentiles, And sing praises to Your name. Great deliverance He gives to His king, And shows mercy to His anointed, To David and his descendants forevermore (Psalm 18:49-50).*

In the midst of the storm, we must give thanks to the Lord. We need to praise Him for the great deliverance and victories that He is freely giving to each of us, His anointed. The Lord will show each of us mercy when we choose to stand firmly upon the Rock of our salvation, trusting in Him to fight on our behalf because we have the liberty to enter into His rest. Praising God in the midst of the storms of life is a wise course of action at this hour.

Psalm 40 is a wonderful promise from the Lord about standing upon the Rock of Christ. It describes how God will help us to overcome the storms or life and enter into His rest.

I waited patiently for the LORD; And He inclined to me, And heard my cry. He also brought me up out of a horrible pit, Out of the miry clay, And set my feet upon a rock, And established my steps. He has put a new song in my mouth-Praise to our God; Many will see it and fear, And will trust in the LORD. Blessed is that man who makes the LORD his trust, And does not respect the proud, nor such as turn aside to lies. Many, O LORD my God, are Your wonderful works which You have done; And Your thoughts toward us cannot be recounted to You in order; If I would declare and speak of them, they are more than can be numbered (Psalm 40:1-5).

When we rest in the Lord, there is a supernatural exchange that takes place. The Lord directs our paths. And by learning to trust in the Lord, we are established and blessed by God. He thinks about us always and is constantly seeking ways that He can help us and protect us. The Lord listens to our prayers and answers when we rest in Him. Choosing to move into the secret place of the Most High God will also enable us to enter into the fullness of rest of the Lord. We will look at keys that will help us to enter into the secret place in the next chapter.

CHAPTER 12

The Storms of Life and the Foolish Man

But everyone who hears these sayings of Mine, and does not do them, will be like a foolish man who built his house on the sand: and the rain descended, the floods came, and the winds blew and beat on that house; and it fell. And great was its fall (Matthew 7:26-27).

As I watched the dark storm from a place of safety upon the Messiah's mighty white charger, I could see many foolish people below me. Their world as they knew it was crashing down and they were panicking. Some were aware of the fact that there was a God. But they just had never taken the time to get to know Him. This was true for not only the lost but also for many of those who knew about Christ. Yet because they had not prepared, they were falling. They were terrified, and they had also lost all hope. Some of the people did not even believe that God exists (see Psalm 14:1).

This will bring forth a great opportunity for evangelism in the midst of the darkness of the approaching storm. The Lord will open unprecedented doors in many formerly unreachable nations for the true Gospel of the Kingdom not only to be preached but also to be demonstrated with the power of God. In the midst of the darkness and the storm, God will begin to raise up men, women, and children who will know Him intimately. They will do great and mighty exploits in the name of the Lord (see Daniel 11:32).

The glory of the Lord will shine upon them and great miracles will be performed in the name of Jesus Christ of Nazareth. As these glorious ones stretch forth their hands, the Lord will work with them and perform great miracles and signs and wonders to confirm the Gospel that they declare and preach to the lost in the middle of the darkness. Many will be saved and learn to enter into the rest of the Lord. They too will learn to rise above the circumstances of the storm and join the rest of the Lord. Power evangelism will explode in the midst of the darkness and multitudes will be born from above and receive the Messiah as Lord and Savior.

There is a grace to call out to our Savior at this season. We should seek the Lord while He may be found. We must seek the Lord while there is still a grace and opportunity to do so. We find a beautiful promise for those who are far away from God in Isaiah 55:6-7: *"Seek the Lord while He may be found, Call upon Him while He is near. Let the wicked forsake his way, And the unrighteous man his thoughts; Let him return to the Lord, And He will have mercy on him; And to our God, For He will abundantly pardon."* Let us return to the Lord!

Yes, we are still in a time and season of mercy and grace. However, the Lord will not strive with us forever. Now is the time for us to return to the Lord with all of our heart, soul, and our entire mind to obtain abundant mercy and everlasting grace. Psalm 103:9 also makes this fact perfectly clear: *"He will not always strive with us, Nor will He keep His anger forever."* (See also Genesis 6:3.)

Move into the Secret Place of the Most High

The Lord has been actively dealing with our hearts for several years seeking to draw and woo us closer to Him. Many who call themselves Christians are far from God. They have sought to go their own ways and make their own plans in these uncertain times. The result has been that many have found themselves sliding and slipping further into uncertainty, unhappiness, and ungodly fear more than ever before.

Many have resisted the Lord's Spirit as He has sought to woo and romance our hearts. Now many feel that they are far from God and

His grace and favor. That is the result of the works of our flesh and not the Lord's perfect heart for each of us. The work of the Spirit will always draw us into a closer place of intimacy and communion with the Lord. That is exactly the place that the Lord's desire is for us to be at this hour. He is calling us to enter into the rest of the Lord. However, when the darkness of the storm approached, those who were not prepared were overcome with fear and anxiety.

In the vision of the dark storm, those who did not know Jesus were lost. They may have known who God was but they did not have any substantial personal relationship with Him. They were not aware of the principles of Christ's Kingdom. They were not well versed in the Word of God. Because of this they were helpless as the onslaught of evil crept out into their sphere of influence as the storm edged closer to them. They did not know or understand how to use the Word of God as a weapon of spiritual warfare. They were like fodder as the demonic hordes of the enemy placed all sorts of ungodly yokes or darkness upon their necks. I was astonished to discover that the majority of these people were unaware of the evil devices with which they were burdened and yoked.

They were not prepared for the spiritual battle because they did not know the Lord Jesus or His Word. They were ill prepared to meet an enemy that was being released by the powers of darkness and spiritual wickedness hidden within the storm. They did not know how to wrestle or fight against the spiritual wickedness and evil. They were not struggling *"against flesh and blood, but against principalities, against powers, against the rulers of the darkness of this world, and against spiritual wickedness in high places"* (Ephesians 6:12, KJV). Many people sought to fight the battle with carnal or intellectual plans and agendas. These will have no substantial effect on the evil powers and principalities within the darkness of the storm. You must begin to learn the Word of God and hide the Scriptures within your heart at this hour.

Praise God there is safety in the midst of the storm! We can choose to make God our refuge and strong tower. When we learn to rest in the Lord, then we empower God All Mighty to fight this evil for us.

We can choose to develop a personal relationship with the Son of God and His precious Holy Spirit. We can personalize the Word of God and say of the Lord,

> *He is my refuge and my fortress; My God, in Him I will trust. Surely He shall deliver me from the snare of the fowler and from the perilous pestilence. He shall cover me with His feathers, and under His wings I shall take refuge; His truth shall be my shield and buckler. I shall not be afraid of the terror by night, nor of the arrow that flies by day, nor of the pestilence that walks in darkness, nor of the destruction that lays waste at noonday. A thousand may fall at my side, and ten thousand at my right hand; but it shall not come near me. Only with my eyes shall I look, and see the reward of the wicked. Because I have made the Lord, who is my refuge, even the Most High, my dwelling place, no evil shall befall me, nor shall any plague come near my dwelling; for He shall give His angels charge over me, to keep me in all of my ways. Amen.*

Pray this scripture from Psalm 91:2-11 in the previous paragraph out loud right now. Make a conscious decision and purpose within your heart to enter into the rest and protection of the Lord today. Choose to dwell in the secret place. Then God is released to fight and war against this evil for you. Then you can rest in Him and His victory! You must learn to stand upon the Word of God, and it will become your Rock as the storm approaches.

New Beginnings

Much of what people are calling "the work of the devil" is actually the Lord shaking the foundations of our lives and ministries and exposing our ungodly beliefs. The Spirit of God is seeking to bring us into a place of protection and safety. The Lord is seeking to position and keep us secure in the approaching darkness and times of uncertainty and upheaval. The Lord is removing some "things" from us to encourage us to rely on Him as our only true source. (See John 15.)

The Lord is removing those things that we have allowed in our lives and ministries that are not of Him. The Lord is also removing those things that we have allowed to become idols in our lives and hearts. These unholy things and beliefs separate us from a holy God. Some of those items are "projects" and agendas that we initiated from within our souls and carnal minds or intellects.

They may have sounded good and looked good to man and they may even appear to be godly, but they were not of God. Therefore, God is removing them. This can even involve ministries and the man-made plans of ministries. This can also involve our personal goals and individual plans. God is redirecting many of our steps at this hour and rearranging the course and structures of our lives. The Lord is giving us a grace to start fresh and new. This shaking will help to position each of us to enter into the rest of the Lord. The Lord is seeking to bring us into geographical obedience. We need to be aware of the gently wooing of the Holy Spirit when He prompts us to move in these times.

We can rebuild by establishing and founding our life and ministries solely upon the Rock of Christ Jesus and the Word of God. For some this seems to be too great of a cost and they are not willing to embrace it; so they will continue to walk and live by their own stamina and power. They will neglect God's best and perfect plans for their lives as a result. (See Numbers 32:13.)

The Lord is allowing strong winds and floods to beat upon our lives. (In some cases this is literal.) Remember the words of Jesus in Matthew 7:24-27: *"Therefore whoever hears these sayings of Mine, and does them, I will liken him to a wise man who built his house on the rock: and the rain descended, the floods came, and the winds blew and beat on that house; and it did not fall, for it was founded on the rock. But everyone who hears these sayings of Mine, and does not do them, will be like a foolish man who built his house on the sand: and the rain descended, the floods came, and the winds blew and beat on that house; and it fell. And great was its fall."*

This parable is a timely and appropriate word for this season. The Lord is allowing His house to be buffered and beaten. (Remember, *we* are His "house.") Everything that we have built that is not founded upon the Rock of Jesus Christ will be demolished and fall. That is great news because we will have ample opportunities to rebuild in God's perfect will if we take the time to allow His pruning and perfect plans to come forth. This is also an important key that we need to understand. We need to be willing to submit to the Lord of the vineyard as we begin to be diligent to enter into the rest of the Lord. We must allow God to prune away everything that hinders us from entering into the fullness of His rest.

There Is a Season of Grace

The Holy Spirit has shown me that there is still a season of grace for us to inspect our foundations and our hearts. I believe that several years, perhaps even decades, remain until we will see a rapid acceleration of this gross darkness and evil spread out into the earth (and throughout America). We are currently in a short season of preparation to cleanse our hearts and our lives in the natural realm. We are entering the hour of Isaiah 60:1-2 when *"darkness shall cover the earth, And deep darkness the people; But the LORD will arise over you, And His glory will be seen upon you."* Of course, the effective fervent prayer of the church can alter this scenario.

The following passage of scripture is very timely for us at this pivotal hour:

> *Likewise the Spirit also helps in our weaknesses. For we do not know what we should pray for as we ought, but the Spirit Himself makes intercession for us with groanings which cannot be uttered. Now He who searches the hearts knows what the mind of the Spirit is, because He makes intercession for the saints according to the will of God. And we know that all things work together for good to those who love God, to those who are the called according to His purpose. For whom He foreknew, He also predestined to be conformed to the image of His Son, that He might be the firstborn among many brethren. Moreover whom He predestined, these He also called; whom*

He called, these He also justified; and whom He justified, these He also glorified. What then shall we say to these things? If God is for us, who can be against us? (Romans 8:26-31).

The Lord is well aware of our weaknesses; and when we fully submit to Him, the Lord is able to transform our weakness into His strength. Jesus Christ has entered into the heavenly places to sit at the right Hand of the Father. Jesus has literally entered into the rest of the Lord as our example. From that place Jesus is praying for you and me. He is making intercession for the saints as one knowing our deepest needs and secret desires (see Romans 8:34).

That is an amazing revelation. When we choose to enter into Christ's rest, we submit to God's preordained purposes and callings for our lives. Then we are perfectly positioned to allow the Spirit of God to transform us into the very image of Jesus Christ. We can grow and mature into our role as a royal priest according to the order of Melchizedek. (If you are a female you can still be a royal priestess!) From that place, what can I say, when God is for us no one, no power, no principality, no demonic being hidden with any dark approaching storm can defeat us! (See Romans 8:35-39.)

On the Day of Atonement in 2012, the Lord Jesus appeared to me in my little prayer room in Moravian Falls. Jesus was dressed in the garments of the royal priesthood. In fact, Jesus was robed in the garments of the royal priesthood according to the order of Melchizedek. As the Lord stood in the room, I became aware of the fact that the mantle or anointing of Melchizedek can only be achieved through entering into the rest of the Lord. And I was given revelation that the rest of the Lord is the key that unlocks the mantle of Melchizedek. Entering into the fullness of Christ's rest is learning to operate and live our lives as a royal priest according to the order of Melchizedek.

One of the aspects of being diligent to enter into the rest of the Lord is beginning to be led by the Holy Spirit. We can learn to allow the Holy Spirit to reveal aspects or dynamics from the spiritual realm to us. This can be called discernment. Discernment is critical to entering into the fullness of the rest of the Lord. As a royal priest according to the order of Melchizedek, you will begin to have the gift of discerning of spirits activated in your life. In the next chapter Paul Cox shares some amazing insights about the mantle of Melchizedek and the gift of discernment. Let's begin to examine this supernatural call upon your life.

CHAPTER 13

Melchizedek and the Gift of Discernment

by Paul L. Cox

In the spring of 2010, I began feeling that we should gather together on the beginning of Pentecost at sundown; so I invited whoever wanted to come and join me at Aslan's Place. I arrived at 7:30 p.m., and a small group assembled as sundown approached. As we waited, we could feel the presence of the Lord increasing; and, as the sunlight disappeared, we felt a slight breeze moving through the room. At 7:50 p.m., the anointing rapidly increased and we felt we were to stand and join hands. But then, all of a sudden, I started running backwards. Now, I want to tell you that I have not even run forward in a long time!

I ran backwards around the living room at a full run seven times. On the final return to my chair, the Lord sat me down, and I asked, "Okay, what was that all about?" Each person had a different idea. One said I was unwinding, another said I was undoing, and another said I was going backwards to something. I was mystified and wondered for many weeks what this meant.

Also during the spring of 2010, the discernment of something new began. I was on the phone with my friend, Pastor Rob Gross from Kaneohe, Hawaii, and together we realized that I was discerning Melchizedek. As I pondered what it meant to discern Melchizedek, I kept saying to others and especially to Rob, "I do not get this." I listened to a set of tapes and read a couple of books about Melchizedek, but I still was not satisfied—I knew that there was something more the Lord wanted me to understand. This was a mystery that I was to comprehend, but what was it?

In searching out the things of God, I often say I need my "aha"—the moment of clarity when all that the Lord is trying to communicate finally makes sense. My aha moment in regard to Melchizedek finally came when I understood that the Lord had taken me back to the very beginning of my training to discern good and evil. And I remembered that the Lord had given me Hebrews 5:14 just after I had conducted my first seminar on discernment, Discerning the Battle. I had returned home from Virginia following that seminar when my friend, Dr. Tom Hawkins, called and said, "The Lord gave me a verse for you." That scripture was Hebrews 5:14; and it became the foundational verse for the call of God on my life to teach discernment. "*But solid food belongs to those who are of full age, that is, those who by reason of use have their senses exercised to discern both good and evil.*" Now, years later, my aha moment occurred when I realized that this verse is right in the middle of the passage about Melchizedek.

After twenty years, the Lord had brought me back to the beginning days and showed me that discernment is really all about recognizing the intercession of Melchizedek. It's about knowing what the Lord Jesus is interceding for in His function as the eternal high priest, Melchizedek, and then doing what the Father is doing. All these years I had been in training, learning to discern many different kinds of spiritual beings; angels, seraphim, cherubim, elders, rulers, elemental spirits, orbs, powers, etc. Now I knew that the purpose of my training had not been just to recognize these beings but also to understand Melchizedek's intercession as the High Priest before the Father. By discerning the spiritual being(s) present, I would be able to see what the Father was doing because He has trained me in regard to their purposes and functions; and I would know how I was to respond based on my discernment. I would understand how to do what the Father is doing.

For years I was told that discernment (the use of the physical senses to know what is going on in the spiritual realm) is not necessary and, indeed, unbiblical. I now understand that not only is discernment necessary but it is *essential* to entering into and understanding the new realms that God has for us.

Who is Melchizedek? Melchizedek is first mentioned in Genesis 14, which tells of nine kings and nations that were warring. Abram became involved in the conflict because Lot, his brother's son, had been taken prisoner. Along with 318 servants, he pursued these enemies, attacking them and rescuing Lot. Then, as Abram returned to the King's Valley with the King of Sodom pursuing him, Melchizedek suddenly appeared before him.

> *Then Melchizedek king of Salem brought out bread and wine; he was the priest of God Most High. And he blessed him and said: "Blessed be Abram of God Most High, Possessor of heaven and earth; And blessed be God Most High, Who has delivered your enemies into your hand." And he gave him a tithe of all (Genesis 14:18–20).*

I believe that Melchizedek is the eternal High Priest who came as Jesus Christ. Melchizedek is the function of Jesus Christ as *THE* eternal High Priest, always interceding for us. As mentioned in scripture, Melchizedek is the King of Peace (Salem) as well as the King of Righteousness.

Melchizedek blessed Abram because the Lord had delivered the enemies of Abram into his hands. Could it be that when we are aware of Melchizedek, it is an indication that the Lord is giving us victory over our enemies? I realized that this is what I had been asking the Lord for. I had been sitting in the Jacuzzi some months before, worn out because I had been battling witchcraft; and I prayed, "*Lord, when do we ever win?*" A righteous anger came up inside me saying, "*How dare these people exercise witchcraft and come against the God Most High?*" I got really angry and asked again, "*God, when do we ever win? Lord, why don't You display Your glory and remove those who come against Your Kingdom plans?"* I prayed for grace and mercy for them; but I also declared, *"O God, arise and destroy Your enemies."*

Isn't it time for God's vengeance against His enemies? Isn't it time for the Kingdom of God to advance? The revelation of Melchizedek would seem to indicate that we are now moving into a period of time in which we will have victory over our enemies.

Melchizedek is a King and a Priest and He belongs to the Order of Melchizedek. Our Heavenly Father has always wanted His people to be an order of kings and priests. In fact, that was His intention for the Children of Israel. However, Israel did not want that—the people refused the position. It was then that the Lord set aside the tribe of Levi to act as priests for the people. But, after the resurrection of Jesus Christ, the Church entered into a new position. Believers are declared to be a "royal priesthood" (1 Peter 2:9)—we are now kingly priests and belong to the order of Melchizedek.

After the brief account of Melchizedek in Genesis, there is no more mention of him until 900 years later during the time of King David, who mentioned Melchizedek in Psalm 110. It is noteworthy that although David was a king, he also once went into the holy place and ate of the table of showbread, therefore acting like a kingly priest. David clearly stated in Psalm 110 that Melchizedek is tied to victory over one's enemies.

> *The LORD said to my Lord, "Sit at My right hand, till I make Your enemies Your footstool." The LORD shall send the rod of Your strength out of Zion. Rule in the midst of Your enemies!... The LORD has sworn And will not relent, "You are a priest forever According to the order of Melchizedek" (Psalm 110: 1-2, 4).*

Now, fast-forward through over 900 additional years before hearing of Melchizedek again. The New Testament book of Hebrews offers the most detailed description of Melchizedek and speaks clearly to us about the High Priestly function of Jesus Christ. In the Hebrews 5-8 we are reminded that Jesus is forever Melchizedek. He is the King of Peace and the King of Righteousness. It is this wonderful Jesus, the Perfect One, who, because of His intercession, enables us to endure and have hope in the future. This Melchizedek is not a priest of the tribe of Levi but of the tribe of Judah. The entire passage crescendos in Hebrews 8:1-2: *"Now this is the main point of the things we are saying: We have such a High Priest, who is seated at the right hand of the throne of the Majesty in the heavens, a Minister of the sanctuary and of the true tabernacle which the Lord erected, and not man."*

But how do we really comprehend Melchizedek? This knowing is not just an "intellectual" knowing but a "discernment" knowing—a knowing that arises through the five physical senses. Melchizedek is difficult to comprehend without physical discernment.

Perhaps it is time to train your senses so that you will know when Melchizedek is interceding so that you may discern the answers of the Father to that priestly intercession. When you discern Melchizedek, then you will understand more fully what the Father is doing. Then, like Jesus, you will be able to do what you see the Father doing. Certainly there is a correlation between Melchizedek and the rest of the Lord. In the next chapter Kevin Basconi will begin to outline this aspect of the rest of the Lord and your role as a royal priesthood according to the order of Melchizedek.

CHAPTER 14

The Rest of the Lord and the Royal Priesthood of Melchizedek

Understanding the rest of the Lord and comprehending how to enter into the rest that Christ has provided is a multifaceted spiritual dynamic. Let's begin to examine more closely the rest of the Lord in a scriptural context. The rest of the Lord refers to a specific day, the Sabbath day (see Exodus 20:9-11). This is the first level of the rest of the Lord. God's preordained rest is both complicated and yet so simple that a child a can attain the peace and divine protection that comes from entering into the rest of the Lord. Scripture sets the example for the rest of the Lord in the second chapter of Genesis.

> *Thus the heavens and the earth, and all the host of them, were finished. And on the seventh day God ended His work which He had done, and He rested on the seventh day from all His work which He had done. Then God blessed the seventh day and sanctified it, because in it* ***He rested from all His work*** *which God had created and made (Genesis 2:1-3, emphasis added).*

The rest of the Lord at times constitutes a spiritual rest.

As with many spiritual aspects of Christ's Kingdom, the rest of the Lord also has many applications and dynamics. Yes, there is a Sabbath rest or Sabbath day. Traditionally in Christ's time the Sabbath day was the seventh day, Saturday. Today many religious people practice the worship of God and recognize the Sabbath day as Sunday. Again, it appears that in the Kingdom of God at times it can be both/and. We will look at the importance of the Sabbath rest in more detail later, but I wanted to mention it here.

However, I believe that the author of Hebrews, under the inspiration of the Holy Spirit, outlined a deeper place that is available to us as we are diligent or labor to enter into the rest of the Lord. Jesus rested from His work when He finalized His mission on earth. The Lord ascended upon High to sit at the right hand of the Father, and Jesus has entered into a season of eternal rest.

The Lord demonstrated for us that we are to enter into a similar lifestyle. We are to rule and reign upon the earth just as the Lord originally intended for us (see Genesis 1:26-28). We are also called and privileged to enter into the rest of the Lord. This dual ability is a facet of our spiritual DNA and our heritage as saints engrafted into the family of God. We can rest in the Lord. We can seek to live our lives as royal priests according to the order of Melchizedek. Once we understand this personal calling, we can literally emulate Christ and enter into the rest of the Lord and also enter into the heavenly places and dimensions (which is another aspect of the rest of the Lord).

We are called to *"come to the unity of the faith and of the knowledge of the Son of God, to a perfect man, to the measure of the stature of the fullness of Christ"* (Ephesians 4:13). We are called to be transformed into the very image of Christ. In other words, we are destined to be transformed by the ministry and power of the Holy Spirit into royal priests according to the order of Melchizedek. Why? So *"that we should no longer be children, tossed to and fro and carried about with every wind of doctrine, by the trickery of men, in the cunning craftiness of deceitful plotting, but, speaking the truth in love, may grow up in all things into Him who is the head—Christ* (vv. 14-15). God is calling you and me to be transformed and recreated spirit, soul, and body until we fully reflect Christ into our spheres of influence. So let's begin to examine the promise of entering into the rest of the Lord by examining God's rest in the Scriptures.

THE REST OF THE LORD AND THE ROYAL PRIESTHOOD OF MELCHIZEDECK

Therefore, since a promise remains of entering His rest, let us fear lest any of you seem to have come short of it. For indeed the gospel was preached to us as well as to them; but the word which they heard did not profit them, not being mixed with faith in those who heard it. For we who have believed do enter that rest, as He has said: "So I swore in My wrath, 'They shall not enter My rest,'" although the works were finished from the foundation of the world. For He has spoken in a certain place of the seventh day in this way: "And God rested on the seventh day from all His works"; and again in this place: "They shall not enter My rest" (Hebrews 4:1-5).

It is important that we understand how we can be transformed and recreated spirit, soul, and body until we fully reflect Christ into our spheres of influence. Therefore, we need to have some basic understanding of the priesthood of Melchizedek. Psalm 110 gives us some powerful insights about Melchizedek and understanding concerning the rest of the Lord.

The author of Hebrews, in chapter 7, verse 17, quotes Psalm 110. I want to look at these scriptures in more detail to help our understanding of our role as royal priests after the order of Melchizedek. Psalm 110 gives us a more detailed description and more information about the dynamics or characteristics of the duties of the royal priesthood according to the order of Melchizedek. Let's examine Psalm 110:1: *"The LORD said to my Lord, "Sit at My right hand, Till I make Your enemies Your footstool."*

We need to understand the magnitude of the invitation given to us here. Yes, this was spoken to Christ by the Father. However, in the prophetic anointing in which King David was writing, he also spoke these words and promises to you and me as joint heirs with Christ. The Scripture is alive. We are born to grow and to mature into the very image of Christ. We are designed to have our minds renewed and transformed into Christlike minds.

King David, who was a type of royal priest according to the order of Melchizedek, penned these words for you and me too. Remember that David was a king and also ministered unto the Lord as a priest. These roles are two of the most important attributes of the royal priesthood after the order of Melchizedek. He carried power, anointing, and authority in the spiritual realm and also in the natural realm. King David understood this dynamic. David was anointed by God to serve Him in two dimensions, as was Elijah, Elisha, Moses, and also Jesus Christ. We too can be anointed by God to serve Him in two dimensions.

Rising above the Storms of Life

When God invites you to sit down at His right Hand, He is asking you to sit down in unity and friendship with Him at His seat of power, both in the spirit and the natural realm. To sit at the right hand of God means to sit with Him at His hand of power, flexibility, or dexterity. He is calling us to sit beside Him upon His throne of power, grace, and glory. We have a standing invitation to enter into the rest of the Lord and rest by God's side. That is the very place that the Messiah is at this moment. Jesus is our example. Jesus Christ is at rest, yet He is also interceding for you at this very instant.

We see this role of Jesus in Hebrews 7:25: *"Therefore He [Jesus] is also able to save to the uttermost those who come to God through Him, since He always lives to make intercession for them."* That is exactly what I saw in the vision of the dark storm. Those who looked upon Jesus Christ could easily reach out and receive His help and salvation. Jesus would empower them to rise up above the storm when they looked to Him. He was inviting them to enter into a place of rest and power with Him in the heavenly realms. Jesus was seeking to empower them in both the natural realm and the spiritual realm or dimension. Remember, God is a multidimensional Being! You could say that God was seeking to release an anointing to those who choose to rise above the storm. That is the hour that we are living in today. We can enter into the rest of the Lord to overcome the storms of this life.

What does it look like to actually rise above the storms of life and to be seated or ascend into the heavenly places? Jesus illustrated this aspect of the royal priest according the order of Melchizedek in Acts 1:9: *"Now when He had spoken these things, while they watched, He was taken up, and a cloud received Him out of their sight."* The Lord actually gave you and I a visual illustration of what it means to minister in the anointing of a royal priest after the order of Melchizedek. The Messiah literally ascended into the heavenly realms and entered into the rest of the Lord. Christ sat down beside the right hand of the Father as outlined in Psalm 110:1. Jesus is at this hour resting from His finished work in triumph and in total victory. The Lord also wants us to rest in triumph and in total victory.

We see Jesus Christ literally fulfill the promise of God found in Hebrews 4:9-16 and Acts 1:9. Let's also look at these passages briefly because Christ demonstrated how we can literally enter into the rest of the Lord by ascending into heavenly places: *"There remains therefore a rest for the people of God. For he who has entered His rest has himself also ceased from his works as God did from His. Let us therefore be diligent to enter that rest, lest anyone fall according to the same example of disobedience"* (Hebrews 4:9-11). The Lord ceased from His work and mission on the earth when we literally ascended into the heavenly realms to sit at the right hand of the Father. This is also the passage of scripture that Jesus spoke to me in the heavenly realms. He instructed me to tell His people to be diligent to enter into His rest at this hour. He cautioned me that many may fall because of their unbelief.

We will learn in Psalm 110 that the right hand of the Father is the place of ultimate power and authority. Remember, Jesus also gave you and me this same ultimate power and authority (see Matthew 28:18-20). When we learn to enter into the rest of the Lord and emulate Christ, we can begin to minister in the anointing of heavenly power and authority. This is a kingly anointing and is synonymous with the anointing or mantle of Melchizedek. God can anoint and empower you with authority in both the natural realm and also in the spiritual dimensions.

The Sword of the Lord and the Refining Work of the Holy Spirit

For the word of God is living and powerful, and sharper than any two-edged sword, piercing even to the division of soul and spirit, and of joints and marrow, and is a discerner of the thoughts and intents of the heart. And there is no creature hidden from His sight, but all things are naked and open to the eyes of Him to whom we must give account (Hebrews 4:12-13).

When we learn to open our hearts and spirits to the living God and allow the Holy Spirit to divide between our soul and spirit, we can begin to learn to enter into the rest of the Lord. One aspect of being diligent to enter the Lord's supernatural rest is permitting the Holy Spirit to help us separate our spirit from our soulish nature. We are really talking about learning to be led by the Lord's Spirit and submitting to the Holy Spirit's refining process of sanctification and cleansing.

When we allow the Spirit of God to minister to the deepest hidden recesses of our soul and heart, we will experience supernatural healing and deliverance. We will be delivered from our ungodly and worldly mindsets and beliefs. We will be set free from hidden yokes of darkness that we may not be aware of. Our souls will be brought into submission to our regenerated (renewed or reborn) spirit, which is created in the likeness of Christ. As a result we will spark and ignite the metamorphosis and transformation process of being recreated in a Christlike character. Then we will have the same privileges and supernatural ability to actually ascend into the heavenly realms to receive revelation and divine direction for our lives and ministries. We will be transformed and empowered to recreate Christ in our spheres of influence. Then we will be empowered to emulate Jesus and pass through the heavens, coming boldly to God's throne of grace, power, and mercy.

This great privilege is outlined in Hebrews 4:14-16: *"Seeing then that we have a great High Priest who has passed through the heavens,*

THE REST OF THE LORD AND THE ROYAL PRIESTHOOD OF MELCHIZEDECK

Jesus the Son of God, let us hold fast our confession. For we do not have a High Priest who cannot sympathize with our weaknesses, but was in all points tempted as we are, yet without sin. Let us therefore come boldly to the throne of grace that we may obtain mercy and find grace to help in time of need." It is in the very presence of God that we can truly begin to enter into the rest of the Lord.

When we enter into God's presence, His glory comes. When we are diligent to rest in His glory, our lives will be supernaturally transformed. In this place our transformation and sanctification will be complete and lacking no good thing. Learning to be diligent to enter into the rest of the Lord and to linger and luxuriate in God's presence will transform us spirit, soul, and body. That can be translated as receiving total salvation. This process is the supernatural ministry of the Holy Spirit.

We will ascend vertically into the heavenly realms and receive supernatural revelation. Then we will pass back into the earthly realm or dimension. We will then be empowered and enlightened as to how we should release the anointing and power of heaven in this dimension upon the earth. At other times we will be empowered to see and discern between two dimensions at once. We will be on the earth and in heaven at the same moment of time.

That is exactly how the Messiah ministered in such supernatural power and anointing of the Holy Spirit. John 5:19-20 outlines this aspect of Christ's ministry as royal priest according the order of Melchizedek, as Jesus spoke, *"Most assuredly, I say to you, the Son can do nothing of Himself, but what He sees the Father do; for whatever He does, the Son also does in like manner. For the Father loves the Son, and shows Him all things that He Himself does; and He will show Him greater works than these, that you may marvel."*

Transformation Glory

That is why Jesus often withdrew in prayer (see Mark 6:46; Matthew 14:23; John 6:15). He needed to enter into the rest of the Lord. Jesus needed to enter into the revelatory realm or the spiritual dimensions of God's glory. Peter, James, and John saw Jesus transfigured by the glory of God on the Mount of Transfiguration (see Matthew 17:2). I believe that was a common occurrence in the life of Christ. In my opinion, Jesus was most likely transfigured by the glory of God on a regular basis. However, those visitations of God's glory upon Jesus are not documented in the canon of Scripture. However, Scripture does document that Moses was visited by the glory of God on many occasions (see Exodus 24:16; 34:33-35; 40:35; Leviticus 9:23; Numbers 20:6; 2 Corinthians 3:7).

We see the fact that Christ was transfigured by the glory of God indicated in the book of Hebrews. This passage is also referring to the Lord's role as a royal priest according to the order of Melchizedek:

> *Therefore, holy brethren, partakers of the heavenly calling, consider the Apostle and High Priest of our confession, Christ Jesus, who was faithful to Him who appointed Him, as Moses also was faithful in all His house.* **For this One has been counted worthy of more glory than Moses**, *inasmuch as He who built the house has more honor than the house. For every house is built by someone, but He who built all things is God. And Moses indeed was faithful in all His house as a servant, for a testimony of those things which would be spoken afterward, but Christ as a Son over His own house, whose house we are if we hold fast the confidence and the rejoicing of the hope firm to the end (Hebrews 3:1-6, emphasis added).*

At this point we need to remember that we are called to do greater works than Jesus Christ accomplished (see John 14:12). And if the Scripture shows that Jesus was counted by God as worthy to experience more of God's glory than Moses, then we too should also expect to experience more of God's glory than Jesus. How can we possibly hope to see this unfold in our lives? It is simple. We need to be diligent to enter into the rest of the Lord. We need to rest in God's tangible glory and allow the Spirit of God to transform our lives just as Christ was transfigured upon the Mount of Transfiguration. We need to rest in the Lord and allow the Father and the person of the Holy Spirit to transform our lives too.

Jesus needed to have intimacy with the Father and the person of the Holy Spirit. Christ needed to ascend into the heavenly realms to see what His Father was doing and saying. Jesus needed to enter into the revelatory realms or dimensions of the Father's glory each day. That is why Jesus often withdrew and prayed (Luke 5:16). Then when He descended back to the earth, He would repeat those same things that He heard and saw.

Let me try to word this more accurately or perhaps more aptly. Jesus would move back into the earthly dimension and repeat those same things that He had heard in the heavenly dimensions. He would reenact the same things that He saw in the heavenlies when He moved back into the earthly dimension or descended or stepped back into the earthly realm. The Messiah perfectly performed the Lord's Prayer in these circumstances by executing and implementing upon the earth the same miraculous things that He saw and heard in heaven or in the heavenly dimensions (see Matthew 6:10; Luke 11:2). In this way, Jesus also entered into the rest of the Lord while He walked and ministered upon the earth. The Father and the Holy Spirit did the miraculous work (see John 14:10). By the way, the heavenly dimensions are not necessarily "up," they are all around each us at this instant. I believe that Jesus abided and lived in the Father's glory every day, twenty-four hours a day. This is possible for us too.

Jesus was on earth but He was also in heaven simultaneously. We are too, but we do not realize it. We do not discern these spiritual dimensions as readily as God desires for us to perceive them. So our minds need to be renewed concerning the reality of the heavenly dimensions. We can emulate this aspect of Christ's ministry as a royal priest according to the order of Melchizedek too. We can also be on earth but in heaven at the same time. This secret or hidden mystery of God's Kingdom is actually quite amazing. Just like the Kingdom of Heaven, it can be both/and for us at times too. This kind of supernatural lifestyle can become normal for us when we learn to enter into the rest of the Lord and abide in His presence and glory.

I believe that Jesus honed His ability to enter into the rest of the Lord and the heavenly realms as He was growing up as a boy, adolescent, young man, and adult (see Luke 2:52). There is no doubt that Christ learned to develop a personal intimate relationship with His heavenly Father and the person the Holy Spirit as He was being trained and prepared for His final mission and ministry upon the earth. The Messiah learned how He could enter into the rest of the Lord and into the very presence and tangible transforming glory of God before He ever began to minister. It is possible that entering into the presence of the Lord and stepping into the rest of the Lord was much more important to the Messiah than any act or miraculous deeds of His ministry, except for the Cross, the Resurrection, and the Ascension.

In the next chapter we will continue to unearth more secrets of the Kingdom of Heaven as we continue to look at hidden mysteries of the royal priesthood according to the order of Melchizedek.

CHAPTER 15

The Author and Finisher of Our Faith

Jesus taught us in Matthew 5:34 that God's throne is in heaven. And we see in Hebrews 12:2 that we are to fashion our faith after Christ's example: *"Looking unto Jesus, the author and finisher of our faith, who for the joy that was set before Him endured the cross, despising the shame, and has sat down at the right hand of the throne of God."* And again, this scripture confirms that through Christ's finished work upon Calvary, Jesus was and is seated by the Father's right hand of power and authority. We have been given this same freedom and access to God's throne of grace and power through the Atonement. We *can* sit with God in heavenly places today (see Ephesians 1:3; 2:6). This scripture in Hebrews is another precious portrait of Christ's ability and anointing to enter into the rest of the Lord. This is a dynamic of the royal priesthood after the order of Melchizedek, the supernatural ability to freely enter into the rest of the Lord.

In the vision of the storm, I saw many people rise above the storm by focusing upon the Lord. They literally ascended into the heavenly realms. That is exactly what the Lord is calling His people to do at this hour. When we focus upon the Messiah and rise above the storm, we are actually entering into the rest of the Lord. As we rest in the Lord, Christ and His heavenly hosts will fight the battle on our behalf. We can rest in and with the Lord in that place of victory. We can enter into the heavenly realms or dimensions while we walk upon the earth. Accessing the heavenly dimensions is one aspect of entering into the fullness of the rest of the Lord.

Returning to the second half of Psalm 110:1, we are told that the fruit of being seated at the right hand of God is that *"I make Your enemies Your footstool."* This is a beautiful portrait of the royal priesthood according to the order of Melchizedek. God will conquer and vanquish our enemies on our behalf! Not only that, Christ and His heavenly hosts will place our enemies under our feet. That is exactly what I saw in the vision of the dark storm.

The truth is that our total triumph and victory over our foes is already finished. The enemy of our soul is already defeated and is, in fact, under our feet. We just need to get the revelation of this fact, and then we need to begin to walk it out in the temporal or earthly realm. We need to learn how we can enter into the rest of the Lord. An important key to entering the rest of the Lord is just realizing that we have the liberty to access the Lord's rest. We can enter into heavenly places or heavenly dimensions that are increasingly invading our personal geographic space. We can seek to obtain God's revelation, power, and delegated authority. That is one aspect of the rest of the Lord—the ability to literally access the heavenly realms.

In Psalm 110:2 it tells us that *"the LORD shall send the rod of Your strength out of Zion. Rule in the midst of Your enemies!"* I find this scripture fascinating. The Father will send out the rod of Christ's strength from Zion and the result will be ruling over our enemies. In this passage the word translated *rod* also means scepter. The scepter represents the delegated authority of a king. When we enter into the rest of the Lord, we will begin to be utilized like a rod or scepter in the Father's hand.

The Levitical Priesthood

The Lord raised up the Levitical priesthood from the tribe of Levi under the Old Covenant. However, the Levitical priesthood was established upon works. The Levitical priesthood offered no opportunity to rest from their work; and, thus, they had no hope of understanding or entering into the rest of the Lord. At this hour the Levitical priesthood no longer exists. The Levitical priesthood needed the temple to be in place in order to perform their priestly duties and works. When the temple was destroyed in AD 72, the Levitical priesthood ceased to exist. Today there is a rabbinical priesthood in its place. The rabbinical priesthood is a manmade form of the Levitical priesthood and is also works based. As such, neither are they able to enter into the rest of the Lord. Nor was the Aaronic priesthood able to cease from their labor and enter into God's rest. Although, it was God's heart and plan for His people to enter into His rest.

At this hour the Lord is now busy raising up a new order of priests from the tribe of the Lion of Judah. The Lord is raising up a royal priesthood according to the order of Melchizedek who will rule and reign with the power and authority of the Father's scepter in their hands. This is a great privilege, and the Lord will not allow just anyone to minister or operate in this kind of anointing or heavenly power. You could call this the mantle of the royal priesthood according to the order of Melchizedek, or the mantle of Melchizedek.

This mantle of Melchizedek is a precious thing that the Father sent His only Son to establish upon the earth. In essence, we are speaking about a God-ordained or kairos moment of time when the Lord will freely give His power to His friends. This heavenly power will be activated within people as they learn that it is possible to enter into the rest of the Lord and are diligent to do so. From learning how to rest in God's presence and in His glory, your life can be supernaturally empowered!

We see this in Psalm 110:3: *"Your people shall be volunteers In the day of Your power; In the beauties of holiness, from the womb of the morning, You have the dew of Your youth."* The language here actually speaks of a set time when an army of God will be cloaked in holiness. Holiness is not optional! It is a very important key to entering into the rest of the Lord. The phrases *"from the womb"* and *"dew of youth"* do not necessarily refer to a chronological age or natural birth. They refer to a rebirth of the spirit or, as Jesus actually said, a set time when Christ's people will be born from above or born from the realms of heaven. It is speaking of a rebirth of the spirit, soul, and body. Again, this work of transformation is the ministry of the Holy Spirit which is sovereignly released in the glory and rest of the Lord.

I believe that this passage also refers to understanding Christ's Kingdom and recognizing your ability to enter into the rest of the Lord. This passage refers to an army or chosen tribe of God's champions. They will be given free access to ascend through the open heavens that Christ has restored to mankind to sit at the right hand of God in holiness, kingly authority, and supernatural power. Psalm 110:4 summarizes this promise and the definition of this free gift from our Father: *"The Lord has sworn And will not relent, 'You are a priest forever According to the order of Melchizedek.'"*

These dynamics are manifesting upon the earth today and will begin to accelerate in the near future. Christ has given us an example to emulate. We are to extend the dominion of Christ's Kingdom as royal priests after the order of Melchizedek who will rule and reign with heavenly power and the authority of heaven upon the earth. When we truly enter into the rest of the Lord, we will understand how to minister as a mediator between the heavenly realm and the temporal or earthly realm. Again, this is yet another facet of the royal priesthood according to the order of Melchizedek: to rule and reign with the delegated authority and sovereignty of God's throne of power and grace. This supernatural delegated authority will be in both the spiritual and natural dimensions.

We are also called to be priests upon the throne. Psalm 110:5-7 illustrates this dynamic: *"The Lord is at Your right hand; He shall execute kings in the day of His wrath. He shall judge among the nations, He shall fill the places with dead bodies, He shall execute the heads of many countries. He shall drink of the brook by the wayside; Therefore He shall lift up the head."* Again, God will conquer our foes and fight our battles as we enter into the rest of the Lord. In the vision of the dark storm, I saw a few people enter into the rest of the Lord. When they entered they would rise above the storm with Christ and His angelic hosts would fight on their behalf. When this occurred they could rest in the midst of the storm. That is what the Lord wants for His people.

We can begin to understand our high calling as priests according to the order of Melchizedek. We can begin to enter the rest of

THE AUTHOR AND FINSHER OF OUR FAITH

the Lord and discern or step into or through the heavenly realms or heavenly dimensions. Then we will begin to see God Almighty fight on our behalf. Very few individuals have ever tapped into this kind of heavenly power and authority. Those who have were all extremely close friends of God.

People like this who overcome and are diligent to enter into God's rest will not always be subject to the laws of nature. Miracles, signs, and wonders will be normal for them. They will live lifestyles of supernatural miracles, signs, and wonders. They *will* be diligent to enter into the rest of the Lord and the very presence of God. They will recreate Christ in their spheres of influence as they learn to release upon the earth the revelatory knowledge and things that they see and hear in heaven or in the heavenly dimensions.

Of course, these overcomers will be regular human beings like you and me. In the coming days there will be times that regular people will be given a supernatural power over the laws of nature. One reason that they will not be subject to the laws of nature is because they will live a supernatural lifestyle and transverse more than one dimension with ease. This supernatural authority will be given from God to His friends for segments of time to help people fulfill mandates and callings of the Lord. This kind of God-given authority will flow directly from the heavenly realms or dimensions and emanate from an understanding of the rest of the Lord.

God is preparing a group or tribe of friends that will not always be not subject to the laws of nature. And at certain God-ordained moments of time, phenomenal miracles, signs, and wonders will be normal for them. These people will not walk in this kind of God-given authority constantly, but at times this mantle of Melchizedek will come upon them to release signs and wonders in the name of Jesus. They will walk in the anointing of a priest and prophet according to the order or anointing of Melchizedek. Of course, this is the identical anointing that Jesus Himself ministered in. It is the anointing of the Holy Spirit. Supernatural authority, signs, wonders, and miracles will be common for these friends of the living God. You are called to walk in this kind of God-ordained intimacy and power too, and it all starts with understanding and utilizing the ability to enter into the rest of the Lord. Remember, God is a multidimensional Being and He can give us revelation and authority of His multidimensional nature and heavenly realms. I find this fascinating!

Going Boldly Behind the Veil

In Hebrews 6 we see more details about the rest of the Lord and the mantle or anointing of Melchizedek:

> *Thus God, determining to show more abundantly to the heirs of promise the immutability of His counsel, confirmed it by an oath, that by two immutable things, in which it is impossible for God to lie, we might have strong consolation, who have fled for refuge to lay hold of the hope set before us. This hope we have as an anchor of the soul, both sure and steadfast, and which enters the Presence behind the veil, where the forerunner has entered for us, even Jesus, having become High Priest forever according to the order of Melchizedek (Hebrews 6:17-20).*

This passage outlines some of the revelation about the mantle or anointing of Melchizedek. First, it is impossible for God to lie. We need to grasp that. God has promised us the ability to enter into the rest of the Lord or the heavenly realms or dimensions and to tap into the mantle of Melchizedek. This is truth. We *can* access this refuge and anchor of hope; that is real, solid, and unchanging. We can live in God's secret place. We can live under God's supernatural protection and favor. We have an immutable and unchangeable promise from our heavenly Father who will never lie to us. What is that promise?

That promise is to enter into the very presence of God by going behind the veil (or through the heavens, the open heavens, or heavenly dimensions). At times these heavenly dimensions will manifest upon earth in our spheres of influence. Understanding this will allow us to come boldly to the very presence of God and enter into His Kingdom and His rest. That is a wonderful portrait of the rest of the Lord. This is not just flowery language or alliteration. This promise is the truth! The Lord promised you and me the right and ability to enter into the very dwelling place of God, the holy of holies, and into the rest of the Lord. We can learn to enter into God's various supernatural dimensions just as we enter into different geographic places in the temporal realms.

That is our anchor. We can go boldly before the very throne of grace and power of God. That is a supernatural dimension or spiritual realm. Why? Because we have an advocate. We have a forerunner. Christ Jesus split open the heavens to restore mankind's relationship with God and our ability to access the rest of the Lord and the heavens or heavenly dimensions so that we can have fellowship, communion, and friendship with Almighty God. Scripture defines this privilege in these terms: *"Having become High Priest forever according to the order of Melchizedek"* (Hebrews 6:20). We could also call it entering into the very rest of the Lord and operating in the anointing or the mantle of Melchizedek.

That is our inheritance. That should be our goal. We need to emulate Christ in this because we are truly called to be transformed into royal priests according the order of Melchizedek who will rule and reign upon the earth. Jesus Christ has entered into the rest of the Lord and we can too. It *is possible* for us to enter into the *Presence* behind the veil where the forerunner has blazed a supernatural trail for us. We *can* learn how to become high priests forever according to the order of Melchizedek today. We *can* enter into the heavenly places or heavenly realms that are beginning to invade our space with increasing frequency. We *can* rest in the Lord and have communion with Christ today and obtain a heavenly perspective, heavenly authority, and God-given power to impact our lives and spheres of influence. We *can* wield the scepter of heavenly power. We *can* rise above the darkness of the storms of the present age and world when we learn to be diligent to enter into the rest in the Lord.

Overcoming Sin

Hebrews 12:1-2 accurately describes what we should seek to do to emulate Christ's example: *"Therefore we also, since we are surrounded by so great a cloud of witnesses, let us lay aside every weight, and the sin which so easily ensnares us, and let us run with endurance the race that is set before us, looking unto Jesus, the author and finisher of our faith, who for the joy that was set before Him endured the cross, despising the shame, and has sat down at the right hand of the throne of God."* (The great cloud of witnesses is another level of the rest of the Lord that I will look at later in the book.) We can also embrace our cross and die to our agendas and seek God's perfect will for our lives. This will also help us to be diligent to enter into the rest of the Lord.

We must overcome the sin in our lives that weighs us down to this temporal or carnal realm. In fact, if you hope to enter into the rest of the Lord and experience the mantle or anointing of Melchizedek today, you will need to seek to walk in holiness and sanctification. Holiness is absolutely necessary to enter into the rest of the Lord and become a priest after the order of Melchizedek. You can become a royal priest according to the order of Melchizedek, but holiness is not optional. You can access the heavenly dimensions in your life and within your sphere of influence.

The blood of Christ has made holiness and sanctification possible for us today. This is because Christ, who through the eternal Spirit, offered Himself without spot to God and has cleansed our conscience from dead works to serve the living God (see Hebrews 9:6-14). It is only through Christ's precious atoning blood that we can hope to enter into the rest of the Lord. The Levitical priesthood did not have this hope or opportunity, but you do. You can enter into the heavenly dimensions and the heavenly realms through the finished work of Jesus upon the Cross of Calvary.

To enter into the rest of the Lord, we must walk in holiness. We must walk blamelessly before our God. The Lord is calling His people to walk in the fullness of Christ's character. In other words, we need to be transformed into the very image of Jesus. Our mind needs to be transformed into a Christlike mind. Our mindset needs to be transformed into a heavenly mindset. What we are speaking of is really a metamorphosis of our spirits and very being as we grow into a mature creature that is shaped and molded into the very image of our Creator. We can be recreated in God's own image; then we can recreate Christ in our spheres of influence. That is God's ultimate plan for you and me and it all flows freely from entering into the rest of the Lord (see Genesis 1:26).

Our minds need to be "stayed" upon Christ and His Kingdom (Isaiah 26:3). In the vision I saw, the people who placed their focus on Christ rose above the circumstances and the storms. We need to count everything that we have learned over a lifetime of education and study of no consequence in order that we might obtain a Christlike mind. We need to seek first the Kingdom of heaven and God's righteousness (Matthew 6:33). We need to take up our cross and put away our sinful natures, mental and intellectual strongholds (16:24). We need this diligent kind of devotion and mindset today, as it will empower us to enter into the rest of the Lord. Praise God, He has sent us a Helper!

The precious Holy Spirit is at work in our hearts and minds transforming us into the very image of Christ. This is a sovereign and supernatural work of grace. However, we must choose to allow the Holy Spirit to minister to us. God will not violate our free will. We need to be mindful that the Lord is gently seeking to reshape our hearts, souls, and minds. It would be wise to submit to the refining forge of the Holy Spirit and His purifying process today. This will also help us to be diligent and to enable us to enter into the rest of the Lord.

Again, this is the season that many find themselves in at this hour. God is preparing His bride. The Lord is raising up a royal priesthood according to the order of Melchizedek. These friends of God will be holy. They will rest comfortable in the Lord. They will minister in the mantle or anointing of Melchizedek. They will mediate between earth and heaven as they realize their supernatural inheritance and understand how to pass between the earthly and the heavenly realms or dimensions. They will work in symphony with the Holy Spirit and God's angelic host to impact the events on earth for Christ's Kingdom and His purposes.

These friends of God will "rend" the heavens over their lives and gain free access to the very courtrooms of God. They will have revelation and understand how to work in harmony with the unction of the Holy Spirit to manifest the Kingdom of God. At times they will also be released to co-labor with God's angels. (For more teaching on this aspect of resting in the Lord please read Kevin's trilogy of books, *The Reality of Angelic Ministry Today*.)

Some people do not believe that it is God's will to have an assembly of priests such as Melchizedek. However, that has always been in the Lord's end-time plan. Jeremiah spells this out clearly:

> *"Behold, the days are coming," says the* LORD, *"that I will perform that good thing which I have promised to the house of Israel and to the house of Judah [Jesus is the Lion born from the tribe of Judah]: In those days and at that time I will cause to grow up to David A Branch of righteousness; He shall execute judgment and righteousness in the earth. In those days Judah will be saved, And Jerusalem will dwell safely. And this is the name by which she will be called: THE LORD OUR RIGHTEOUSNESS"* [The Hebrew meaning of this is Jehovah-Tsidkenu, a symbolical epithet of the Messiah]. *For thus says the* LORD: *"David shall never lack a man to sit on the throne of the house of Israel; nor shall the priests, the Levites, lack a man to offer burnt offerings before Me, to kindle grain offerings, and to sacrifice continually"* [This speaks of the appointed feasts of Israel, and firstfruits offerings on the weekly, monthly, and yearly appointed and God-ordained times]. *And the word of the* LORD *came to Jeremiah, saying, "Thus says the* LORD: *'If you can break My covenant with the day and My covenant with the night, so that there will not be day and night in their season, then My covenant may also be broken with David My*

servant, so that he shall not have a son to reign on his throne, and with the Levites, the priests, My ministers. As the host of heaven cannot be numbered, nor the sand of the sea measured, so will I multiply the descendants of David My servant and the Levites who minister to Me'" (Jeremiah 33:14-22).

This passage speaks prophetically of the hour in which we live. God promised that through the tribe of Judah He would raise up a priesthood that would minister to God and offer sacrifices to God continuously. This group of priests would be innumerable, *"as the host of heaven cannot be numbered, nor the sand of the sea measured"* (v. 22). This is the promise of the royal priesthood according to order of Melchizedek. This innumerable priesthood is being birthed from the blood of Jesus Christ. You are called to be a royal priest according to or modeled in a like manner as the order of Melchizedek—a priesthood who will rule and reign with the power and authority of the Father's throne. This will be a priesthood that will perfectly reflect and emulate Christ in their spheres of influence.

Jesus is standing at the door of the heavens and knocking. It is our responsibility to hear Him and to answer. It is our responsibility to be diligent to enter into the rest of the Lord. He has given you and me authority to release His Kingdom upon the earth as we learn to minister under the open heavens that Christ restored to mankind. The days of the restoration of all things is at hand, and we can now live our lives in the fullness of Christ and His finished work of Calvary and the Lord's total atonement. We can serve a living God in power and authority. We can enter into the rest of the Lord and into the associated heavenly realms or spiritual dimensions here on earth!

On the Day of Atonement in 2012, the Lord appeared to me again in my little prayer room in Moravian Falls, North Carolina. This propelled me on a supernatural journey of learning more about the rest of the Lord. In the next chapter, I begin to share with you the amazing things that Jesus showed me that constitute the other amazing levels and characteristics of the rest of the Lord.

CHAPTER 16

The Day of Atonement 2012—More Revelation Revealed

The supernatural experiences described in the previous chapters of this book changed the course of my life. I have been on a mystical journey searching the Scriptures and the heart of God concerning the rest of the Lord. It has taken me a full year to summarize and document the revelation that the Lord has released to me in reference to the importance of understanding and entering into the rest of the Lord. However, I am certain that I do not have the full understanding of this mystery of Christ's Kingdom.

This season of seeking began to culminate on September 25 and 26 on the Day of Atonement 2012. The Lord appeared to me in my prayer room as a royal Priest according to the order of Melchizedek. In fact, I relived much of the supernatural experience that had occurred on the Day of Atonement in 2011. I once more found myself in the heavenly places with Christ. It seemed Jesus wanted to make sure that I fully understood the message that He was revealing to me about the importance of the rest of the Lord.

During the previous twelve months, the Lord had patiently taught me and led me to many places to receive further revelation about the rest of the Lord and the importance of this Kingdom principle for each of us at this hour. The encounter with the dark and evil storm and being lifted up with Jesus above the storm on the Day of Atonement 2011 was pivotal for me. I was certain that the Lord had revealed five levels of the rest of the Lord to me. On the Day of Atonement of 2012, Jesus released more revelation to augment those things that I had been diligent to search out over the past year.

I have already written about the first level: The rest of the Lord, the fullness of God's rest, and the mantle of Melchizedek. In the remainder of the book I will seek to elaborate on the other four levels for you. My goal is to help the reader understand the importance of being diligent to enter into the rest of the Lord. This is a critical issue at this day and hour. I have also asked Paul Cox to write about the importance of the royal priesthood according to the order of Melchizedek and his revelation concerning the importance of rest of the Lord and how it relates to the anointing of Melchizedek. Since I do not have a full understanding on the subject of the rest of the Lord, I have asked Paul Cox to share his revelation on this subject. I pray that together we can impart revelation to you on some important keys that can help you to be diligent to enter into the rest of the Lord. There is no question about the importance of this issue.

We must learn to enter into the Lord's rest at this pivotal time. In fact, your very life may depend upon your ability to enter into God's rest and to understand that you can live permanently in the fullness of the rest of the Lord. On the Day of Atonement in 2011, Jesus spoke to me about these five aspects or levels of the rest of the Lord. The Lord has continued to build upon the amazing concepts that were birthed within my spirit that day. Again, the five levels of the rest of the Lord are:

1. The rest of the Lord, the fullness of God's rest, and the mantle of Melchizedek
2. The rest of the Lord, the Sabbath rest
3. The rest of the Lord, the heavenly hosts, the rest of God's family
4. The rest of the Lord, resting in His glory and allowing Him to work on our behalf
5. The rest of the Lord, the hidden and mysterious treasures in the Kingdom of God

THE DAY OF ATONEMENT 2012—MORE REVELATION REVEALED

Since we have already examined the fullness of God's rest and the mantle of Melchizedek, we will look at the final four in the next several chapters. During this season the Lord began to instruct me about the importance of learning about His yearly cycles and the feasts of the Jewish calendar. Many Christians already know and understand the need to observe these feasts, but it has been an amazing discovery for me. I was not aware of the importance of recognizing and keeping the yearly feasts. Since I have started to honor these feasts, the blessings that the Lord God Almighty has begun to pour out upon my life have been truly miraculous! Furthermore, I am thoroughly convinced that the Lord also wants to bless you in a supernatural way in every aspect of your life too.

An important key to unlocking this door of supernatural blessing is to recognize and keep the Lord's weekly, monthly, and yearly cycle of the feasts pertaining to the Jewish calendar. Some of you reading this may think that since you are saved and know Jesus Christ as your Lord and Savior that you do not need to observe the Jewish feasts. Perhaps you think that these feasts are antiquated and religious dogma. However, I urge you to consider this. Jesus is Jewish, and the Lord Jesus Christ was faithful to rigorously observe the feasts as directed and commanded in the Law of Moses and the Torah.

Jesus observed and kept the appointed Jewish feasts His whole life. Several of them, from His birth to His growing up years, are recorded in Luke 2.

We should also remember what Jesus taught us about the Law of Moses in Matthew 5:18: *"For assuredly, I say to you, till heaven and earth pass away, one jot or one tittle will by no means pass from the law till all is fulfilled."* In other words, the Lord was saying that the laws of the Old Testament or the Old Covenant are still valid and will never be totally replaced by the laws of the New Testament or the New Covenant. Today many Christians do not recognize these important appointed feasts of the Old Testament, but that does not invalidate them. In fact, there are great blessings that can come to you as you begin to embrace these appointed times to fellowship with the Creator of the heavens and earth.

There are three key cycles or sequences of times that God requires His people to draw close to Him in the yearly calendar. We need to also understand that today most people operate exclusively on the Greco-Roman, now the Gregorian, calendar. However, the Lord still keeps time according to the Hebrew calendar. Therefore, we need to understand this fact and meet God at these appointed times or feasts according to the Hebrew calendar. These fall into weekly, monthly, and yearly categories. When we are diligent to keep the feasts and come to present ourselves before the Lord, there are incredible blessings that the Father seeks to pour out upon us. Of course, we must be walking circumspectly and in righteousness as we come before the Lord.

Over the past year I have begun to learn more about the essence of the Sabbath rest. I have discovered as I have researched the Scriptures and sought additional revelation that the Lord is a chronological God. As I stated earlier, the Lord began to establish a weekly cycle of rest in Genesis 2. After the Lord completed His work of creation, He rested. Then God established and appointed a weekly day of rest for His creation. This principle was so important that God Almighty even included it in the Ten Commandments (Exodus 20:8-10).

The Mulberry Tree

In 2001 while I was in Africa, the Lord told me to go to Tennessee when I returned to America. I was diligent to be geographically and chronologically obedient to the Lord. Because I was in the right place at the right time, I had a God-ordained meeting with a woman under a mulberry tree in Nashville. Her name was Anna (I have changed her name for the sake of anonymity). At that time I was very zealous for the things of God. I had traveled from Africa to Nashville to attend a School of the Supernatural hosted by Encounters Network and James Goll.

After one morning session I was preparing to leave to invest my last three dollars on a hamburger when the Lord spoke to me. He said, "Go and have lunch with that woman." So I turned off the ignition of my car and walked over to meet Anna for the first time. She

THE DAY OF ATONEMENT 2012—MORE REVELATION REVEALED

offered me a sandwich and something to drink. Anna was sitting in the shade of a mulberry tree resting and praying as she ate her lunch. Looking back on this incident now, I can see the prophetic symbolism of this divine appointment!

During our conversation I received a word of knowledge for the healing of her right rotator cuff. She allowed me to pray for her, and the Lord did heal her under that mulberry tree. Interestingly enough, mulberry trees prophetically symbolize knowledge, wisdom, and healing. Since that time Anna promised to pray for me. In fact, she has prayed and interceded for me for over a decade as of this writing. Her prayers and intercession have been amazing! God has used her to prophetically decree the things that she both saw and heard in the spiritual dimension of the Kingdom of God. Anna has decreed these things over and into Kathy and my lives in a Christlike manner. If you are beginning in the ministry, allow me to encourage you to ask the Lord to send you a true intercessor with God's heart like Anna. One of the things that she saw and prayed for five years without my knowledge was that the Lord would connect me with Paul Cox.

I am certain that Paul's help and participation in this book were birthed by Anna's prayers. The other reason that I mention Anna is that since 2001 she has encouraged me to invest time studying the Jewish calendar. As with most young Christians who are full of zeal, it has taken me years to heed her sage advice. You see, the Hebrew calendar is extremely important in reference to understanding and entering into the rest of the Lord.

Having said all of this, I want to share a brief history of the appointed feasts of Israel and the Hebrew calendar. These are some of the things that Anna sought to help me to understand over the years. Today I am glad that Anna helped Kathy and me to understand more about the Jewish feasts. And I pray that this little study will help those of you who read this book. We will briefly explore seven of the appointed feasts of Israel in addition to the weekly Sabbath rest.

Let's look at the seven prominent appointed feasts of Israel. Hopefully this will help those who are not acquainted with the importance of these feasts to consider recognizing and observing them each year. Please understand that this is a very rudimentary look at the feasts, and I am by no means any expert on this subject. However, I want to touch on them as a way of helping you to understand the importance of timing in God's Kingdom.

The Lord Is Chronological

Today we can only enter into the rest of the Lord because Jesus Christ fulfilled every feast with the exception of the Feast of Tabernacles. The Feast of Tabernacles will be fulfilled in the Messianic Kingdom that is to come, or perhaps is at hand. However, understanding the appointed chronological feasts of Israel will certainly help you to be diligent to enter into the rest of the Lord. That is an important key. Many people in the Body of Christ are not aware of these seven feasts that God has commanded us to observe in addition to the weekly Sabbath. These feasts are found in Leviticus 23. Understanding more about the Jewish feasts will help us to appreciate and to be aware of the fact that the Lord is a chronological God. The Lord speaks to us as a Body (corporately) and as individuals at specific times. God expects specific responses from us at these appointed times each year. These specific times are outlined chronologically on the Jewish calendar. The seven feasts come in chronological order and are related to the seasons. These appointed feasts are: (1) the Passover; (2) the Feast of Unleavened Bread; (3) the Feast of Firstfruits; (4) Pentecost, Feast of Weeks, or Shavout; (5) the Feast of Trumpets or Rosh Hashanah; (6) the Day of Atonement or Yom Kippur; (7) and the Feast of Booths, Tabernacles, or Sukkot.

What I have realized is that as I have been obedient to honor the Lord with the firstfruits of my day, each and every day, He has honored my efforts by releasing amazing grace and favor upon my life. As I have sought to honor the Sabbath Day to keep it holy every week, the Lord has given me real understanding and breakthrough into His rest. From that place I began to learn to honor the Lord on a

THE DAY OF ATONEMENT 2012—MORE REVELATION REVEALED

monthly basis at Rosh Chodesh. Rosh Chodesh marks the beginning of the new month, and it is a time to hear from the Lord for His plans for you for the next four weeks.

As I have recognized this monthly day of rest and celebration, the level of His rest and favor in my life has dramatically escalated. I believe that the grace and favor of God can multiply in your life in a similar way as you learn to enter into the rest of the Lord too. We must be diligent to enter into the Lord's rest on a daily, weekly, monthly, and yearly basis. Understanding the appointed annual feasts can help us to walk in God's abiding rest or the fullness of God's rest. This is absolutely critical to living a victorious life.

It is important to state that we do not want to observe these appointed feasts in a religious manner. We should seek to celebrate these in the Spirit (Ruach HaKodesh) and not legalistically. There should be freedom in the way that you recognize and honor these appointed feasts. I believe that God looks upon our hearts. I am also sure that if you choose not to observe the feasts, your choice will be acceptable to the Lord. In other words, not honoring or observing these appointed feasts is not sinful. However, I also believe that by ignoring them you may limit the Lord's ability to pour out the full measure of His blessings upon you. This is a matter of personal choice.

An important reason to understanding God's timing is because the enemy has sought to change the times and seasons. In addition to this, he has tried to deceive us and works to blind our eyes. And he works to limit our ability to hear and understand what the Lord is seeking to say to us at God-ordained or kairos moments of time. This device of the enemy gained strength when the Roman calendar was first instituted by King Romulus around 700 years before Christ. It was later modified and replaced by Julius Caesar not long before Christ was born and is called the Julian calendar. In the late 1500s, Pope Gregory XIII revised it again. This calendar, called the Gregorian calendar, has become the calendar that we observe today with some minor modifications.

God never switched over to the modern calendar. Today most of us live our lives based upon the Gregorian calendar. What we need to keep in mind is that this calendar is not based upon God's appointed times and feasts. This fact can keep us from being in sync with the Lord and His appointed annual feasts. The Lord has His own chronological timetables for seasons and appointed feasts. These are also appointed times for us, His people. There are preordained or appointed times for each of us to "do business" with God as individuals.

God Is a Chronological God

If we are not aware of God's timetables, then we live our lives out of sync with the Lord. This is one way that the enemy seeks to kill, steal, and destroy God's people. If he can keep us out of sync with the Lord's timing, we have a very difficult time receiving God's blessings. In addition to this, we will have a tendency to run to and fro seeking the Lord at the wrong time and in the wrong place. If we do this, we live without God's grace and purposes in our lives and we wear ourselves out working diligently at religious activities and unfruitful works. When we get on this out-of-sync and out-of-time treadmill, we cannot possibly enter into the rest of the Lord.

So a very important key to being diligent to enter into the rest of the Lord is knowing the Lord's times and seasons. We must walk and live our lives in sync chronologically with the Lord. We must recognize that our God is a chronological God. When we seek to live our lives in His perfect timing, then His perfect plans and purposes come forth easily in our lives and we can enter into the rest of the Lord. We need to be chronologically and geographically obedient to the Lord at all times. Having said all of this, let's look briefly at the seven the appointed feasts of Israel. Again, we should honor these feasts in the Spirit (Ruach HaKodesh) and not legalistically. There should be freedom in the way that you recognize and honor these appointed feasts.

The first of the seven yearly feasts is Passover. This appointed feast usually comes in the spring and is observed in the Jewish month of Nisan. The Passover is a time to recognize and to remember the release of the Jewish people from the bondage of slavery in Egypt. Each household was told to sprinkle the blood of an unblemished lamb on the doorposts of their homes so that the angel of death or "destroyer" would "pass over" them (see Exodus 12). They were protected by the blood of the lamb just as we can be protected by the blood of the Lamb today (1 Peter 1:19). Christ's blood redeems each of us from the bondage to sin and makes atonement for us today.

The second of the seven yearly feasts is the Feast of Unleavened Bread. This appointed feast runs concurrently with the Passover. The Feast of Unleavened Bread starts the day after the Passover evening and lasts for seven days. During this time the Jewish people put away all leaven from their houses and only eat unleavened bread. This feast speaks of repentance of sin. The Jewish people usually eat a matzo type of bread. This kind of bread is prophetic in nature. It represents the coming Messiah who would take away the sin (leaven) of the people. Matzo bread prophetically represents the Lord Jesus Christ who takes away all of our sins. Matzo bread is striped in the baking process; these stripes symbolize the stripes that Jesus Christ took upon His back for the healing of our bodies (see 1 Peter 2:24; Isaiah 53:5). Of course the Passover is symbolic of the Lord's Supper or the Communion table as well. I recommend that you practice taking the Lord's Supper each and every day as a way to be diligent to enter into the rest of the Lord.

The third of the seven yearly feasts is the Feast of Firstfruits. This appointed feast is directly related to Passover and Unleavened Bread as it is recognized and celebrated on the day after the regular Sabbath. In the times of Jesus, this holiday was a feast of thanksgiving. It was a celebration of the first harvest of grain in the year. The Feast of Firstfruits celebrated and recognized that God, who gave the weather and rain to bring forth a harvest of the first crop, was going to also release the rain and good weather for the harvest of a greater and much larger grain harvest later in the year. This too speaks prophetically of the Messiah, who would be a Firstfruit whom God would raise from the dead. Through the finished work of Jesus Christ, there will be a great harvest of souls that will come into the Kingdom of God in the last days. Giving a firstfruit offering to the Lord is another important key that can help you supernaturally enter into the rest of the Lord. Be diligent to give a firstfruits offering to God each day, week, month, and year. I will look at this aspect of entering into the rest of the Lord in the next chapter in much more detail.

The fourth of the seven yearly feasts is Pentecost or the Feast of Weeks. This appointed feast comes chronologically exactly fifty days after the Passover Sabbath. The name, Pentecost, is translated from the Greek word for fifty. The Jewish people also call this feast Shavuot, which is the Hebrew word for weeks. This feast is a celebration or harvest festival that honors and gives God glory for the wheat harvest. Tradition states that Shavuot is celebrated with the priests offering to God two loaves of bread baked from the newly harvested grain. This too, is pregnant prophetically as this act represents both Jew and Gentile who will be reconciled to God as one new man through the Messiah (see Ephesians 2:15).

The fifth of the seven yearly feasts is the Feast of Trumpets, also referred to as Rosh Hashanah. This feast celebrates the beginning of the civil year and is the Jewish New Year's Day. In Leviticus 23:24 the Lord calls for the blowing of trumpets on this day. Jewish scholars refer to this day as the beginning of the days of judgment. During this time all people are called to pass before the Lord. The righteous have their names written into the book of life and the wicked receive condemnation. For those who find themselves in the middle, this feast gives them ten days to repent and to seek the Lord asking for forgiveness. Jesus is the One who is able to give us total salvation through His finished work on the Cross of Calvary. Because of the Cross we can find our names written in the Lamb's Book of Life. The blood of the Lord Jesus Christ gives us atonement for our sins. Those who have received Jesus Christ as Messiah will also celebrate the mighty trumpet sound of the Angel of God at the return of Christ (see 1 Thessalonians 4:16).

The sixth of the seven yearly feasts is the Day of Atonement. It is considered to be a time of fasting and prayer. It was the one day of the year that the high priest was allowed to enter into the holy of holies to make atonement for the people's sins. The high priest entered behind the veil with the blood of the scapegoat to seek the Lord's forgiveness of the people's sins. Jesus Christ was the Lamb without spot or blemish that was offered once and for all. The blood of Jesus makes perfect atonement for our sins, and through the blood of Jesus we have a way into the holy of holies. We can follow the forerunner who has blazed a trail for us into the heavenly realms. The sacrifice of Jesus upon the Cross of Calvary has made a way for us to enter into the very presence and glory of God. As I have written, the visitations of the Lord Jesus Christ on the Day of Atonement birthed this book. For me the Day of Atonement is a very special day each year. We can enter into the rest of the Lord today because Jesus fulfilled the requirements of the Day of Atonement for each of us.

The seventh of the seven yearly feasts is the Feast of Booths, also known as Tabernacles or Sukkot. In biblical times this feast celebrated the final harvest of the growing season. It was a time to congregate together in Jerusalem to celebrate the goodness of God and His provision. The Jewish people would build booth-type structures and live in these during this feast. The booth-type structures are meant to remind the people of the times that they lived in tents in the wilderness. However, this feast also speaks of the season of abundant blessings and of the rest that the Hebrews would have when they reached the Promised Land. These booths were decorated with harvest fruit and branches of trees. This feast prophetically symbolizes the fullness of entering into God's rest.

So an important aspect of recognizing and celebrating the seven appointed feasts of Israel is to help us to ultimately enter into the fullness of the rest of the Lord. There is a supernatural significance to these dates and appointed feasts. As we learn to recognize, honor, and celebrate them, we will learn to walk in sync with God. As a result we can live our lives in God's perfect timing and receive His revelation and grace that will empower us to enter into the rest of the Lord.

In the next chapter we will continue our journey by looking at what I have learned about the rest of the Lord that we know as the Sabbath rest. Then we will add to that understanding by looking at the importance of the monthly cycle and Rosh Chodesh and the role observing these two appointed times plays in your ability to be diligent to enter into the rest of the Lord.

CHAPTER 17

Understanding the Sabbath Rest

God has ordained a weekly cycle of rest. This is the most basic and perhaps most important aspect of being diligent to enter the rest of the Lord. The Sabbath Day was and still is called the Shabbat in the Hebrew language. The Sabbath is a commanded weekly day of rest required by God. This is a weekly occasion for each of us to reserve time for the Lord. We are called to have communion and fellowship with the Lord. We are called to cease from our work just as the Lord, Elohim, did when He created the heavens and earth. We see this scriptural principle and Kingdom commandment in Genesis 2:2: *"And on the seventh day God ended His work which He had done, and He rested on the seventh day from all His work which He had done."*

This is the model given to us by our God. Work six days and rest on the seventh, which is the Shabbat. The Shabbat is a time to draw near to God. The Shabbat is a time to celebrate life and God's goodness. We are to consider the works of God's hands and relish in His blessings that He has ordained for you and me to experience and to walk in. The Shabbat is to be a festive time of loving God and those in our sphere of influence. The Shabbat is a time to celebrate God and His goodness to each of us. Unfortunately, I had never heard this taught to any significant degree in most of the churches that I attended.

In July, 2012, I had the opportunity to minister at a Messianic Church in Riga, Latvia. It was an amazing experience for me. They celebrated the Shabbat with singing, dancing, and feasting. It was a real party. And even though the people at the Messianic gathering seemed to be poor by Western standards, the love of God that emanated from the congregation and the love that they demonstrated for each other were truly amazing.

The Lord was faithful and miracles were worked in the name of Yeshua HaMashiach. This resulted in a Jewish woman who was visiting receiving the Lord Jesus Christ as Savior as she saw the love of her Jewish God demonstrated through this wonderful group of Jewish Messianic believers. Yeshua became real to her when she saw the miracles and experienced the love of God that was poured out upon the group on the Shabbat celebration. This was an epiphany for me!

The Lord greatly desires to pour out His blessings and nature upon us each and every Sabbath day. In my opinion, it does not matter which day you celebrate the Sabbath during the week. The most important thing is that you observe the Sabbath and rest in the Lord on that day. Celebrate God!

The Sabbath rest is the principle and most basic way that you can enter into the rest of the Lord. The Lord has promised to bless those who keep the weekly Sabbath day. In fact, it is so important to the heart of God for us to set one day a week aside to love and recognize Him that this principle is included in the Ten Commandments:

> *Remember the Sabbath day, to keep it holy. Six days you shall labor and do all your work, but the seventh day is the Sabbath of the LORD your God. In it you shall do no work: you, nor your son, nor your daughter, nor your male servant, nor your female servant, nor your cattle, nor your stranger who is within your gates. For in six days the LORD made the heavens and the earth, the sea, and all that is in them, and rested the seventh day. Therefore the LORD blessed the Sabbath day and hallowed it (Exodus 20:8-11).*

What God is saying here is that we need to work on the first six days of the week, but the seventh we are to give it totally or wholly to Him. No one in our immediate sphere of influence is to work. To hallow the Sabbath day means to keep an appointed time holy and sanctified unto the Lord.

Why? Because we are commanded to rest in the Lord! We are designed to rest and to celebrate God's goodness towards us on the Sabbath. This aspect of God's very nature is inherent in our spiritual DNA.

God commands us to rest in the Lord on the Sabbath or the Shabbat. This is God's day! He commands us to rest and to enjoy time fellowshipping with Him and meditating on His goodness and bountiful provision found in the earth, the sea, and all that is upon the earth. God's creation was given to each of us, and we are to have dominion over it. This is actually an aspect of the fullness of the rest of the Lord, which I will share more about later. However, observing the Sabbath and keeping it holy is a huge prerequisite to receiving the supernatural abundance and blessings that God desperately desires for each of His children to have. Resting in the Lord on the Sabbath is a basic principle of entering into the rest of the Lord. It is mandatory!

Many in the Body of Christ do not walk in God's blessings because we do not honor the Lord by keeping the Sabbath day holy. It is the Lord's Day, literally, so we need to give it to Him and learn to rest in the Lord on the Sabbath day. Resting on the Sabbath day can be life changing. However, we need to discipline ourselves to do it.

God's rest is tied to His chronological season of blessings. These come in weekly, monthly, and yearly times to rest in the Lord and to seek His guidance and grace. Again, the most basic way that we can enter into the rest of the Lord is through observing the Sabbath day on a weekly basis. Resting in the Lord is also inseparably spiritually connected to sowing and reaping in the natural realm or earthly dimension. We sow into the spirit but we reap in the natural as we learn to rest in the Lord. We are called to sow into the Lord's rest on daily, weekly, monthly and yearly cycles and appointed times.

During this season of learning and discovering God's desire to meet with me on a regular basis, I made an amazing discovery (for me, anyway). I discovered that when I gave the Lord the firstfruits of my time, He began to respond in amazing ways. Therefore, as I sought to learn more about the rest of the Lord, I began to honor the

Sabbath day to keep it holy as best I could. At these times that I set aside to meet with the Lord each week, He began to show up! His glory began to invade my space! Usually I would sequester myself away with the Lord in my prayer room in Moravian Falls and the glory and presence of the Lord would come and fill me and refresh me. Another amazing thing also began to happen; the Lord began to speak to me in a very clear and direct way. This is an added benefit of resting in the Lord on the Sabbath day. God will speak to you very clearly and you can begin to exercise your spiritual senses by reason of use (Hebrews 5:14).

When we were traveling and ministering, I would still seek to enter into the rest of the Lord on the Sabbath. At times that meant that I would honor the Sabbath day as I was on an international flight. However, that did not seem to negate the power and presence of the Lord that would come and rest upon me. You see, when I began to seek the Lord of the Sabbath, He began to come and rest upon me. It did not seem to matter where I was. Nor did it seem that God was religious about meeting me for Shabbat on a specific day of the week. When I chose to rest in Him, He chose to rest upon me. This revelation and understanding of the rest of the Lord is truly life changing.

When you seek to rest in the Lord, He will seek to rest upon you. In fact, the anointing and glory of God is resting upon me even as I write this. Perhaps you can feel the power of the Holy Spirit upon you now. If you do, just set this book down and go find a quiet place to wait upon the Lord. Tell Him that you want to have Shabbat. Tell Him that you want to rest in Him. Invite the presence and the glory of God to rest upon you as you rest in the Lord even now.

Shabbat with the Lord

Soon I discovered that it did not seem to make a difference where I was or what day of the week that it happened to be. When I purposed in my heart to have Shabbat with the Lord, He would come and rest upon me. This revelation was life changing! As a result I began to practice Sabbath every day. In other words, I began to wait upon the Lord every day. I began to rest in the Lord every day. I began to ask the Lord to rest upon me every day, and He has been very faithful to do so. My life is being transformed by investing time waiting and resting in the Lord. His glory comes and I just rest in His glory. You can too. This is an elementary type of entering into the rest of the Lord.

Purpose in your heart to invest time resting in His presence and soon you will discover that the Lord is transforming your life and circumstances in supernatural ways. In fact, you will discover that your spiritual DNA will begin to be transformed into the very DNA of Christ. Your character will begin to change. Your mindset will begin to change. Your mind will be transformed into a Christlike mind, and your spirit will begin to become dominant in terms of your perception in your every waking moment.

Once you begin to enter into the rest of the Lord regularly, be it daily or weekly, you can expect to begin to see the Lord's hand move in your life. I want to encourage you to observe the weekly Sabbath rest or Shabbat. By seeking and being diligent to enter into the rest of the Lord each week and day, you will be initiating a metamorphosis in your life and sphere of influence. Actually, you will be following an example that was given to us by the Lord Jesus Christ. Remember, Jesus often withdrew and prayed. He invested time resting in the Father's presence. *"He Himself often withdrew into the wilderness and prayed"* (Luke 5:16).

What was the result, the fruit, of Jesus resting in the Lord? We see the fruit of the Lord's waiting upon the Father in the very next verse. *"Now it happened on a certain day, as He was teaching, that there were Pharisees and teachers of the law sitting by, who had come out of every town of Galilee, Judea, and Jerusalem. And the power of the Lord was present to heal them"* (Luke 5:17). Resting in the Lord will release the Kingdom of God and the power of God into your life.

Resting in the Lord during the weekly Shabbat will release true revival in your life and within your sphere of influence. Resting in the Lord will empower you to demonstrate the Kingdom of God with miracles, signs, and wonders everywhere you go. But, as amazing as those things are, they are only elementary compared to the power that can be released into your life as you begin to enter into the fullness of the rest of the Lord. Let me begin to lay a foundation for that dynamic of the rest of the Lord as we look at how recognizing and honoring the monthly feasts can release even more power and authority into your life.

CHAPTER 18

Understanding the Monthly Rest

Along this journey I have discovered that there are other times that the Lord is seeking to meet with me. I have waited upon the Lord for several years on the Day of Atonement. As I wrote earlier in 2011, the Lord began to speak to me about being diligent to enter into His rest. I soon discovered that in addition to the weekly Sabbath rest there are other appointed times or cycles on the Lord's calendar of celebrations and feasts when God seeks our attention. Again, these fall into three categories: weekly, monthly, and yearly feasts. Each of these chronological seasons is designed for us to approach a holy God and to seek His will and blessings for our lives. During these appointed times, God speaks to us and often ministers to us by supernaturally releasing blessings and favor into our lives.

It was during this process that I began to recognize and observe the monthly celebration on the Jewish calendar called Rosh Chodesh. Rosh Chodesh is a monthly celebration of the Jews on which they bring their firstfruits unto the Lord.

I was already having wonderful encounters with the Holy Spirit each week as I waited upon Him on the Sabbath day seeking to enter into His rest. I had purposed in my heart to seek Him early each day by giving the Lord the firstfruits of my day. Since I did not actually have literal fruit to give to the Lord, I chose to give to the Father, the Son, and the Holy Spirit the firstfruits of my time each day.

I began to enter into my little prayer room the first thing each morning and pray this prayer found in Ephesians 3:

> *I bow my knees to the Father of our Lord Jesus Christ, from whom the whole family in heaven and earth is named, that He would grant you, according to the riches of His glory, to be strengthened with might through His Spirit in the inner man, that Christ may dwell in your hearts through faith; that you, being rooted and grounded in love, may be able to comprehend with all the saints what is the width and length and depth and height—to know the love of Christ which passes knowledge; that you may be filled with all the fullness of God. Now to Him who is able to do exceedingly abundantly above all that we ask or think, according to the power that works in us, to Him be glory in the church by Christ Jesus to all generations, forever and ever. Amen (Ephesians 3:14-21).*

As you will read later, God has been answering this prayer in amazing ways in my life!

Basically, through this prayer we can seek the Lord each day to be empowered by His Spirit, asking that we can know the fullness of His power and receive revelation about the fullness of His Kingdom. In my heart, that very much includes the ability to enter into the rest of the Lord. Remember, Jesus had told me to *"be diligent to enter into My rest, lest you fall according to the same example of disobedience"* (Hebrews 4:11).

Once I discovered that the glory and presence of the Lord would rest upon me each day as I gave God the firstfruits of my day, some amazing things began to happen in my life. These supernatural signs and wonders occur with regularity and often manifest on a daily basis. These include favor with both God and man. We have experienced an incredible multiplication of the finances coming into our personal life and into the coffers of King of Glory Ministries International. God has multiplied our finances as we have rested in His presence each day, week, and month. We have experienced an incredible multiplication of revelatory knowledge from the hidden mysteries of Christ's Kingdom. I will share more with you about this awesome benefit of resting in the Lord, receiving hidden revelatory knowledge regularly, later in this book too.

So as Kathy and I have sought to observe the monthly cycle of Rosh Chodesh, we have sought the Lord's heart on firstfruits and firstfruits offerings. For us firstfruits offerings have taken the form of resting in the Lord's presence and waiting for the glory of God to come or to rest upon us. This is another way that you can rest in the Lord, and I will look at this in great detail later. Once the glory has come, we invite the Lord to speak to us. During the day of Rosh Chodesh each month, the Lord has been faithful to speak to us very clearly. At times the Lord has told us to give away money or to sow money into certain ministries or other individual needs. I call this sowing into the glory, and I will share with you about this amazing aspect of the rest of the Lord later in the book. However, I mention it to you here as it is an important aspect of resting in the Lord and allowing Him to guide your firstfruits giving on a monthly basis during Rosh Chodesh. Firstfruits offerings are not to be confused with tithing. Firstfruits offerings are giving above and beyond the customary ten percent tithes.

Rosh Chodesh is a very important time on the Lord's calendar. It is a time for us to hear clearly from the Lord concerning His direction for our lives and ministries for the coming thirty days. We need to learn to be in sync with the Lord. We must walk in obedience to the Spirit of God. We must learn to be both geographically and chronologically obedient. In other words, we need to have revelatory knowledge from the Lord as to when and where we are called and ordained to work and minister on a weekly and monthly basis. This is a huge aspect of the rest of the Lord. God will give you revelation about your call for the times and seasons (see 1 Chronicles 12:32). Only from waiting and resting in His presence and His glory can we gain His heart and insight for the ministry assignments and the missions that He has ordained for us each season.

We have an acquaintance, Bobby Connor, who lives near us, who says, "If you are not in the place that God has called you to be, there is no grace to be in the place where you are." I like to say that we need "grace for our place." You see, at times we can have an understanding that we are to be at a specific place. However, if we are in the right place prematurely or too late we can still miss God's intended plan or blessings for us. God is a chronological God. He has certain preordained things that He wishes to accomplish in our lives at preordained times and seasons at specific geographic places. That is why observing the Lord's appointed feasts of the Hebrew calendar are critical to entering into the rest of the Lord. Again, we must learn to be both geographically and chronologically obedient.

That is one reason that so many people in the Body of Christ are still laboring to bring all of their prophetic words to pass in their lives. People like this do not have 20/20 spiritual vision nor do they tend to hear the Lord very well. As a result, they do not understand why the promises of God have not come forth. Another reason may well be that they have not honored the Lord by observing the Sabbath properly each week. It is also possible that they have not recognized nor honored the monthly and yearly feasts as required by the Lord. They may have neglected to present themselves to the Lord at the appointed times and may have missed their windows of opportunity each week, month, and year. As a result, many are going around the proverbial mountain again year after year.

Rest = Multiplication / $E = mc^2$!

At specific times in specific geographical places, God will open spiritual gates. It is important that we recognize these spiritual doors and walk though these supernatural openings in God's perfect timing. That is the beauty of learning to enter into the rest of the Lord. When we present ourselves to the Lord at the appointed times each week (the Shabbat) and each month (Rosh Chodesh), we position ourselves to hear the Lord. We honor the Sabbath and the Lord's designated feasts and position ourselves to receive the blessings of God. The Lord's blessings, by the way, come in multiples. Jehovah is a God of multiplication. He wants to bless us and multiply us. We see this principle in Genesis 22:17. God says, *"Blessing I will bless you, and multiplying I will multiply your descendants as the stars of the heaven and as the sand which is on the seashore; and your descendants shall possess the gate of their enemies."*

You see, God *is* a God of multiplication. As we learn to enter into the rest of the Lord, we will begin to position ourselves to receive His blessings of multiplication. That is an aspect of the rest of the Lord that is designated to be celebrated each month at Rosh Chodesh. That is why our firstfruits offerings are so important on Rosh Chodesh. When we give God our firstfruits offerings, He can and will do amazing things with them as we position ourselves to receive His blessings. Especially when you give according to the instructions given to you when you rest in Him and wait for the Lord to speak to you from the midst of the glory. I call this giving into the glory, and I will share more on this dynamic of the rest of the Lord later in this book. Understanding how to sow into the glory of God is very important!

Another amazing aspect that is released in our lives and in our sphere of influence as we are diligent and seek to learn to truly enter into the rest of the Lord is that the Lord will allow us to *"possess the gate of our enemies."* I will write more about this later as we discover the abundance and miraculous things that we can step into as we learn to enter into the rest of the Lord. So, honoring the Father during the monthly feast or celebration of Rosh Chodesh is critical to entering into the rest of the Lord.

In addition to the weekly and monthly appointed times, feasts, and celebrations that we need to observe, we also need to honor the Lord's yearly cycles and be diligent to recognize these too. By observing these yearly cycles of feasts, we can enter into a deeper place in the rest of the Lord. This process was instituted in my life quite innocently by the Holy Spirit. Several years ago the Holy Spirit asked me to wait upon the Lord, or to rest in the Lord, on the Day of Atonement. What I experienced was amazing and life changing. Without realizing what I was doing, I began to seek the Lord and position myself in a state of rest each year on the Day of Atonement. Amazingly the Lord began to speak to me in a very clear and straightforward manner over the years.

In hindsight, I believe that it was my innocence and obedience to wait upon the Lord on the Day of Atonement that birthed the trilogy of books, *The Reality of Angelic Ministry Today*. My obedience to write these books transformed my life and King of Glory Ministries International. It was allowing the Holy Spirit to lead me to rest in the Lord on the Day of Atonement and at other appointed feasts times that released the blessing of God into my life in a greater level. In fact, the Lord continues to multiply the intensity and level of His blessing upon my life as I am diligent to wait upon Him and to rest in His presence daily, weekly, and at the yearly appointed times. I feel certain that the Lord will also release a similar multiplication and acceleration of His blessings in your life as you learn to rest in Him and seek Him at the appointed weekly, monthly, and yearly feasts too. These kinds of supernatural and miraculous multiplications are mind blowing!

The Lord is seeking those from among His people who He can fellowship, empower, and bless to make the covenant of His Son known among the nations of the earth. Are you willing? Then you will need to begin to seek to understand and be diligent to enter into the rest of the Lord. When Jesus appeared to me in the midst of the glory of God, He encouraged me with the following scripture:

> *Therefore, since a promise remains of entering His rest, let us fear lest any of you seem to have come short of it. For indeed the gospel was preached to us as well as to them; but the word which they heard did not profit them, not being mixed with faith in those who heard it. For we who have believed do enter that rest, as He has said: "So I swore in My wrath, 'They shall not enter My rest,'" although the works were finished from the foundation of the world. For He has spoken in a certain place of the seventh day in this way: "And God rested on the seventh day from all His works"; and again in this place: "They shall not enter My rest." Since therefore it remains that some must enter it, and those to whom it was first preached did not enter because of disobedience, again He designates a*

certain day, saying in David, "Today," after such a long time, as it has been said: "Today, if you will hear His voice, Do not harden your hearts." For if Joshua had given them rest, then He would not afterward have spoken of another day. There remains therefore a rest for the people of God. For he who has entered His rest has himself also ceased from his works as God did from His. Let us therefore be diligent to enter that rest, lest anyone fall according to the same example of disobedience (Hebrews 4:1-11).

Once we become diligent to enter into His rest, we can begin to grow in favor with both God and man. As we seek to rest in the Lord by honoring the weekly, monthly, and yearly appointed times that God has ordained, we can begin to enter into the fullness of God's rest. The fullness of God's rest is a place of victory. The fullness of God's rest is a place of triumph and prosperity. It is a place of intimacy, fellowship, and communion with God. As we rest in Him, we can watch as He orchestrates and releases amazing increase in our lives. As we learn to understand this revelation, it can be life changing!

Honoring these weekly, monthly, and yearly feasts and appointed yearly times on God's calendar is crucial to entering into the rest of the Lord. Scripture tells us in 2 Corinthians 3:18 that *"we all, with unveiled face, beholding as in a mirror the glory of the Lord, are being transformed into the same image from glory to glory, just as by the Spirit of the Lord."* We can all go from glory to glory! We can move into greater levels of glory within Christ's Kingdom!

One of the most important keys that the Lord has given us is the ability to understand that we *can* enter into or access deeper levels of His rest. In the next chapter I will describe how the Lord Jesus visited me in a dream to help me understand the importance of His appointed feasts.

CHAPTER 19

Another Visitation of Jesus and Understanding That Jesus Honored the Feasts

During the process of writing this book, I was visited in a dream once again by Jesus. The Lord stood beside my bed in my little prayer room in Moravian Falls, North Carolina. He said, "You have been seeking and asking about the appointed feasts of Israel. I want you to know that I kept all of the feasts even from childhood." When the Lord spoke these words to me, I was released into a vision within my dream. Perhaps this may sound unusual to you, but I have been hearing God through dreams, trances, and visions for years.

In this succession of visions I saw Jesus as He grew from a babe in swaddling clothes to the Messiah upon the Cross. I saw Him step out of the tomb of Joseph of Arimathea. I witnessed the Lord ascend into the heavenly realms as depicted in Acts 1:9. In this dream I saw many scenes from the Lord's earthly life unfold before my eyes. It seemed as if I was actually there with Him. All of the events that I saw in my dream were directly related to Christ's observance of the appointed feasts of Israel.

Jesus was dedicated at the temple in Jerusalem by His earthly parents, Joseph and Mary, as commanded by the Jewish Law. Jesus was a Jew, so Jesus was required by Jewish Law to honor and observe the appointed feasts and God's appointed times. As a Hebrew man, an indispensable part the Lord's religious Jewish lifestyle was His observance of God's appointed times. Jesus certainly attended synagogue on a weekly basis; Jesus certainly observed the Shabbat or Sabbath day to keep it holy. Here is one example from Scripture:

> *When the Sabbath had come, He began to teach in the synagogue. And many hearing Him were astonished, saying, "Where did this Man get these things? And what wisdom is this which is given to Him, that such mighty works are performed by His hands! Is this not the carpenter, the Son of Mary, and brother of James, Joses, Judas, and Simon? And are not His sisters here with us?" And they were offended at Him. But Jesus said to them, "A prophet is not without honor except in his own country, among his own relatives, and in his own house." Now He could do no mighty work there, except that He laid His hands on a few sick people and healed them. And He marveled because of their unbelief. Then He went about the villages in a circuit, teaching (Mark 6:2-6).*

Jesus told His disciples to wait in prayer after His Resurrection: *"Being assembled together with them, He commanded them not to depart from Jerusalem, but to wait for the Promise of the Father, 'which,' He said, 'you have heard from Me'"* (Acts 1:4). As the disciples were chronologically and geographically obedient, the Lord confirmed His promise of the Holy Spirit on the appointed Jewish Feast of Pentecost. This proves that Jesus honored and recognized the Jewish feasts even after His Resurrection. That fulfillment of God's promise is seen in Acts 2:

> *When the Day of Pentecost had fully come, they were all with one accord in one place. And suddenly there came a sound from heaven, as of a rushing mighty wind, and it filled the whole house where they were sitting. Then there appeared to them divided tongues, as of fire, and one sat upon each of them. And they were all filled with the Holy Spirit and began to speak with other tongues, as the Spirit gave them utterance (Acts 2:1-4).*

The story of the disciples at Pentecost is a perfect portrait of waiting on God or resting in the Lord. This is a wonderful prophetic example of waiting on God or resting in the Lord at a specific geographical place at a God-ordained time that released a supernatural impartation of Kingdom power and strength to the 120 or so disciples. By their chronological and geographical obedience, the disciples received an impartation and the tangible anointing of the Holy Spirit came upon their lives. You can still receive this same kind of supernatural empowerment as you wait or rest in the Lord today.

We also see from a study of all four Gospels that Jesus observed the Passover according to the commanded Jewish law. Jesus had all of the elements in place and made sure that His disciples understood the prophetic significance of "The Last Supper" as they took the bread and wine as recorded in Matthew 26:17-30 and Mark 14:12-26. We see this illustrated clearly in Matthew:

> *Now on the first day of the Feast of the Unleavened Bread the disciples came to Jesus, saying to Him, "Where do You want us to prepare for You to eat the Passover?" And He said, "Go into the city to a certain man, and say to him, 'The Teacher says, "My time is at hand; I will keep the Passover at your house with My disciples"'" (Matthew 26:17-18).*

It is clear from searching the Scriptures that Jesus observed all of the appointed feasts rigorously as a Jewish man.

In the Old Testament, God commanded the Jewish people to observe the appointed feasts and celebrations throughout all generations (see Leviticus 23). As Christians, you and I are a genealogical part of this covenant and commandant too. We are engrafted into Christ's family through the blood of Jesus. The Lord's appointed times are an intricate component of His covenant with the Israelites. It was and is imperative that the Jewish people observe the appointed feasts each week, month, and year. The observance of these times helps to keep the people of Israel in good relationship with God; and by honoring the feasts, the Jews are distinguished and also set apart as God's chosen people. No other group of people on earth, except Christians, has this privilege to celebrate God by honoring the appointed feasts and celebrations of the Jews.

As the Lord stood over me in this dream, I was certain that if He had not observed the Jewish appointed holidays and feasts it would be very clearly spelled out in the Scriptures. However, the Gospels clearly indicate and demonstrate the Jesus observed all of the appointed feasts and celebrations throughout His entire earthly life. What's more, I am certain that the Lord continues to honor and observe all of the appointed feasts and celebrations from His throne of mercy and grace in the heavenly realms and dimensions. I believe that God blesses us when we choose to honor and observe all of the appointed feasts and celebrations too.

I firmly believe that the Lord's disciples and the first- and second-century church also observed and celebrated the Jewish appointed feasts and celebrations. The disciples saw Jesus keep and honor the holy days, and they were taught by Jesus to do the same things that He did (see John 13:15; 2 Peter 2:21). It was not until about 200 years after the Lord's Resurrection that the church ceased to honor the appointed Jewish holidays and feasts. The Gospels and the Epistles do not mention or teach a lot concerning appointed holidays and feasts because it was a forgone conclusion that the church would always understand the importance of these appointed times to meet with God. However, today we know that as the Body of Christ we have lost this revelation and our understanding of the importance of the appointed feasts for the most part. However, there are a lot of believers in the Body of Christ who are returning to the Jewish roots of Christianity by honoring and celebrating appointed holidays and feasts. This makes Jesus smile!

Paul, using an analogy, speaks of Christ as the Passover in 1 Corinthians 5:7: *"Therefore purge out the old leaven, that you may be a new lump, since you truly are unleavened. For indeed Christ, our Passover, was sacrificed for us."* There is no question that the early church observed and recognized these feasts. In my opinion, it is also important that we as individuals should seek the Lord about the importance of celebrating appointed holidays and feasts too.

There are great blessings and empowerments that can come from the heavenly realms as we learn to observe the feasts of Israel. As we are diligent seek the Lord at the weekly, monthly, and yearly times, as Jesus did, we will receive a blessing from the Creator of Heaven and earth. This is some of the revelation revealed to me the dream.

Ruach HaKodesh

However, we need to understand clearly that we do not want to observe the feasts in a religious way. Rather, we should seek to honor and celebrate the feasts in the spirit. We should observe the appointed holidays and feasts as led by the Holy Spirit—not in a rigorous religious manner but by the Ruach HaKodesh. The literal translation of this Hebrew phrase is "the Spirit of holiness." The Holy Spirit exemplifies Christ's love, and that is how we should observe the feasts. Of course, this has been a very basic and rudimentary look at the feasts. However, this concept can be life changing for you if you do not now recognize the Jewish feasts and appointed times. I pray that basic understanding will help you to step into a secret place in Christ and His Kingdom and that it will propel you deeper into the rest of the Lord.

As Jesus stood over me in my dream, I looked up at Him to see the Lord smiling broadly at me once more. This always brings such pleasure and acceptance into my heart. As I looked into the eyes of Jesus in this dream, it seemed that I began to relive my past. And through revelation I understood that there were times when I was a new Christian that the Holy Spirit had told me to read, rest, fast, and pray. As Jesus stood over me in my little prayer room, I continued to dream about His childhood, adolescence, and adulthood. I saw how Jesus and His earthly family observed the Jewish feasts and appointed times on God's calendar. Suddenly, as I looked into the eyes of Jesus in the dream, revelation flooded into my spirit.

I had the sudden realization that the Lord had led me to observe the Jewish feasts and appointed times unwittingly in the past decade. It was this unconscious observance and honoring of the appointed times that transformed my life. I had honored the feasts without realizing it with my mind or soul. I did not realize what I was actually doing. I was just being led by the Holy Spirit. Today people all over the world ask me how God could transform my life in such a miraculous way when they hear my testimony. (Kevin's testimony, *From the Gutter to Glory*, is available for free in our online Resource Center, www.kingofgloryministries.org/store.) Today I realize that I sparked the blessings of God in my life as I had unwittingly honored the appointed times on the Lord's calendar.

In fact, after the dream, I searched out the times of certain events in my journals and notes. Then I correlated them to the Jewish feasts and appointed times on God's calendar. I discovered that the Lord had spoken to me to read, rest, fast, and pray on Rosh Chodesh on several occasions. However, two of the most significant miraculous breakthroughs in my life came in 2002 when the Lord spoke to me to rest in Him and wait for Him to speak to me on Passover of that year. That event happened in March of 2002. I rested in the Lord for about seven consecutive days. However, I did not realize that it was during the celebration and feast of Passover that I was resting in the Lord. I read God's Word as led by the Holy Spirit. I prayed and repented as led by the Holy Spirit. I rested in His glory and presence, and the whole time I was fasting with water only. I was unknowingly observing the Passover feast at the proper time.

Easter Sunday fell on March 31, 2002. At that time I did not know about the Jewish Passover feast. It was in the middle of the Passover feast that the Holy Spirit led me in a time of waiting, resting, and seeking the Lord. On the way to church that Easter Sunday, the power and glory of God filled my vehicle and God spoke to me in what may have been an audible voice. He said, "You are about to see My Hand move in your life. I will speak to you today in the service. Do not doubt that it is Me. For I have seen and observed your heart towards me. And today I will begin a new chapter in your life. You will travel to Africa and minister there, and this will launch you into you destiny in My Kingdom." I arrived at Deliverance Temple under the influence of the Holy Spirit. I was totally drunk in the Holy Ghost!

During the service the Lord spoke to me again, telling me to go and kneel at the altar.

When I knelt there someone spoke in an utterance in the gift of tongues. As this utterance was being spoken, the power of God once more fell upon me and washed over me in waves. There was an interpretation of the tongues, and it seemed that God was speaking directly into my heart through this gift of the Spirit (see 1 Corinthians 12:10). He answered every question that I had asked Him during the past few days of prayer, repentance, and fasting. One of the things that the Lord had spoken to me was that He would supernaturally supply all of the money that I needed to travel to Africa. He did. All of the money was actually in my bank account within seventy-two hours: $3,800.

The Lord told me that He would make sure that I was accepted on the team for the missions trip even though the opportunity was closed at that time. God worked in a miraculous way; when I returned to my little house after church that Easter Sunday, there was a message waiting on the answering machine. The message informed me that I had been accepted on the team for the missions trip to Africa. God uses missions trips! The miracles that God started to work in my life are numerous and too many to share here. However, I write about many of them in my trilogy of books, *The Reality of Angelic Ministry Today*.

On October 13, 2012 (Shabbat), I awoke from my dream to see Jesus still standing there smiling over me in my little prayer room in the natural realm. Jesus was actually standing over me. He was paying me a visit. Jesus lingered there for several moments and then He vanished leaving a wonderful fragrance of fresh cut roses. Incredibly, I understood that I had been blessed by God Almighty over a decade ago as I had unwittingly honored God by recognizing His appointed times as the Holy Spirit led me. You see, you don't have to have perfect theology or intellectual understanding of the feasts of God. God will release blessing upon your life as you are faithful and diligent to seek to observe the appointed holidays and feasts as led by the Holy Spirit. Through your simple decision to recognize the

Lord's appointed times and to seek Him at the correct times, God will observe your heart in this. God will look upon your heart and will reward you according to the thoughts and intents of your heart (see Psalm 44:21; Jeremiah 17:10).

When we seek God with clean hands and a pure heart, God will hear us. Psalm 24:4-5 states this fact very clearly: *"He who has clean hands and a pure heart, Who has not lifted up his soul to an idol, Nor sworn deceitfully. He shall receive blessing from the LORD, And righteousness from the God of his salvation."* This visitation of the Lord confirmed for me that God Almighty truly releases blessings to those who seek Him with clean hands and a pure heart. Clean hands and a pure heart come from diligent prayer and a lifestyle of repentance. They can come by observing and honoring the Jewish feasts and appointed times on God's calendar. I lay there in my little prayer room luxuriating in the fragrance of roses as the fragrance of the Lord lingered in the air. Tears of joy trickled from my eyes. How amazing is our God and *"what is man that He is mindful of him?"* (Psalm 8:4).

Later I researched the revelation that Jesus had given to me about these things. I searched in journals and looked though other documents to confirm what the Lord had shown me. I was astonished to see that what Jesus had told me about the dates in 2002 was exactly right. How beautiful for the Lord to visit me and to give a missing piece of revelation to place in this book concerning the ways that we can recognize, celebrate, and honor the Jewish feasts and appointed times on God's calendar. I searched the Scriptures most of the day, and they confirmed all of the events that I had observed about the life of Christ in my dream. There is no doubt that Jesus observed and honored all of the appointed yearly feasts of the Jewish calendar. Jesus was faithful to honor His Father each year during the appointed yearly feasts as He grew from a Jewish child into a Jewish man.

It is not by our intellectual knowledge or our doctrine that God releases these magnificent blessings into our lives as we seek His face at the correct times. No, it is by *His Spirit*. It is through and by *His mighty merciful Spirit* that God honors and looks upon our spirit to release supernatural manifestations of His Kingdom and His King into our life.

The Messiah, Jesus Christ of Nazareth, is the one who gives us the privileges and ability to approach a holy God at His appointed times. These are all grace gifts from God to all of His children, and I am very grateful to be an heir of these supernatural privileges and to have the right to honor and celebrate the Jewish feasts and appointed times on God's calendar.

One of the most important ways that we can be diligent to enter into the rest of the Lord is to walk in obedience and observe the yearly feasts. This is also one of the most powerful keys that the Lord has given to us to appropriate the power of His blessings in our lives. Let's look at how honoring these appointed yearly feasts consistently releases supernatural blessings into our lives. In the next chapter I will examine the difference between entering into the rest of the Lord and entering into the fullness of the rest of the Lord.

CHAPTER 20

The Sabbath Rest and the Fullness of God's Rest

As we begin to understand the rest of the Lord and become diligent to enter into His rest, we come to a place of trust in the Lord. We step into a new place. Usually by this time our whole life has begun to be transformed and recreated by the power of Christ as we learn to rest in Him. When we learn to enter into the rest of the Lord for more than short periods of time, the grace and favor of God begin to rest upon us or abide upon us consistently. Remember, when we learn to rest in God, God begins to rest upon us.

This dynamic of the rest of the Lord is truly life changing. We move from a place of occasionally entering into the rest of the Lord to a place of abiding in the rest and presence of the Lord. We step fully into Christ's Kingdom and begin to walk in dominion authority. We begin to walk in the kingly anointing. God begins to fight our battles for us as we learn to fully trust Him and to fully, or constantly, rest in the Lord. We choose to abide in God and He abides upon us (see Psalm 91:1-2, 9). As we learn to rest in His glory, His glory arises upon us daily.

From this place we step into the fullness of the rest of the Lord. In this place God's Spirit, the Holy Spirit begins to lead and guide us in our every waking moment. We rest and trust in the Lord to guide us and to lead us in His paths of righteousness every second of every day (see Psalms 23:3; 37:23). This is a dynamic of actually allowing the Lord to be our true Shepherd and allowing the Spirit of God to become dominant in terms of our perception at all times. This is resting in the fullness of the Lord. The Apostle Paul spoke of this as spiritual maturity.

When we learn to rest fully in the Lord, we find that our soul—our mind, will, intellect, and emotions—is in submission to the Spirit of God. Our flesh (our body) is also brought into submission to the Spirit of God as we allow the Lord to lead us and guide us continually. The Holy Spirit who dwells within us leads us. We grow into mature sons and daughters of God as we learn to be led by our regenerated spirits (see Romans 8:14). We learn to trust in God totally.

Another important aspect of subjecting our bodies to the Lord is to bring our tongues into submission to God or to learn to or allow the Holy Spirit to bridle our tongue. This is critical to resting in the fullness of the Lord. We need to learn to speak life at all times. We need to speak God's heart at all times into each and every situation. We need to learn to speak life into all of those who cross our paths each day.

The Apostle Paul understood this dynamic of entering into the fullness of the rest of the Lord. He writes about it in Romans:

> *I beseech you therefore, brethren, by the mercies of God, that you present your bodies a living sacrifice, holy, acceptable to God, which is your reasonable service. And do not be conformed to this world, but be transformed by the renewing of your mind, that you may prove what is that good and acceptable and perfect will of God. For I say, through the grace given to me, to everyone who is among you, not to think of himself more highly than he ought to think, but to think soberly, as God has dealt to each one a measure of faith (Romans 12:1-3).*

The perfect will of God is for each of us to enter into the fullness of His rest and learn to trust Him in every situation.

We must allow the Lord to transform our mind (our soul) and learn to bridle our tongue with the help of the Holy Spirit who is within us. This is a key to entering into the fullness of the rest of the Lord. The Lord's earthly brother James taught about this too. In James 1:26 he said, "If *anyone among you thinks he is religious, and does not bridle his tongue but deceives his own heart, this one's religion is useless.*" When we fully rest in the Lord, we allow the Holy Spirit to orchestrate our speech. Many times this means that we do NOT speak at all. We do not allow our soul to speak through us with our intellectual knowledge, but rather we allow the Holy Spirit to speak God the Father's heart through our words and lips. We begin to see the best in all people and the possibilities for the Kingdom of God to shine forth in seemingly impossible situations. The Lord loves it when we begin to rest in Him and see things like He sees them. "*For with God nothing is impossible*" (Luke 1:37)!

God created us in His image. As such our words are powerful. We can create life or we can create death. We can speak forth life or we can speak forth death. Job 22:28 teaches us this powerful scriptural principle: "*You will also declare a thing, And it will be established for you; So light will shine on your ways.*" It is vital to learn to speak life with our tongues. We must train our tongues to bless and not to curse. We must learn to call those things that do not exist as though they do (Romans 4:17). One of the greatest hindrances that keeps many people from entering into the rest and glory of God is their words and their unbridled tongues. It was the words of the children of Israel that hindered them from entering into the rest of the Lord. I want to encourage you that you can learn to speak life and blessings with your words, and this will help you to enter into the fullness of the rest of the Lord.

We see this aspect of resting in the Lord again in James 3:2: "*We all stumble in many things. If anyone does not stumble in word, he is a perfect man, able also to bridle the whole body.*"

Learning to allow the Holy Spirit to lead us and guide us continuously is a process. It is a learning curve, and that is why it can take a season to learn to enter into the rest of the Lord on a daily basis. It can take even longer to learn to live our lives in the fullness of the rest of the Lord. However, the Lord is merciful and kind and He is seeking friends who truly wish to enter into His rest. God is seeking those who will be diligent to enter into the fullness of the rest of the Lord. And it is through those individuals that He will release transformation and revival in the coming years. I find that exciting! Learning to bridle our tongues is a critical key to being diligent to enter into the rest of the Lord. Learn to speak blessings and life!

Remember that Jesus taught us that He only did what He saw His Father doing. In other words, Jesus rested in the Father. He rested in the Lord. Look at John 5:19-20 where Jesus says, *"Most assuredly, I say to you, the Son can do nothing of Himself, but what He sees the Father do; for whatever He does, the Son also does in like manner. For the Father loves the Son, and shows Him all things that He Himself does; and He will show Him greater works than these, that you may marvel."*

Jesus saw into more than one dimension simultaneously. From a place of rest, the Lord Jesus Christ was able to see on earth (in this dimension) what His Father was doing in Heaven (in a heavenly dimension). This is an important aspect of the rest of the Lord. Resting in the Lord will help you develop your ability to both see and hear clearly from the heavenly realms or dimensions. I will talk about this more later, but I mention it here for you to consider. Remember that Jesus was and is *the* royal Priest according to the order of Melchizedek. Jesus set an example for us to follow in terms of resting in the Lord and speaking only what the Holy Spirit revealed to Him.

Total Victory Is in the Fullness of the Rest of the Lord

When we learn to enter into the fullness of the rest of the Lord, we position ourselves so that the Lord can fight our battles for us. The Lord will defeat our enemies, and we will experience a season of supernatural prosperity and peace on all sides. The outworking and effects of the rest of the Lord in your life are an aspect of the anointing or the mantle of Melchizedek. Melchizedek was the king of peace. We see this referred to in Genesis 14:18: *"Then Melchizedek king of Salem* [peace] *brought out bread and wine; he was the priest of God Most High."*

Melchizedek was both a king and a priest of the Most High God. When you begin to enter into the fullness of the rest of the Lord, you will enter into the anointing of the kingly priesthood. In other words, you will begin to function and live your life as a royal priest according to the order of Melchizedek. However, before you can obtain that place, you must enter into the fullness of the rest of the Lord. To receive the mantle or anointing of Melchizedek you must understand and enter into the rest of the Lord just as Jesus did. You must be diligent to enter into the fullness of the rest of the Lord.

Koinonia and the Rest of the Lord

Another amazing aspect of the mantle or the anointing of Melchizedek is the communion found in Genesis 14:18: *"Melchizedek king of Salem brought out bread and wine."* This passage of scripture represents the Communion table and foreshadows the Cross of Calvary. God gave us eternal rest through the finished work of Jesus Christ on the Cross. As we learn to enter into the rest of the Lord through communion with God, our lives can be transformed. Again, this is another aspect of the rest of the Lord.

Communion is developing an intimacy and fellowship with the Spirit of God. It is koinonia with God. Paul speaks of it in 2 Corinthians 13:14: *"The grace of the Lord Jesus Christ, and the love of God, and the communion of the Holy Spirit be with you all. Amen."* The Greek word *koinonia* used in this scripture means to have friendship, communion, or intimacy with another. That is what the rest of the Lord is all about, friendship. Entering into the fullness of the rest of the Lord is having intimacy and communion with God at all times. Jesus lived like this. Jesus walked in the fullness of the rest of the Lord at all times. Jesus trusted the Father even when He was separated from the Father for the first time ever (see Matthew 27:46). We must learn to fully trust the Lord.

Of course, communion is also about the Communion table and the Lord's Supper (see Matthew 26:26; Mark 14:22). Again, this is a wonderful way that we can help to activate our ability to enter into the Lord's rest every day. There is something supernatural that is released in our lives as we partake of the Lord Supper on a regular basis. Contrary to some denominations' religious doctrinal beliefs, you do have the privilege of taking communion in the privacy of your own home.

Jesus did not teach that you need to have a priest, pastor, or other spiritual leader to take the bread and wine and bless the elements to have communion. No, Jesus instructed us through His example that *"when He had given thanks, He broke it* [the communion bread] *and said, 'Take, eat; this is My body which is broken for you; do this in remembrance of Me'"* (1 Corinthians 11:24). Jesus said to *"you, do this in remembrance of me"* (Luke 22:19). We have the right and the privilege to take the Lord's Supper as individuals. We can partake of the Lord's Supper or the Communion table every day as individuals. Kathy and I seek to have Communion each day, and most of the time the peace and glory of God fall upon us as we eat the bread and drink the wine/juice in remembrance of the Lord Jesus Christ's atoning work for us. Taking the Lord's Supper consistently and correctly is an important key to entering into the rest of the Lord.

Communion is a wonderful privilege that we have that can help to accelerate the understanding of the rest of the Lord in our lives. I highly recommend that you begin to practice taking Communion or the Lord's Supper regularly with your friends and family. It can be life changing and can also help you to draw closer to the Lord and enter into the fullness of the rest of the Lord. Again, this is a dynamic or an aspect of the ministry or anointing of Melchizedek. Melchizedek was one who carried the peace or presence of God. Melchizedek lived his life in the rest of the Lord; and as a result, the blessings of the Lord God Almighty were upon him. He had spiritual authority. Melchizedek also had authority in the natural realm as an earthly king.

Sowing into the Glory

Genesis 14 tells the story of a battle and great victory won by Abram. Afterwards Melchizedek blessed him (vv. 19-20). Again, this is a picture of entering into the rest of the Lord. Abram was blessed by

Melchizedek after they partook of bread and wine together, which is a type or foreshadow of the Lord's Supper: "Then *Melchizedek king of Salem brought out bread and wine; he was the priest of God Most High*" (v. 18). Another way to say this is that Melchizedek was a friend of God and lived his life in the blessings of the Most High God, Jehovah. Melchizedek was anointed to carry the peace of God and the authority of God, and he abided in the rest of the Lord. The favor of God and the anointing of God were evident upon Melchizedek's life.

Abram recognized this. Abram acknowledged the anointing and the higher level of favor and relationship with God that Melchizedek walked in. Abram most likely felt the tangible anointing and the power of the Spirit of God that rested upon Melchizedek. Abram discerned that the favor of God or the rest of the Lord was abiding upon Melchizedek. So he acted on that knowledge. He gave a tithe to Melchizedek. We see this in Genesis 14:19-20: "*And he* [Melchizedek] *blessed him* [Abram] *and said: 'Blessed be Abram of God Most High, Possessor of heaven and earth; And blessed be God Most High, Who has delivered your enemies into your hand.' And he* [Abram] *gave him* [Melchizedek] *a tithe of all.*"

This is huge! This is perhaps the most important key to entering into the rest of the Lord. You must learn to sow into the anointing or sow into the glory. Abram recognized the anointing of God upon Melchizedek and gave him a tithe. Abram gave Melchizedek an extravagant amount of goods and wealth. We need to learn that are times when the Lord will call for us to sow extravagantly into other men or women of God who carry some Kingdom treasure that we would like to possess. If we want to see the anointing, favor, grace, power, revelation, and goods of the Kingdom of God in our lives, we need to sow into the glory as the Spirit of God leads us.

I will talk to you more about sowing into the glory or sowing into the anointing later. However, at times when we are resting in the Lord and the presence and the glory of God visits us, the Lord will often times speak to us to give into other ministries or individuals who have a higher level of the anointing of the Holy Spirit or who walk with a greater revelation and closer relationship with the Lord than we do.

To see the manifestation of the reaping or harvest of your "glory seed," you need to sow it into a greater anointing than you are currently carrying. However, you need to sow these glory seeds as directed by the Spirit of God. In the rest of the Lord, God will reveal to you exactly when and where you are instructed to sow your glory seeds. Please allow me to encourage you to sow extravagantly. When the Lord is resting upon you and speaks to you to sow into the glory, you can expect an incredible increase in the seed that you sow. Remember, our God is a chronological God. Sowing into the Kingdom is absolutely critical to entering into victory in your finances whether as an individual or as a ministry. Seek to sow your glory seeds into the right place at the right time.

The fruit of Abram's tithe to Melchizedek was a generational blessing released into Abram's generational line. Once we begin to experience the rest of the Lord and God begins to prosper us and to win our battles for us, just as He did in this instance with Abram, we must be obedient and remember to tithe and give generous alms. We need to ask the Lord to whom we are to give, and usually it is to those who are walking in a greater level of anointing than we are.

Recently the Lord told me to sow $1,000 into another anointed ministry's building fund. Because I had recently given away $1,000 to another place, I hesitated. But then I remembered what I had learned about giving into the glory. So I gave $1,001. Almost immediately after this "glory seed" was sown, King of Glory Ministries International received a 4,000 square building on 5.3 acres of land on which we are establishing our new Ministry Equipping Center. The MEC will soon begin functioning to raise up a royal priesthood according to the order of Melchizedek.

God will send His people from the ends of the earth to Moravian Falls to be trained and equipped to do the work of the Lord. We will send them out in the Acts 13 model, and the Lord will use them in great and mighty ways for His glory. We are expecting saints from age eight to eighty-two to come and be empowered by the Spirit of

God at the Ministry Equipping Center. Now, that is a supernatural harvest and it is happening supernaturally fast! The result is an advancement of God's Kingdom, as we will soon be training individuals to preach the Gospel of the Kingdom to reach the ends of the earth from Moravian Falls. That is just one testimony of a glory seed bearing supernatural fruit. Praise the Lord!

This is a prophetic picture of entering into the fullness of God's rest. Kathy and I have been amazed as the Lord has supernaturally multiplied our glory seed offerings. I am sure that the Lord will also release a similar supernatural reaping on your glory seeds as well. Learning to be obedient to the Lord as He asks us to sow into His Kingdom is another way that we can learn to trust the Lord and enter into the fullness of Christ's rest. Many times the Lord will ask you to sow extravagantly after you receive a victory as you learn to rest in the Lord. Abram did with Melchizedek.

These kinds of glory seeds always bring in an accelerated supernaturally fruitful harvest. In my mind I thought that it would take about five years for the ministry to get a property like this. However, when I was obedient to sow into the glory, God released in five weeks what my soul thought would take five years. Now, that is a supernatural harvest! God provided the land and the financing to pay for it before He even spoke it into being in my spirit. It is amazing how God is doing things like this to advance His Kingdom at this hour. What is more, He wants to release these kinds of financial miracles to you too. They come from understanding and entering into the rest of the Lord and being obedient to sow as instructed by the Lord into the glory with your glory seeds.

Supernatural Rest

Another benefit of these extravagant gifts into God's Kingdom is that we establish the fullness of the rest of the Lord in our lives—spirit, soul, and body. At this point the Lord begins to release to us supernatural prosperity in all aspects of our lives. We see this kind of rest in the Scripture. Let's look at a few examples now.

The Lord gave Joshua a supernatural rest after He allowed the Lord to fight the battle for the children of Israel. In Joshua 21:44 it tells how *"the LORD gave them rest all around, according to all that He had sworn to their fathers. And not a man of all their enemies stood against them; the LORD delivered all their enemies into their hand."*

Again, we see that when the people of Israel allowed the Lord to fight their battles and learned to trust the Lord, or rest in the Lord, God delivered their enemies into their hands. The other amazing thing that unfolded rather effortlessly was that the Lord gave them rest all around. That is a prophetic portrait of what the Lord wishes to do for you when you learn to enter into the fullness of His rest and wait for Him to fight your battles for you. Trusting in the Lord releases the rest of the Lord. The greater your trust in the Lord is, the greater the level of your rest in the Lord.

We see this dynamic of entering into the fullness of the rest of the Lord unfolding in the life of King David as told in 1 Chronicles 22:18: *"Is not the LORD your God with you? And has He not given you rest on every side? For He has given the inhabitants of the land into my hand, and the land is subdued before the LORD and before His people."* Again, we see the benefits of learning to rest in the Lord as God gave King David overwhelming grace, favor, peace, and ultimate victory. Learning to enter into the fullness of the rest of the Lord releases supernatural favor and peace in your life. God defeated Israel's enemies and gave the people rest on every side during King David's reign.

This same dynamic of the rest of the Lord is evident in David's genealogical line. Just like God blessed Abram, who was King David's genealogical predecessor, God also released a generational blessing into King David's seed. King David's generational seed was blessed by God, and through that supernatural favor we are also blessed as joint heirs of Christ. Learning to enter into the fullness of the rest of the Lord releases a genealogical blessing of grace and favor into our generational line. That is why we can leave an inheritance to our children's children (see Proverbs 13:22). David walked in this kind of supernatural favor and this anointing of genealogical blessings.

Look at the life of Solomon in 1 Kings 5:4: *"But now the LORD my God has given me rest on every side; there is neither adversary nor evil occurrence."* David's son (seed) Solomon was blessed with supernatural peace and prosperity. Again, we should note that Solomon gave an extravagant offering to the Lord. Solomon sowed into the glory (see 2 Chronicles 7:1-16). This extravagant giving moved the Lord to release additional favor upon Solomon's life. This enabled him to enter into the fullness of the rest of the Lord and to experience rest on every side. It is also true that during his reign Solomon also ruled and reigned in the mantle or anointing of Melchizedek. God gave him rest on every side. In other words, Solomon entered into the fullness of the rest of the Lord.

The fullness of God's rest is truly entered into when your enemies are defeated by the Lord on your behalf. You submit to God and allow Him to fight the battles for you. Actually, when you enter into the fullness of the rest of the Lord, you come to a place of breakthrough or to the spiritual gate of breakthrough.

Spiritual Gates

King David came to such a place recorded in 2 Samuel:

> *The Philistines also went and deployed themselves in the Valley of Rephaim. So David inquired of the LORD, saying, "Shall I go up against the Philistines? Will You deliver them into my hand?" And the LORD said to David, "Go up, for I will doubtless deliver the Philistines into your hand." So David went to Baal Perazim, and David defeated them there; and he said, "The LORD has broken through my enemies before me, like a breakthrough of water." Therefore he called the name of that place Baal Perazim (2 Samuel 5:18-20).*

When we have been diligent to enter into the fullness of the rest of the Lord, we will come to a place of breakthrough. Our Baal Perazim will be a place where we choose to rest in the Lord and allow Him to fight our battles for us. When the victory is gained through the Lord's power and His Spirit, we will transition into and through a spiritual gate into a place of peace. We will step into a place where we are completely resting in the Lord and He will give us peace on every side. A key to this is chronological and geographical obedience.

The fullness of God's rest manifests in our lives as we rest in God and become mature in our discernment to understand the times of the seasons of our lives. When we walk according to God's chronological cycles of blessings, we will learn to enter into the fullness of His rest at the appropriate time and in the perfect place; we will come to our own Baal Perazim. We will come to a gate of breakthrough, and we will break into the fullness of the rest of the Lord. We will come to a place of spiritual blessings and unlimited breakthrough.

These spiritual gates can be called open heavens or portals of God's glory. The key to entering into them is chronological obedience. This ability to discern the times and seasons of our lives only comes from becoming a mature son or daughter of God and allowing the Holy Spirit to lead us into the fullness of the rest of the Lord. Once we enter into the fullness of the rest of the Lord, we will be entrusted with dominion authority and dominion power. At this point we will have passed through our gate of breakthrough, our personal Baal Perazim, and God will break through for us and give us rest on every side!

It is important to remember that disobedience will hinder you from entering into the fullness of the rest of the Lord. We can learn from the example of the Israelites in Psalm 95. God did not allow Israel to enter in to His rest. The Lord desired for the whole nation to enter into the fullness of His rest so that they would have peace and prosperity on every side. But the people of Israel were disobedient. The Lord gives a warning for our benefit:

> *For He is our God, And we are the people of His pasture, And the sheep of His hand. Today, if you will hear His voice: "Do not harden your hearts, as in the rebellion, As in the day of trial in the wilderness, When your fathers tested Me; They tried Me, though they saw My work. For forty years I was grieved*

with that generation, And said, 'It is a people who go astray in their hearts, And they do not know My ways.' So I swore in My wrath, 'They shall not enter My rest'" (Psalm 95:7-11).

There is a direct correlation between sowing and spiritual gates of breakthrough. Although this spiritual dynamic of the Kingdom of Heaven is difficult to articulate, it is nonetheless real. Sowing as we are directed by the Holy Spirit in specific places at specific times (chronological and geological obedience) is critical to opening the heavenly realms over your life. Some people call this principle "open heavens." When we are obedient with our "first fruit" offerings and sow into the Kingdom as the Lord leads, we often will experience an immediate breakthrough in our lives.

Supernatural sowing, or sowing into the glory, is an important key to unlocking spiritual gates of breakthroughs in your life, your family, and within your personal sphere of influence. This is yet another aspect of being diligent to enter into the rest of the Lord. In fact, this aspect of sowing into the glory or obedient giving is a key that can help you to be diligent to enter into the *fullness* of the rest of the Lord. In the next chapter we will begin to look at another amazing hidden mystery of the Kingdom of God and the rest of the Lord: the heavenly hosts—the rest of God's eternal family. We will touch on how the Lord is releasing angelic ministry to help His friends who will operate in the anointing or mantle of the royal priesthood according to the order of Melchizedek.

CHAPTER 21

The Heavenly Hosts— the Rest of God's Eternal Family

On the Day of Atonement in 2012, I seemed to relive the entire experience from the Day of Atonement 2011 over again. Once again I sat upon Christ's mighty white charger and watched carefully as millions of God's angels maneuvered all around the Lord Jesus and me. I was astonished at the multitudes of angelic beings that had accompanied the Lord Jesus Christ as He had led the charge through the supernatural rip in the atmosphere. The powerful glory of God was palatable and felt like a heavy, weighty tangible substance that had been poured out upon the earth. I watched many angelic leaders approach Jesus to receive battle instructions. At one point there was a short gap in the action, and the Lord spoke to me very sternly.

The Lord turned and leaned out to His left upon His charger and looked deeply into my eyes. Frozen by the proximity of Jesus, I was at a loss for words and my mind became absorbed by the majesty of the Messiah. I must have looked stunned. I remember the beautiful smile upon the Lord's face. Jesus asked me a question: "Do you understand?"

I seemed to be immobilized by the power that emulated from the Lord. I found it hard to think, much less speak. But as I gazed into the eyes of my Savior, His love covered me once more. Once again I felt the power of His unconditional love for me and for all of mankind. Tears began to stream from my eyes. And I remember thinking, *Why am I weeping?* But I could not stop crying. Through it all Jesus just continued smiling at me while waves of His glory washed over me. I remember looking in to the Lord's beautiful eyes. I became lost in His glory. I became enamored looking at the reflections of the glory of God that was being reflected in the Lord's pupils. I must have gazed into the eyes of Jesus for a long time. At least it seemed that way, but perhaps time as I know it had ceased to exist at that instant.

It seemed that the Lord allowed my stare to linger for a time. My concentration of observing the glory in the Lord's eyes was broken by the sound of metal upon metal. Suddenly I was aware that Jesus was once more unsheathing His mighty sword. I remember thinking, *I hope that He shows me His sword to me again.* You see, by now I had witnessed the reflection of the glory of God dancing and pirouetting on the gleaming blade of Christ's beautiful sword. It seemed that the Lord's smile broadened as with His right hand Jesus drew His sword once again from its sheath. The sword made a crisp sound as it was freed from the scabbard on the Lord's right thigh, and there was a beautiful ringing of the metal for a moment. Once more the Lord's sword gleamed in the manifest glory of God.

Jesus held up His magnificent sword and allowed me to see the words "The Rest of the Lord" once more. Once again, Christ's sword was very close to my face. Suddenly Jesus wielded the sword in a practiced, expert, fluid sweeping motion and pointed the tip of His sword at multitude of angelic beings that were maneuvering around us. With great authority and intensity, Jesus said very loudly, *"Be diligent to enter into My rest"* (Hebrews 4:11).

As I looked into the eyes of Jesus for one more fleeting second, revelation flooded my mind. At that instant I understood that the angels who were maneuvering around us were also made up of the great cloud of witnesses. Those who rode upon the horses were saints who had preceded me into the heavenly realms. It was apparent to me that Jesus regarded and considered these heavenly residents, these angelic beings, to be the "rest of the Lord." They were a part of God's family (see Ephesians 3:15).

Once more it appeared that Jesus was speaking to me in a parable. It seems that the Lord often speaks to me in parables; but why should I expect Him to do speak to me any other way? My gaze left the Lord's magnificent eyes to follow the steel of the blade of the Lord's sword to the direction that He was now pointing it. I once more saw the glory of God dancing around the words "The Rest of the Lord" that were inscribed into the shaft of the blade. The power and glory of God fell upon me in a fresh and new way and revelation continued to pour over me in waves.

It was not so much that I received this in words, because the amount of information was too great to comprehend in mere human words. It was a supernatural understanding, or perhaps it was because of the spirit of wisdom and revelation that may have been upon the enormous pair of mighty white horses that were at that moment galloping up to the Lord's position. These two stallions carried angelic beings, perhaps these were the spirits of wisdom and revelation. Subconsciously I clung to the Lord's waist as this outpouring of knowledge fell upon me and was absorbed effortlessly into my mind. Jesus did not seem to mind that I was clinging to Him so tightly. I could feel the power of Christ's mighty charger between my legs.

Beyond the tip of Christ's sword were millions of angelic beings. The sounds and fragrances that were surrounding us at that moment were overwhelming. These mighty warriors were all equipped with the accoutrements of war. There were angelic beings like I have never seen. Not all of them were in human form. This shocked me but did not surprise me. Yet others were humans. Both of these were members of the great cloud of witnesses. They too were members and an element of the rest of the Lord. As this avalanche of revelation poured into my spirit, the scripture from Matthew 24:30-31 flowed into my mind: *"Then the sign of the Son of Man will appear in heaven, and then all the tribes of the earth will mourn, and they will see the Son of Man coming on the clouds of heaven with power and great glory. And He will send His angels with a great sound of a trumpet, and they will gather together His elect from the four winds, from one end of heaven to the other."*

I began to wonder if I was alive or dead. I questioned myself wondering if I was still in my prayer room in Moravian Falls. Had I joined the great cloud of witnesses? Were the millions of angelic beings that were moving all around me the same ones that are described in Hebrews?

> *Since we are surrounded by so great a cloud of witnesses, let us lay aside every weight, and the sin which so easily ensnares us, and let us run with endurance the race that is set before us, looking unto Jesus, the author and finisher of our faith, who for the joy that was set before Him endured the cross, despising the shame, and has sat down at the right hand of the throne of God (Hebrews 12:1-2).*

Once more I seemed to be lost in an instant of time. In fact, time seemed to stand still. It seemed that hours passed as I looked at millions upon millions of angelic beings maneuvering past upon mighty white horses. In fact, I seemed to relive the entire experience from the Day of Atonement 2011 over again. The angelic hosts rode above the terrified masses of humanity who were huddled some distance below us.

Within my field of my vision to the left was the hand of God with His mighty sword pointing to the angelic hosts as they passed by in amazing formations. The glory of God continued to dance upon the sword of the Lord. A thought came into my mind: *It is impossible to count all of these angels.* After a long time I wondered within my heart: *Is this it? Is this the end? Is the Son of God coming from heaven to earth today? Is that what I am seeing in the people below me? Are the people of the earth in such great anxious and fear because they see You coming back, Jesus? Do they see You coming on the clouds of heaven with all of this power and all of this great glory? Lord, are you sending all of your angels with the mighty sound of that shofar that I heard earlier? Are these angels here to gather together Your elect from the four winds, from one end of heaven to the other?* "O Lord, have mercy on us," I prayed.

A Supernatural Angelic Ballet

By now I was covered in sweat. The Lord continued to hold His sword firmly in His right hand. I could see the nail scar that is upon His hand. I looked at the beautiful signet ring that is upon the Lord's ring finger. I watched as Jesus slowly moved His sword from left to right and from right to left revealing a panoramic view for me to witness this massive swirling multitude of angelic beings. My attention was transfixed upon the sword of the Lord for a long time. Shivers began to run up and down my spine. When I glanced away from the pageantry of the supernatural angelic ballet that was unfolding in the manifest glory of God, I saw the huddled masses below trembling in fear and horror. By now the dark and evil storm had engulfed many of them. My mind was racing as I continued to look down the wide shaft of the Lord's sword. Glory continued to dance and pirouette upon the metal of Christ's sword.

In the glory of God, it appeared as if the words "The Rest of the Lord" were actually alive. It felt as if an eternity had passed. However, when Jesus spoke I understood that it had only been a moment and the twinkle of an eye. Once more I was lost in my thoughts as I gazed upon the words "The Rest of the Lord" that were inscribed upon the Lord's sword. As the glory seemed to luminesce throughout this heavenly dimension from the rip in the earthly sky, the Lord's sword seemed to be alive with luminescent colors that danced upon the blade. The pirouetting of these supernatural colors was mesmerizing. I became lost in my thoughts again. I gazed upon Christ's living sword for several moments as time itself seemed to be supernaturally suspended.

Once more I looked at every detail of the sword of the Lord, and I became lost in the spirit and lost within my own thoughts: *Is this the end of the world as we know it?* I remember thinking, *Are all of those people down there going to be lost? There was so much more that I should have done!* The words "The Rest of the Lord" once more became supernaturally etched upon my mind like they were engraved into the heavenly metal of the Lord's mighty sword. The Lord allowed me to watch an innumerable number of angels pass by our position. It seemed as if I was in a trance within a vision. Honestly, I am not sure. The Lord's mighty white charger whinnied and moved slightly forward. It appeared that this supernatural beast was ready to bolt up higher into the heavenly realms. I seemed to be in a state of shock, and my mind was so full of revelation that I could not comprehend it all. I seemed to have trouble forming thoughts, although I wanted to ask the Lord several questions.

However, in the glory I could not think. I just continued to gaze upon the Lord's sword and the angelic pageantry that was continuously passing by. After I had observed these amazing things unfold for a very long time, I was finally able to form a sentence and these words tumbled childlike from my month: "Lord, I thought that the rest of the Lord was a scripture from Hebrews chapter 4." At that instant it seemed that the pleasure of the Lord enveloped me and the uneasiness and concern that I had felt evaporated. I thought that I was witnessing the end of the world, so I was overwhelmed. Perhaps I was in a state of shock. My heart was pounding within my chest as sweat tricked from my hair across my forehead and onto my robe. I began to breathe more easily.

The peace of God flooded my spirit and understanding filled my heart that there is still time! I looked up to see Jesus smiling at me with great love and compassion. His eyes were ablaze as He said, "Yes, but My rest is much more than that. The rest of the Lord is the Kingdom of Heaven. When you learn to enter into the rest of the Lord, you can enter into the rest of the Lord." With that Christ once more pointed at the multitudes of angels that were still moving in choreographed formations around us. I looked again into the beautiful eyes of Jesus. In an instant more revelation filled my spirit, and I understood that there is another aspect or realm of Christ's Kingdom that constitutes the "rest of the Lord." That is the angelic host of God's Kingdom. This angelic host that I was witnessing is the rest of the Lord too.

There are secrets and hidden mysteries of God which very few are able to unlock or discover on this side of eternity. However, I understood that we are living in a God-ordained moment of time when the Lord is empowering ordinary people to comprehend and discern the great cloud of witnesses. Angels are an important part of God's end-time plans, and the Lord is in the process of equipping regular people to understand this aspect of the rest of the Lord. God's angels are a very important part of "the rest" of the Lord.

Now it became perfectly clear to me why the Lord had told me back in 2004 to write the trilogy of books, *The Reality of Angelic Ministry Today*. God wants His people to understand this aspect of the rest of the Lord. The great cloud of witnesses is a part of the rest of the Lord. Again, it seemed as if the hidden and mysterious things in Christ's Kingdom often come in parables. Sometimes it is just both/and. Hebrews 12:1 reveals one aspect of the rest of the Lord; *"Therefore we also, since we are surrounded by so great a cloud of witnesses, let us lay aside every weight, and the sin which so easily ensnares us, and let us run with endurance the race that is set before us."* Jesus and I were surrounded by a great cloud, a great multitude of angelic beings. There are many different kinds of angels in God's Kingdom. What is more amazing is that they are all on our side.

As I wrote in the trilogy of books, *The Reality of Angelic Ministry Today*, we have stepped into a God-ordained moment of time when God is opening up this realm of heaven to His friends. God is empowering ordinary people to understand that there is a great multitude or cloud of angelic beings from the heavenly realms or the heavenly dimensions that the Lord is allowing to work in harmony and unity with us today. The Lord is releasing these angelic beings to impact the earthly realms today. Perhaps God's angels like these are ready to work for you too. The key to entering into the aspect of the rest of the Lord (the help of the angelic hosts) is to look *"unto Jesus, the author and finisher of our faith, who for the joy that was set before Him endured the cross, despising the shame, and has sat down at the right hand of the throne of God"* (Hebrews 12:2). We need to look at Jesus who is seated in the heavenly realms.

We need to learn to enter into the rest of the Lord and understand that the God of the universe is allowing you and me to also be seated in the heavenly places with Him. God is releasing His people to learn to enter into the rest of the Lord in order that we can minister in the anointing or the mantle of Melchizedek. When we begin to understand this, we can rest in the Lord and allow His great cloud of witnesses to work on our behalf according to Hebrews 1:14: *"Are they not all ministering spirits* [angels] *sent forth to minister for those who will inherit salvation?"* That was exactly what I was seeing in this vision. Jesus was coming as the Lord of Hosts, He was coming as the King of Glory, and He was releasing His angelic host to minister for those who would receive His free gift of salvation!

We learn from Colossians 1:16-17 that *"for by Him* [Jesus] *all things were created that are in heaven* [angelic beings] *and that are on earth, visible* [humans] *and invisible* [angels and demons], *whether thrones or dominions or principalities or powers. All things were created through Him and for Him. And He is before all things, and in Him all things consist."* God created the multitudes of the angelic beings that I was seeing swirling around me at that instant. God's angels were created by Him, and God's angels were created for His purposes. It all made perfect sense as I sat upon the Lord's mighty white stallion high above the turmoil below.

Jesus was encouraging me to be diligent to enter into the rest of the Lord. In this case, the angelic host of God that was all around us at that instant constituted the rest of the Lord. In fact, I realized that God's angels are always around each of us at every moment of every day. And we are living in a kairos moment of time when God is allowing His children to understand this and to work or co-labor with His angelic hosts. That is one way that we can enter into the rest of the Lord. Another is that we can make sure that we are saved and will go to heaven.

So when Jesus pointed His sword at the angelic host and said, *"Be diligent to enter into My rest"* (Hebrews 12:1), He was referring to the great cloud of witnesses. You see, when we are diligent

THE HEAVENLY HOSTS—THE REST OF GOD'S ETERNAL FAMILY

to enter into the rest of the Lord, at times we will actually enter into the heavenly places or heavenly realms (see Ephesians 1:20). Again, the Lord was speaking to me in a parable. He was also saying, "Be sure that your salvation is real and true so that you can join or enter into the rest of my family" (see Ephesians 1:14-15). There will be people who believe that they are saved or born again who may not make it to heaven. I saw many people like that in the vision of the dark and evil storm. We need to be sure that we are going to make it into heaven at this hour.

I understood that another aspect of the rest of the Lord is the Lord's angelic host. We can enter into this great cloud of witnesses when we learn to be diligent to enter into the rest of the Lord. Again, this is an attribute of the mantle or anointing of the royal priesthood according of the order of Melchizedek. We can literally be raised with Christ and seek those things which are above (the power of the heavenly realms or dimensions). We can access the very throne of grace and mercy where Christ is sitting at the right hand of Father God. We can do this by setting our minds or renewing our minds by looking on things above and not on things on the earth (Colossians 3:1-2). This happens when we die to our plans and self-seeking agendas and our lives become hidden with Christ in God. *"When Christ who is our life appears, then we also will appear with Him in glory"* (v. 4). And I suppose that is what I experienced as I was sitting on the Lord's mighty white stallion on the Day of Atonement.

I am certain that Jesus wanted me to understand that the angelic hosts of heaven also make up an element of the rest of the Lord. I found this understanding and revelation quite comforting. I hope that you also find comfort with the revelation that the entire hosts or God's angelic family are ready willing and able to stand alongside of you in every aspect of your life. What can I say then, *"If God is for us"* (along with all the angelic hosts of heaven), then *"who can be against us?"* (Romans 8:31). One of the most important keys to being diligent to enter into the rest of the Lord is a lifestyle of prayer. I want to begin to examine this in the following chapters and share a few keys that the Lord has revealed to me over the years. Perhaps these keys and my experiences will help you to be diligent to enter into the rest of the Lord and experience the glory of God for yourself.

CHAPTER 22

Diligent Prayer and the Rest of the Lord

Psalm 140:13 is pregnant with a wonderful promise of being diligent to enter into the rest of the Lord: *"Surely the righteous shall give thanks to Your name; The upright shall dwell in Your presence."* The language here seems to indicate that we can sit down beside the Lord and dwell under the shadow of His covering allowing God Almighty to protect us. In this place of the fullness of God's rest, He will be our true Shepherd and we can receive all of the promises to be found in Psalm 23 and Psalm 91. There is a great, great grace and multiplied blessings that come from dwelling in God's presence. This speaks of resting in the Lord's protection and provision continuously. This is a wonderful portrait of entering into the fullness of the rest of the Lord. I have unwittingly done this since 2001 by allowing the Holy Spirit to lead me to read (God's Word), rest (in the glory and presence of the Lord), fast (seek the Kingdom of Heaven with violent spiritual action), and pray (seek the Lord in outer and inner court prayer). The results have been amazing!

As I have shared previously, when I have been faithful to begin my day in God's presence, He has been faithful to come and to rest upon me. This is yet another aspect of being diligent to enter into the rest of the Lord. Earlier I wrote about how I purposed in my heart to give the Lord the firstfruits of my time each day. We have sought to give the Lord the Sabbath day each week by recognizing it and contended to keep it holy. (That does not necessarily mean attending a church service on Sunday, although attending church can be a way to honor the Shabbat.) Kathy and I have also sought to give the Lord a monthly firstfruits offering on Rosh Chodesh. And we have begun to recognize and observe the yearly feasts as outlined upon the Jewish calendar. Again, all of these are actually very elementary but critical aspects of being diligent to enter into the rest of the Lord.

During the vision of the dark and evil storm, Jesus sternly and very clearly instructed me personally to "be diligent to enter into My rest." The Lord also instructed me to tell His people that they (that means you), too, need to be faithful and diligent to seek to enter into the Lord's rest at this hour. Over the last year, the Lord has continued to amaze me as I have sought to practice these elemental ways of being diligent to enter into the rest of the Lord. There has been a marked increase of the grace and favor that the Lord releases into my wife, Kathy's, and my lives as we are diligent to invest time in waiting or meditative prayer. I am sure that the Lord will also begin to do amazing things in your life as you are diligent to wait upon Him or rest in His presence as you start each day, week, month, and year. Listen and allow the God of the universe to speak to you and into your life during these times. Then be obedient to do what you hear.

This process, learning to rest in the Lord in this way, is a learning curve. One analogy that the Holy Spirit gave me about this type of resting in the Lord parallels the temple. The holy temple was made up of three parts; the outer court, the inner court, and the holy of holies. It was in the tabernacle of Moses or the temple that the Aaronic and the Levitical priesthoods performed their priestly duties. In the temple the priests worked and offered sacrifices to mediate between a sinful people and a holy God. These priests offered the blood of animals to make atonement for the sins of the people. These men were never able to enter into the rest of the Lord because the covenant that they had with God was incomplete and not perfect. The works and ministries of the Aaronic and the Levitical priesthoods required those men to work constantly. They had to offer unending sacrifices to make atonement for sin.

God has given us a better covenant through the sacrifice of His only begotten Son, Jesus Christ of Nazareth (see Hebrews 7:22;

8:6; 12:24). Jesus offered His blood once and for all to make perfect atonement for the sins of all of mankind. Jesus Christ's prophecies about the destruction of the temple were fulfilled in AD 72 when the temple in Jerusalem was destroyed by Roman soldiers (see Matthew 24:2; Mark 13:2). There is no further need for the Aaronic and the Levitical priesthoods to perform their priestly works; there is no longer a temple for them to minister in or a place where they can offer their sacrifices.

Jesus Christ came and established a better covenant based upon a greater blood sacrifice, the blood of God. Christ's perfect sacrifice has empowered and enabled you and me to enter into the rest of the Lord. The finished work of Christ empowers you and me to become royal priests according to the order of Melchizedek. God has ordained for this priesthood to replace the Aaronic and the Levitical priesthoods in this new dispensation of grace. As such, we have the liberty to enter into God's rest just as Jesus finalized His work as a royal Priest according the order of Melchizedek and entered into the God's eternal rest.

Jesus literally ascended into the heavenly realms or the heavenly dimensions to sit at the right hand of the Father (see Acts 1:9; Hebrews 4; Psalm 110). The Father sent His only begotten Son to empower us. The finished work of Jesus Christ upon the Cross of Calvary authorizes and enables us to enter or pass behind the veil (through the heavenly realms or dimensions) just as the Lord did. God has ordained that only sanctified priests can enter into the holy of holies.

Because of Christ's perfect atoning work we can enter into the tangible, weighty presence of God Almighty as individuals (see Hebrews 6:19-20; 9:3-7; 10:20-39). We do not need a priest to mediate between God and man for us. We can come boldly before the throne of mercy and grace (Hebrews 4:16). We can approach God behind the veil of the holy of holies because the blood of Jesus makes us righteous, holy, and sanctified (see Revelation 1:5-6; 5:9-10; Hebrews 10:10). We can enter into the rest of the Lord and luxuriate in the very presence of Almighty God. We are God's temple, and His glory can rest upon just us as His glory abided between and rested upon the cherubim in the tabernacle of Moses and the temple of Solomon (see Hebrews 9:1-5; Exodus 25:17-22).

Hebrews 6:19-20 speaks about this type of ministry that is available to you and me today: *"This hope we have as an anchor of the soul, both sure and steadfast, and which enters the Presence* [glory] *behind the veil, where the forerunner has entered for us, even Jesus, having become High Priest forever according to the order of Melchizedek."* Scripture defines this supernatural privilege that we have to enter into the very presence and glory of God and to rest in His glory because Jesus became High Priest forever according to the order of Melchizedek.

That is what the Lord is calling us to today. That is why Jesus told me in no uncertain terms to tell His people to *"be diligent to enter into My rest, lest anyone fall according to the same example of disobedience"* (Hebrews 4:11). We have this privilege today, and we can enter into the rest of the Lord in this way. We can go behind the veil and rest in the presence and glory of God. This kind of waiting or meditative prayer can be life changing and is another aspect of being diligent to enter into the rest of the Lord. Let me take a moment to describe the things that the Holy Spirit has taught me about entering into the rest of the Lord in personal prayer times like this.

The Temple Model of Prayer

Again, this kind of prayer is modeled by the temple. The outer court of the temple was a place for repentance. When we first begin to seek to enter into the rest of the Lord in this manner, we must first move into the outer court which is a place of repentance of dead works and sins (Hebrews 6:1). Pray for the forgiveness of your sins: *"If we confess our sins, He is faithful and just to forgive us our sins and to cleanse us from all unrighteousness"* (1 John 1:9). It is good to ask the Lord to guide you as you pray for forgiveness as it is His nature to help us in this way (see Luke 11:1-13; Matthew 6:5-15; Romans 8:26). Ask the Lord show you any areas that you need to release to Him, release and repent, and then ask Him to forgive you for your sins.

These can include sins of omission or sins of commission. These may include sins like unrighteous judgments, unforgiveness, or the works of the flesh. *"Now the works of the flesh are evident, which are: adultery, fornication, uncleanness, lewdness* [pornography, ungodly entertainment on TV or the Internet, etc.], *idolatry* [we looked at this earlier], *sorcery* [this can include sinful intercession or manipulative prayers, which is Christian witchcraft], *hatred, contentions, jealousies, outbursts of wrath, selfish ambitions, dissensions, heresies, envy, murders, drunkenness, revelries, and the like"* (Galatians 5:19-21).

Ask the Holy Spirit to show you any areas where the words of your mouth (word confessions) and the meditation of your heart or ungodly mindsets (soul-mind, will, and emotions) were sinful in God's sight. Then repent and ask the Lord to forgive you and to redeem you (see Psalm 19:14). Doubt and unbelief fall into this category, and these two attitudes can hinder you from entering into the rest of the Lord. Doubt and unbelief were two of the reasons that the Israelites could not enter into the Promised Land and into the rest of the Lord.

As you are diligent to repent in this way, you will begin a supernatural process of restoring your soul with the help of the Holy Spirit (see Psalm 23:3). This process may take some time. And as you are diligent to practice this model of prayer, your ability to enter into the rest of the Lord will exponentially increase over time. Once you have "prayed through" all of your personal issues, then you will need to pray for the things that God's Word commands for us to pray. This is inner court prayer.

We enter into the inner court in our times of resting in the Lord. Then we pray for the president and those in authority in our sphere of influence (city, county, state, and nation). We pray for our family. We pray for the issues that the Holy Spirit places upon your heart. We pray for those in our sphere of influence, such as our families, our children, our friends, the prayer requests that we receive, etc. We pray as led by the precious Holy Spirit. Pray for the Body of Christ and the church; pray for *all* churches in your sphere of influence regardless of their denominational affiliation. God loves them all, and so should we (see 1 John 3:14).

And please allow me to state that it is critical to pray for the peace of Israel and the peace of Jerusalem. In fact, there is a promised blessing that comes from praying for the apple of God's eye (see Zechariah 2:8; Psalm 122:6-7). Ask the Holy Spirit to help you and to guide you as you rest in the Lord and pray in the inner court. Once you have prayed through all of these commanded prayers, you can allow the Holy Spirit to pray through you (see Romans 8:26-31).

Next, pray in the Spirit until you feel a release to stop interceding this way. This can take a few minutes or it can take a few hours. Again, this practice takes diligence and determination on your part. Don't give up. You are building yourself up spirit, soul, and body as you pray like this in the Spirit (Jude 20). If you are not filled with the Holy Spirit, then just pray in the way that you normally intercede and ask the Holy Spirit to help you as you seek the Lord. Of course, the Lord can help you to develop your own personal prayer model. I only suggest this one for your edification. It is best to be led by the Holy Spirit in this venture.

As you become diligent to pray in this fashion each and every day, you will soon discover that you will have to invest less and less time in the outer court and in the inner court. You will not need to repent as often for your sinful nature because the Lord will begin a supernatural process of sanctification and transformation in your life. Again, these are attributes and blessings that come from being diligent to enter into the rest of the Lord. As you are diligent to enter into the rest of the Lord each day by investing and giving or offering your time to God in prayer like this, the Lord will become faithful to rest upon you. That is when you begin to move from the inner court and the outer court into the holy of holies.

It is in the holy of holies where you find the glory of God. It is in the holy of holies where you cease from your labors and enter into the rest of the Lord. It is in the holy of holies that you find the cherubim and the glory of God resting between them. It is in the holy of holies where you find true rest for your soul. It is in the presence of

Jesus, in the presence of the Holy Spirit, in the presence of the Father that the weighty, tangible glory of God will rest upon you. And when you are diligent to enter into the rest of the Lord and come to Him regularly in the holy of holies, your life will be transformed as you rest in the Lord and rest in the glory of God.

Eventually you will find that God's glory will be waiting for you even before you begin to pray. *"Surely the righteous shall give thanks to Your name; The upright shall dwell in Your presence"* (Psalm 140:13). At times the presence and the glory of God will start to fill you and to rest upon you the instant that you step into your prayer room and close the door behind you. At times like this you may just want to worship and adore the Lord. Worshiping the Lord in the glory realm can be life changing. Worshiping God in the atmosphere of glory can accelerate your ability to enter into the rest of the Lord. I wrote about this kind of experience with the Holy Spirit in the books *Dancing With Angels 1* and *2.* This is still another wonderful blessing that can come upon you as you learn to be diligent to enter into the rest of the Lord. By resting and worshiping in the holy of holies, you position yourself to receive God's supernatural grace and favor. Let's look at how God's supernatural provision, favor, and grace will begin to unfold in your life in the next chapter.

CHAPTER 23

Supernatural Transformation Transpires by Resting in the Glory

It is impossible for me to articulate how this supernatural transformation transpires. I can only say that when we are diligent to enter into the rest of the Lord in this manner, God will start a metamorphosis in our lives. The Lord begins the process of recreating us in the very image of Christ. We will be transformed in a moment and in the twinkle of an eye and changed into the very image of the Son of God. God knows exactly when your moment will come. You just need to rest in Him and wait for His timing. You will begin to grow in grace and favor with both God and man. You spark a God-ordained process of being transformed into a royal priest according to the order of Melchizedek.

You see, when we choose to remain and rest in the glory and presence of God, a supernatural exchange takes place. We become like the boy Samuel who rested near the tabernacle and the Ark of the Covenant (see 1 Samuel 3). Samuel grew in favor with both God and man (1 Samuel 2:26). We become empowered to grow and mature into overcomers like Joshua in the following scripture when we linger in the glory of God. We see our lives transformed by staying and lingering in the holy of holies of the tabernacle and in the glory of God. (Remember that *we* are the temple or tabernacle of God today.)

We see another scriptural example of this in Exodus:

> *So it was, whenever Moses went out to the tabernacle, that all the people rose, and each man stood at his tent door and watched Moses until he had gone into the tabernacle. And it came to pass, when Moses entered the tabernacle, that the pillar of cloud [this pillar of cloud was the glory and presence of Almighty God] descended and stood at the door of the tabernacle, and the LORD talked with Moses. All the people saw the pillar of cloud [glory] standing at the tabernacle door, and all the people rose and worshiped, each man in his tent door. So the LORD spoke to Moses face to face, as a man speaks to his friend. And he would return to the camp, **but his servant Joshua the son of Nun, a young man, did not depart from the tabernacle** (Exodus 33:8-11, emphasis added).*

In this passage of scripture we see two important attributes of the rest of the Lord. First, in the glory of God, the Lord spoke to Moses as a man does to a friend. I want to encourage you that the God of the universe, the Creator of heavens and earth, is seeking to tabernacle with you. God wants to speak to you as His friend. When you are diligent to enter into the rest of the Lord, God will begin to speak to you and to manifest to you in a very clear and distinct way (see John 14:21). The second attribute we can learn is that when we linger and rest in the manifest presence of God, our lives are transformed. We are supernaturally empowered to be overcomers like Joshua.

Joshua lingered in the glory. He rested in the presence of the Lord for extended periods of time. This is a great key and example for us and illustrates how we should invest time lingering in God's glory and presence. You can be assured that God also spoke to Joshua as the young man lingered and rested in the presence and glory of the Lord. Joshua started and sparked a supernatural exchange in his life. It was from resting in the Lord that Joshua was empowered to lead the children of Israel into the Promised Land. However, because of disobedience the children of Israel were not permitted to enter into the fullness of the rest of the Lord. But you can.

SUPERNATURAL TRANSFORMATION TRANSPIRES BY RESTING IN THE GLORY

By being diligent to rest in God's glory, you can initiate a similar process of supernatural and God-ordained transformation in your life. You can receive amazing impartations from Christ's Kingdom by simply resting and waiting in the glory of God. When you are diligent to rest in the Lord on a regular basis, you will be empowered to be transformed into an overcomer. Learning to enter into the rest of the Lord will help you to be changed into an overcomer. Jesus made this amazing statement about overcomers:

> *He who overcomes shall be clothed in white garments, and I will not blot out his name from the Book of Life; but I will confess his name before My Father and before His angels....He who overcomes,* ***I will make him a pillar in the temple of My God, and he shall go out no more.*** *And I will write on him the name of My God and the name of the city of My God, the New Jerusalem, which comes down out of heaven from My God. And I will write on him My new name (Revelation 3:5, 12).*

When God gives you a new name, it is because you have been transformed into a new person. You will dwell in the presence and glory of God continually.

That is an amazing promise from the Lord that speaks of the direct and immediate blessings that come from being diligent to enter into the rest of the Lord. Along this line, Jesus also says in Revelation 21:7: *"He who overcomes shall inherit all things, and I will be his God and he shall be My son."* Actually, what these scriptures are describing is entering into the fullness of the rest of the Lord. In the fullness of the rest of the Lord, we cease from *our* works and allow God to work on our behalf. It is in the rest of the Lord that we can receive our supernatural inheritance. We begin to supernaturally inherit incredible things as sons and daughters of God. The Lord releases His grace and blessings into our lives and into our spheres of influence in miraculous ways. To state it simply, we are transformed into royal priests according to the order of Melchizedek. We are recreated as new men and women with Christlike natures. We receive a new anointing, a new mantle.

Allowing God to Work on Your Behalf

I have prayed and sought the Lord about this dynamic of the rest of the Lord for over a year. And as I have waited and rested in the Lord and in His presence and glory, the Holy Spirit has spoken into my heart about this amazing spiritual dynamic and this supernatural exchange that takes place as we rest in His glory. As I mentioned earlier, I have rested in the presence of the Lord since 2001 when the Lord instructed to me to "read, rest, fast, and pray." When we cease from *our* work and are diligent to enter into the rest of the Lord, we release and empower God to begin to work on our behalf.

At this point Jesus Christ begins to make intercession for us as a royal Priest according to the order of Melchizedek. We see this role of Jesus as a royal Priest according to the order of Melchizedek in Hebrews chapter 7. You see, when we cease from our work and when we cease from our work of intercession, we empower Jesus to intercede and pray for us. That, my friends, is an amazing exchange! I am sure that you will agree that Jesus Christ, who is seated at the right hand of the Father, has an empowered prayer life; and He is willing to pray for you and your needs *if* you allow Him.

When we reach this place of resting in the Lord by allowing Jesus to intercede for us, we are set free. We begin to enter into the "fullness" of the rest of the Lord. Then we only have to step into or walk out in the natural realm the wonderful things that the Son of God is praying into existence for us from His throne of power, mercy, and grace from the spiritual realm or dimension. Hebrews gives us some details concerning the role of Jesus as a royal Priest according to the order of Melchizedek:

> *And inasmuch as He was not made priest without an oath (for they have become priests without an oath, but He with an oath by Him who said to Him: "The LORD has sworn And will not relent, 'You are a priest forever According to the order of Melchizedek'"), by so much more Jesus has become a surety of a better covenant. Also there were many priests, because they were prevented by death from continuing. But*

> *He [Jesus], because He continues [ministering and interceding for us] forever, has an unchangeable priesthood. Therefore He is also able to save to the uttermost those who come to God through Him,* **since He always lives to make intercession for them** *[those who are born again, born from above, or saved] (Hebrews 7:20-25, emphasis added).*

I found this to be an amazing epiphany! When we enter into the fullness of the rest of the Lord, we are only doing the things that our Lord is doing. We become Christlike as we only do those things that we see and hear our Father doing, just as Christ did (see John 5:19). We rest in the Lord by allowing God to work on our behalf. This supernatural exchange is illustrated in scripture in Zechariah 4:6: *"'Not by might nor by power, but by My Spirit,' Says the LORD of hosts."*

In this passage of scripture, the Hebrew words translated "might" and "power" can be defined as the force or means of man, human flesh and resources, human military strength, wealth, virtue, valor or courage, physical strength and/or man's physical ability. We could also say it means man's intellectual knowledge or the schemes and philosophies of the human mind. So the Lord is declaring or prophesying to the seer prophet Zechariah through an angelic being, "This miraculous transformation of the Kingdom of Israel [the church] is not going to happen because of your physical abilities or your military resilience. This miraculous exchange is not going to happen because of your intellectual way of life, worldly mindsets, or philosophies. It is not coming through your doctrines. This miraculous exchange happens when you rest in Me and allow the Holy Spirit to move upon your behalf." That can be difficult unless you learn to be diligent to enter into the rest of the Lord.

At this point Israel was in captivity and held in bondage. It can be said that the church and the Body of Christ are also in captivity and bondage to a degree at this season. Perhaps you are in bondage to some sort of sin or generational iniquity as you read this. Resting in the Lord can set you free from stubborn generational sins and iniquities in a supernatural and effortless way. In the rest of the

Lord, you can be set free from religion and a religious spirit. So we could say that the amazing and miraculous transformation of your life and personal circumstances will not come from your ability to earn money or work with the strength and abilities of your hands. Your miraculous transformation is not going to manifest because of your superior intellectual ability and carnal mindsets of intellectual knowledge or the philosophies of psychology, scientists, politicians, or theologians. Neither will the Body of Christ be transformed into a Christlike character by any of these human attributes.

The Lord of Hosts is saying that these kinds of miraculous transformations will come to pass supernaturally by the Spirit of God. These miraculous transformations are initiated by the *ruwach* of God. *Ruwach* is the Hebrew word translated for Spirit in Zechariah 4:6. *Ruwach* is the breath, exhalation, or the breathed word of God. Remember that God breathed into the dust and created the creature man (see Genesis 2:7). In fact, it was the *ruwach* of God, or the Spirit of God, that was lingering or resting over the waters that supernaturally birthed all of creation in Genesis 1:2: *"The earth was without form, and void; and darkness was on the face of the deep. And the Spirit [ruwach] of God was hovering over the face of the waters."*

We are talking about the word decrees and prayers of God. This is the very breath of God, or we could say God's breath of life. To say it another way, when Jesus Christ prays for you as a royal Priest according to the order of Melchizedek, He releases the *ruwach* of Father God or the God-ordained destiny or God-inspired prophetic word into and over your life. Jesus declares your destiny in the heavenly realms or dimensions. These decrees or *ruwach* of God then supernaturally manifest in the temporal or earthly dimension. Of course, we need to walk in chronological and geographical obedience to God to position ourselves to receive these blessings. However, when God begins to speak from His throne of mercy, power, and grace, it is not by our might or our power but by the power of the Holy Spirit of the living God that this supernatural exchange takes place. The key to this process is resting in the fullness of the Lord.

When we learn to be diligent to enter into the fullness of the rest of the Lord with meditative prayer and waiting in the glory of God, we release Jesus to intercede for us. When the Lord Jesus prays for us, then it is simply a matter of allowing the Lord's prayers to manifest as the Father releases the wonderful Holy Spirit to go forth and move upon our behalf. Sometimes we just need to wait and rest in the Lord while the Holy Spirit and the breath of the Holy Spirit is working on our behalf. The Holy Spirit will honor our God-ordained destiny when we enter into the rest of the Lord. The Father rested and allowed the *ruwach* of the Holy Spirit to work in the beginning of creation as we saw in Genesis 1:2. Again, this passage of scripture is the very foundation for the Sabbath rest. This is basic "being diligent to enter into God's rest 101" stuff.

At other times the Lord will also release His angelic hosts to go and to make our paths straight and to co-labor or minister *for* us, who are to inherit Christ's salvation. We see this in Psalm 103:20: "*Bless the Lord, you His angels, Who excel in strength, who do His word, Heeding the voice of His word.*" At times God releases angels to help bring the intercession of Christ to come to pass in our lives (see Hebrews 1:14). The reason for this is that God's angels recognize the *ruwach* or breath of God on His words and work steadfastly to help those prophetic decrees manifest in your life. It is really very simple. We rest in the fullness of the Lord and allow God to work on our behalf. When we enter into the fullness of His rest, we learn to totally trust God by allowing the Spirit of God to work on our behalf in any form or fashion that the Lord chooses.

This aspect of the rest of the Lord is spelled out for us in scripture. Hebrews 4 illustrates how Jesus Christ will intercede for us as a royal Priest according to the order of Melchizedek from His throne of rest and power to work on our behalf:

> *There remains therefore a rest for the people of God. For he who has entered His rest has himself also ceased from his works as God did from His. Let us therefore be diligent to enter that rest, lest anyone fall according to the same example of*

> *disobedience [Jesus Christ spoke this exact scripture to me in the heavenly dimensions]. For the word of God is living and powerful, and sharper than any two-edged sword, piercing even to the division of soul and spirit, and of joints and marrow, and is a discerner of the thoughts and intents of the heart. And there is no creature hidden from His sight, but all things are naked and open to the eyes of Him to whom we must give account. Seeing then that we have a great High Priest who has passed through the heavens, Jesus the Son of God, let us hold fast our confession. For we do not have a High Priest who cannot sympathize with our weaknesses, but was in all points tempted as we are, yet without sin. Let us therefore come boldly to the throne of grace, that we may obtain mercy and find grace to help in time of need (Hebrews 4:9-16).*

How do we come boldly before the throne of grace? By resting in His glory and allowing His Spirit to work while we rest. Is it by our constant intercession and works? No, we come into the Lord's presence by resting in His presence and waiting in the midst of His glory. We come boldly before the throne of grace; and in that place, the holy of holies, our lives can be transformed. We can be recreated so that we can recreate Christ in our lives and to those whom we meet.

Entering into the fullness of the rest of the Lord will empower us to do the greater works that the Lord Jesus Christ has called us to do (see John 14:12). We can accomplish those miraculous works just like Jesus. We can rest in the Lord just like Jesus. We too can do those things that we see our Father doing because we learn to live and linger in a place of intimacy and the fullness of God's rest. When we understand that the Kingdom does not manifest in our lives by our power nor our strength but by the power of the Spirit of God and the *ruwach* that is released when we allow Christ to intercede and to decree His plans for us into our spheres of influence, then our lives will be supernaturally transformed. Resting in the Lord allows the Holy Spirit to work on our behalf.

In the next chapter I will examine another facet of the benefits of being diligent to enter into the fullness of the rest of the Lord. As we grow and mature in Christ's Kingdom, we can better understand how God can prosper and bless us. Being diligent and resting in the Lord will begin to release amazing blessings into our lives. As I sat upon Jesus Christ's mighty white charger high above the dark and evil storm in 2011, the Lord released revelation to me about the hidden mysteries of God's Kingdom that are to be found in the rest of the Lord. In fact, these hidden mysteries are a portion of the rest of the Lord. Next we will look at the keys to unlock these hidden treasures of the Kingdom of God in your life.

CHAPTER 24

The Hidden and Mysterious Treasures in the Kingdom of God

As I sat upon Christ's mighty white charger with the manifest glory of God vaulting all around me, more revelation continued to flood into my spirit. The sounds of the angelic hosts that were maneuvering around me were bewildering. The hordes of angelic beings that were in fluid motion around us were truly beyond belief, and my senses were overcome with the profusion of auditory and visual stimulation. I was in a trance, yet I also seemed to be in a state of shock. Jesus had just said to me; "Yes, but My rest is much more than that. The rest of the Lord is the Kingdom of Heaven. When you learn to enter into the rest of the Lord, you can enter into the rest of the Lord." Jesus was still pointing His amazing sword at the multitudes of angels moving in semicircular patterns all around us.

As I peered into the mesmerizing eyes of the Messiah, at that instant more revelation permeated my spirit with supernatural understanding. I realized that Jesus was speaking to me in parables once more. I smiled and I saw Jesus smile back at me with a grace and love that I had not encountered before. His eyes sparkled with love as He discerned that I had received the revelation that He was seeking to release to me about the Kingdom of God. Another epiphany bubbled up within my spirit and into my mind. I was given a supernatural understanding of the hidden and mysterious things that are concealed within Christ's Kingdom. This is the fifth level of the rest of the Lord.

At that precise moment there was another extraordinarily loud blast of a shofar that seemed to place a spiritual punctuation mark on this revelation. My gaze lingered for a few moments more as I allowed this new understanding of the Kingdom to matriculate into my spirit, soul, and every fiber of my being. I was transfixed by the Lord's countenance in the glory realm as I looked into the Lord's eyes. It seemed that Jesus took great pleasure in the fact that I understood the parable He had just spoken to me. He returned my gaze with a gentle look of love and compassion. Once more I became lost in my thoughts. This was amazing. Again, I began to wonder where I was.

I was certain that I was seated with Christ in the heavenly places (Ephesians 2:6); however, I was unsure at exactly *which* heavenly place. My mind was blown. And once more legions of angelic beings maneuvered nearby as if to highlight this celestial spectacle that was unfolding around me physically and within the confines of my human mind. It was almost too much. Christ turned to His left and again spoke an order to one the angelic leaders in a language that I did not understand. All the while the sword of the Lord was still pointed at the innumerable hosts of angels that were flowing all around us. Once more my eyes landed upon the words inscribed into the sword of the Lord: "The Rest of the Lord."

I again watched the glory of God dancing and pirouetting upon the shiny polished metal of the Lord's sword. Once more I became lost in my thoughts as I contemplated the revelation that Jesus had just imparted to me in the heavenly realms. There is another aspect or realm of Christ's Kingdom that constitutes the "rest of the Lord." In the heavenly dimensions there are hidden mysteries that have been reserved for you and me to discover. There are innumerable secrets and hidden treasures of God which very few are able to unlock or discover on this side of eternity. However, they are available to us at this kairos God-ordained moment of time. God has supernatural secrets to share with us. These hidden mysteries are special treasures that God gives to His children. This kind of revelatory knowledge is in the form of hidden pearls the Father has reserved for us at this hour.

As this thought came into my mind, I was reminded of the parable from Matthew 13:44-46 where Jesus was speaking about the Kingdom of Heaven. He said, *"Again, the kingdom of heaven is like treasure hidden in a field, which a man found and hid; and for joy over it he goes and sells all that he has and buys that field. Again, the kingdom of heaven is like a merchant seeking beautiful pearls, who, when he had found one pearl of great price, went and sold all that he had and bought it."* It occurred to me that the Kingdom of God really is like that.

There really are pearls of great price that are hidden with Christ in God's Kingdom. In fact, at that moment I realized that our *lives* need to be *"hidden with Christ in God"* (Colossians 3:3). That is one of the hidden mysteries of the Kingdom of God. I am referring to the secret of the rest of the Lord which is hidden in plain sight. When we rest in God, we are hidden in Christ. This pearl of great price seemed so simple yet so few find it. God's rest is right there in the Scriptures. Yet, the concept of entering into the rest of the Lord is somehow difficult to grasp with our carnal or earthly mindsets.

As I sat there with the Lord in that amazing atmosphere of glory and power, I understood that we are living in a God-ordained moment of time. Elohim, the Creator of the heavens and the earth, is empowering ordinary people to comprehend and discern hidden and mysterious treasures in His Kingdom. The Creator is empowering the creature with revelatory knowledge and with the supernatural grace to enter into His Kingdom and enter into the fullness of the rest of the Lord. As these wonderful thoughts percolated through my spirit, I continued gazing at the Lord's sword. Jesus was still holding up His magnificent sword and allowing me to see the words "The Rest of the Lord." Indeed, these hidden mysteries that are concealed like pearls of great price are still available to God's friends today. I understood that the key to unlocking this kind of revelatory knowledge is the rest of the Lord. In fact, this kind of knowledge is a part of the rest of the Lord.

I continued to gaze upon the words "The Rest of the Lord" inscribed upon the Lord's sword. Time seemed to pass without end and more understanding filled my spirit. As the glory poured out through the atmosphere from the rip in the sky, the Lord's sword seemed to be alive with luminescent colors that danced upon the blade. I was lost once more in my thoughts. I seemed to be in a vacuum of time and space, and it seemed that time as I know it ceased to exist. The pirouetting of the glory on Christ's sword was mesmerizing. The revelation that was flowing into my spirit as I sat with Christ in the heavenly places was mesmerizing.

I was now totally lost in the spirit for an extended segment of time. Subconsciously I continued to scrutinize every detail of Christ's living sword for what seemed like an eternity. And it seemed as if time itself was supernaturally suspended. As I realized this, it occurred to me that one of the hidden mysteries of the Kingdom of God is just that. In the spiritual dimension or the heavenly places time does not exist as we understand it. That is why God's people will be given supernatural revelation and grace to be translated forward into the future in the coming days. In addition to this, there will also be other times when the Spirit of God will allow God's friends to suspend time (see Joshua 10:13). At other instances of time it will seem like time as we know it will be expanded. It will be actually manifesting *"on earth as it is in heaven"* (see Matthew 6:10). At other times God's friends will be translated from one geographic location to another place like Phillip (see Acts 8:39-40). Somehow I understood that this secret of the Kingdom was a dynamic and function of the glory of God. It was an amazing revelation. This is yet another hidden treasure of the Kingdom of God.

As the glory continued to pour forth through the rip in the atmosphere, I looked at every detail of the sword of the Lord and remained lost in the spirit and within my own thoughts. The words "The Rest of the Lord" were branded upon the retinas of my eyes just like they were inscribed into the heavenly metal of the Lord's mighty sword. I understood that Jesus had an important purpose for allowing and orchestrating this experience.

I observed the sword of the Lord for what seemed to be hours as revelation continued to flood into my mind. Later I spoke to the Lord about the rest of the Lord. Then, as I shared earlier, I took my gaze from Christ's sword to look once more into the beautiful eyes of Jesus. The Lord was smiling at me with what seemed to be great pleasure and understanding. The Messiah's eyes burned with love and compassion as He spoke to me about His rest. Jesus said, "The rest of the Lord is the Kingdom of Heaven. When you learn to enter into the rest of the Lord, you can enter into the rest of the Lord." Jesus was referring to the secrets and mysteries hidden in His Kingdom and within the spiritual dimensions.

With these words came more revelation, and in an instant I understood that there are even more aspects, realms, or dimensions of Christ's Kingdom that constitute the "rest of the Lord." The scripture from Ephesians 3:14-21 exploded in my spirit with this understanding. I saw that Jesus once more beamed with pleasure with my comprehension of this mystery. In the Kingdom of God there are many dimensions or heavenly places. That is why we will invest our eternity discovering more about our God and His Kingdom. We will invest eternity exploring the different realms and dimensions of heaven. (I write about this aspect of Christ's Kingdom in the book *Angels in the Realms of Heaven*.)

I had been praying the prayer from Ephesians in my firstfruits offerings of my time and prayers to the Lord for an extended season. However, as I sat with the Lord in the heavenly places on the Day of Atonement, the hidden meaning of this passage filled my spirit.

> *For this reason I bow my knees to the Father of our Lord Jesus Christ, from whom the whole family in heaven and earth is named, that He would grant you, according to the riches of His glory, to be strengthened with might through His Spirit in the inner man, that Christ may dwell in your hearts through faith; that you, being rooted and grounded in love, may be able to*

> *comprehend with all the saints what is the width and length and depth and height—to know the love of Christ which passes knowledge; that you may be filled with all the fullness of God. Now to Him who is able to do exceedingly abundantly above all that we ask or think, according to the power that works in us, to Him be glory in the church by Christ Jesus to all generations, forever and ever. Amen (Ephesians 3:14-21).*

As I sat there in the heavenly places with the Lord Jesus, revelation continued filling me. Suddenly I realized that in the Kingdom of God there are many dimensions or heavenly places. That is what this passage refers to when it says, "C*omprehending with all the saints* [those who comprise the great cloud of witnesses, the rest of the Lord's family] *what is the width and length and depth and height of God's love,"* it refers to knowledge of the hidden and mysterious things that the Father has preserved and withheld for us within His Kingdom. Amazing!

This passage speaks about four characteristics of the Kingdom of God. It reveals four levels of the spiritual dimensions of the Kingdom of God: width, length, depth, and height. Again, our God is a multidimensional God. We live in a three-dimensional realm or world. Our understanding and discernment is often limited to those three dimensions. Three-dimensional space is a geometric model of the physical universe in which we live. Of course, God created this universe. Scientists refer to these three dimensions as length, width, and depth, and they comprise the temporal realm or earthly realm. But scientists are not all knowing; their intellectual understanding and knowledge is incomplete. However, in the Kingdom of God in the spiritual realm or dimensions there are innumerable dimensions. This passage lists four. The word used here by the Apostle Paul for "depth" is the Greek word *bath'os*. It can mean by implication an extensive mystery (hidden mystery) or a very deep and mysterious thing, like concealed treasures.

As I sat upon the mighty white charger with Jesus and revelatory knowledge continuing to flood my mind, I had another epiphany. It

THE HIDDEN AND MYSTERIOUS TREASURES IN THE KINGDOM OF GOD

is the understanding of the love of God. God's love releases to us the revelation and understanding of the hidden mysteries of God's Kingdom. Through resting in the unmerited love of God, which we cannot comprehend with our human minds, we can be filled with all of the fullness of God. I realized that the unmerited love of God is a type of God's glory. I understood that there are many types and degrees of God's glory, just as there are many levels and dimensions in the Kingdom of God. Each type of the glory of God has been given a specific purpose and function by God.

The fullness of God is the hidden and mysterious treasures that are concealed in the realms of heaven or in the heavenly dimensions. That was what I was experiencing at that precise instant! The love of God was pouring out through Jesus Christ and filling me with revelatory knowledge that Jesus wanted me to share with His people. I was being filled with the *bath'os* or hidden understanding of a few of the mysteries of the Kingdom of God. There are secrets and hidden mysteries of God which very few are able to unlock or discover on this side of eternity. It would take an entire lifetime to just understand all of the attributes and idiosyncrasies of each of the different types of God's glory and their purposes alone. And this is only one of the hidden mysteries in the Kingdom of God.

These kinds of supernatural treasures constitute and comprise the "rest of the Lord" in the heavenly realms. These are secret places and special treasures of God. The Father has hidden treasures and secrets to give to His friends. I recall thinking, *"It is your Father's good pleasure to give us the kingdom"* (Luke 12:32). When I thought this, the Lord laughed and a shofar blast sounded nearby as if to punctuate this Kingdom principle. Taking my eyes off of the glory that was dancing on Christ's sword, I looked once more into the eyes of the Jesus. His eyes appeared to be ablaze with passion and love (see Revelation 19:12).

For just an instant I was able to perceive again just a tiny portion of the unconditional love and passion that Jesus has for the lost and the huddled masses that were being tormented below. It was this same power of love that is released to us as we rest in the Lord.

The love of God is a tangible form of the glory of God. God's love is truly life changing, even when we only comprehend a tiny portion of it with our carnal senses. It is this same love of God that helps to unlock the hidden mysteries of the Kingdom of God for His children. It is this same love that enabled the Father to send His only begotten Son to make perfect atonement for our sins. The love of God is the most powerful thing in the universe and is epitomized by the blood of Jesus.

It seemed as if I was coming out of a trance. In fact, it appeared that I was experiencing a trance within a vision. I was undone; and as I peered into the beautiful eyes of Jesus, revelation continued to percolate into my heart from the Son of God. The love glory of God was fueling this exchange. I was amazed that I had the ability to understand these marvelous things. I had never had this kind of understanding before. As this thought came into my mind, the Lord smiled at me once more and the scripture from Proverb 25:2 filled my heart: *"It is the glory of God to conceal a matter, But the glory of kings is to search out a matter."* That is what the hidden and mysterious treasures in Christ's Kingdom are. Somehow I understood that this scripture referred to the fact that God does in fact hide treasure for us to discover. It is our glory to reveal or uncover God's hidden secrets. Later I discovered that the word *conceal* in this scripture means to literally conceal, hide, or to keep secret a valuable article or treasure.

We are living in that day and hour. God has chosen us to be alive for such a time as this. By learning to rest in the Lord, we can begin to receive revelatory knowledge and empowerment to discover the hidden mysteries from God's Word and from His Kingdom. There are hidden treasures concealed by God in His Kingdom and hidden by Christ in the heavenly realms or in the spiritual dimensions. We can learn to access these as we are diligent to rest in the Lord. Once we allow the Lord to transform us as we wait in His glory, we will be able to minster in the anointing or the mantle of Melchizedek. We will be transformed into royal priests according to the order of Melchizedek. And as we have learned, Melchizedek was both a priest and a king.

Therefore, there are amazing promises given to us when we are diligent to enter into the rest of the Lord and allow the Holy Spirit to transform us into kings and priests according to the order of Melchizedek. As kings we can discover treasures that are hidden by God. As it tells us in Proverbs 25:2, "*It is the glory of God to conceal a matter, But the glory of kings is to search out a matter.*" Jesus shed His blood to make you and me kings and priests before God the Father. We see this in Revelation 1:4-6: "*Grace to you and peace from Him who is and who was and who is to come, and from the seven Spirits who are before His throne, and from Jesus Christ, the faithful witness, the firstborn from the dead, and the ruler over the kings of the earth. To Him who loved us and washed us from our sins in His own blood, and has made us kings and priests to His God and Father, to Him be glory and dominion forever and ever. Amen.*" Our God wants for you to be a king and a priest.

We see this wonderful blessing again in Revelation 5:9-10 as heavenly beings are singing to Jesus: "*You are worthy to take the scroll, And to open its seals; For You were slain, And have redeemed us to God by Your blood Out of every tribe and tongue and people and nation, And have made us kings and priests to our God; And we shall reign on the earth.*" It is the love and glory of Jesus that makes you and me able to become kings and priests (if you are female, a queen or priestess). In other words, it is only through the finished work of Calvary and the shed blood of the Messiah that you and I can be transformed into royal priests according to the order of Melchizedek.

Once you understand this fact, that you are a priest and a king, you then have the liberty and the God-given right to search out hidden and mysterious treasure that can be found in the heavenly realms of Christ's Kingdom or within the spiritual dimensions of the Kingdom of God. As I was seated with Christ in the heavenly places, this understanding and this epiphany dropped into my spirit and I grasped this secret with my mind. When this happened, the love and power of the Lord multiplied and I found myself coming back to my senses there in the heavenly realms. As I looked up, I saw the Lord continuing to stare gently into my eyes as a loving father might look into the eyes of his firstborn son.

The Lord spoke to me and told me to write these things down and to encourage His people to be diligent to enter into the rest of the Lord. By now the maneuvering of the angelic armies around us seemed to be coming to a crescendo. I was not sure how long I had been lost in the spirit there in the heavenly dimensions. I was sure that the love of God surpasses our ability to comprehend and is much more powerful that we can possibly imagine. I now think of it as love glory. Before I dismounted from the Lord's steed, Jesus looked deeply into my eyes for a moment. It seemed that He was satisfied that I had understood the hidden secrets that He had sought to release to me on the Day of Atonement.

Once more the love of God washed over me in waves and refreshed me. I was shocked that my time with the Lord was coming to an end. It seemed that this experience lasted for several hours; but I was not sure because then again it seemed like this encounter had just begun. I was torn; I wanted to stay with Jesus in the heavenly realms but I also knew that I needed to be obedient to do the things the Lord was instructing me to do. Jesus helped me and I dismounted from the side of Christ's magnificent white charger. My time with Jesus was ending. The Lord held up His sword once more to allow me to look at it one last time. Once again the words "The Rest of the Lord" danced in the heavenly light show.

Jesus smiled at me and said, "Now go and learn what this means!" A shofar sounded and I found myself back in my prayer room in Moravian Falls. I was totally undone. I was filled with so much of the Lord that it took me a long time to process it all. After a time I journaled the events as best as I could, remembering that the Lord had charged me to write down the vision and to tell His people the things that He had spoken and revealed to me about the rest of the Lord. It has taken me over a year to document everything that is contained in this book. The Lord was very stern when He instructed me to tell His people that they need to be diligent to seek to enter into the Lord's rest at this hour. That is what this book is all about.

You must be diligent to enter into the rest of the Lord!

One of the ways that you can accomplish Christ's mandate is by developing your spiritual vision. As you are diligent to enter into the rest of the Lord, there is an activation of your spiritual senses. The eyes of your understanding become alive and enlightened to the things of the Kingdom of God. This can also be called the seer anointing. (For more information or teaching on the seer anointing, see Kevin's new book, *Unlocking the Mysteries of the Seer Anointing*.) As I shared earlier in this book, it is absolutely critical that we develop our ability to hear the voice of God for ourselves at this hour. We need to see what our heavenly Father is doing. In the next chapter, I will share some of the keys that I have learned about how resting in the Lord can help to activate you spiritual senses and how you can be diligent to refine and perfect your spiritual senses that can help you to enter into the fullness of the rest of the Lord.

CHAPTER 25

Your Spiritual Senses and the Rest of the Lord

One of the themes that I have sought to reiterate throughout this book is the importance of hearing God. As I sat upon the Lord's mighty white charger in the heavenly realms, I was certain that the most important key to entering into the rest of the Lord is to develop your ability to hear what God is saying to you personally. We must also hone our spiritual senses so that we can "see" what the Lord is showing us. Remember, Jesus only did those things that He saw His Father doing (see John 5:19). As I have stated, sometimes in the Kingdom of Heaven it is both/and. The Lord is seeking to *both* speak to you *and* show you important things. God is revealing hidden treasures within His Kingdom to His friends at this hour.

Developing these two aspects of your spiritual senses is absolutely critical today. Hearing what God is saying to you and seeing what God is leading you to do are perhaps the most important keys and basic elements to entering into the rest of the Lord. Therefore, I want to highlight several things that the Lord has revealed to me recently about our spiritual senses. In chapter 8, *Good News in the Midst of the Storm*, I shared the parabolic testimony in the subheading Mice or Men—Small Acts of Obedience Can Open Huge Doors. In that testimony I described how, as a new Christian, I had allowed my vain imagination to run wild. As a result, I had turned two small and harmless mice into gigantic monsters. In the end, I sought the Lord and God spoke to me clearly and gave me His wisdom concerning how to fight this personal battle.

Also in chapter 8, I shared another parabolic but true testimony about the prophet and the snowstorm. In that testimony I shared about how one man stood on the plan that God had spoken into his heart during a season of prayer, even though a seasoned prophet had spoken a prophetic word contrary to what he had heard the Father speaking to him. In the end the man stood on what he had heard from the Lord. This course of action ultimately saved the man a lot of fear and anxiety. Hearing God clearly for himself also saved the man a lot of money and hard work.

Many people in the man's community never questioned the prophetic word about a terrible snowstorm. As a result some of them worked very hard preparing for a situation that never came to pass. The prophecy spoken about the storm did not come as prophesied. None of the people's preparations were sinful or actually wrong. They were just not necessary. When we are diligent to judge prophecies, we are actually learning to be diligent to enter into the rest of the Lord. By judging prophecies, we can many times avoid a lot of unnecessary anxiety and work. Sometimes we invest a lot of unnecessary time and energy preparing to fight battles that never exist. We can also overestimate the strength of our enemies, like I did with the two small mice (this is deception), instead of allowing God to fight our battles.

We need to be diligent to enter into the rest of the Lord. We need to trust the Lord and build our house on the Rock. It is possible that great storms may come and that we *will* need to make preparations. However, it is also very important that we seek to hear the voice of the Lord clearly for ourselves. That is the best course of action. Listen to the prophets, but judge each prophetic word individually. Prophecy should only confirm what God has already spoken or placed into your spirit. Allow the Holy Spirit to guide you and lead you as you learn to be led by Him. This is a better way. Develop your ability to hear the Lord for yourself as these dark and evil storms approach. Do not allow fear generated by prophetic words to transform you into a "doomsday prepper." Rather, allow the Spirit of God to speak to you and guide your steps (see Psalm 119:133).

As I waited upon the Lord on the Day of Atonement, the Lord spoke to me about these matters. I want to reiterate what Jesus said to me about these two testimonies. He said: "This dark storm is a lot like that. People believe that it is going to be overpowering, but '*I have overcome the world*' [John 16:33]. I have overcome the storm. Even though many of My people believe the lies of the enemy, he is defeated. Just like Hobo defeated those little mice quickly, so shall I quickly overcome and calm the approaching darkness and storm [see Mark 4:39]. However, it is imperative that My people keep their eyes focused upon Me in the midst of the storm.

"There are many people today who know about Me, but they do not know Me. Just like My disciples continued to cower in fear even after I came into the boat with them, so do these people cower in fear from the storm [see Mark 4:36-41]. Like My disciples, they do not know Me yet. Therefore, they must begin to learn My ways. '*My yoke is easy and My burden is light*' [Matthew 11:30]. Just like the snowstorm that was prophesied failed to come as expected, so too shall this dark storm fail to manifest as many people believe and teach. Just like the snowstorm came in the spring and then quickly melted, so shall this dark and evil storm melt away with little or no effect for those whose eyes are focused upon Me."

Hear and Obey

We must learn to hear the voice of God and then obey His instructions. We must learn to see what the Lord is doing and then do only those things. Perhaps the Lord will lead you to prepare for the end times by gathering and hording supplies and learning how to grow potatoes and mushrooms. If the Lord shows you to do these things, then by all means be obedient. However, make sure that you are not motivated by fear. Make sure that you are being diligent in your work because the Lord is leading you by faith. It is a season to begin to develop your spiritual senses. In this way you can avoid being distracted. We can resist the enemy and avoid being pushed on to the wrong track by the devil through fear and deception (see James 4:7). However, we must be diligent to cultivate our ability to hear the voice of God.

Hebrews 5:14 tells us that "***solid food*** [the hidden or mysterious principles or weightier matters of God's Kingdom] ***belongs to*** *those who are of full age, that is,* ***those who by reason of use have their senses exercised to discern both good and evil***" (emphasis added). We can grow and mature our spiritual senses in the same way that a weight lifter builds his biceps as we use our spiritual senses seeking to comprehend the spiritual elements of the Kingdom of God. This will enable us to discern between good and evil. Understanding this will be very important in the coming days. We can no longer live our lives by allowing others to hear God for us. We need to receive divine directions for our lives directly from God's throne of mercy and grace.

The Lord has endowed or given everyone spiritual senses. Some people have just worked a little harder to develop their ability to see and hear what God is doing and saying. They can hear God at a higher level than some others. But it is God's heart for all of His people to see and hear what He desires for them without question. The Apostle Paul understood this and teaches us about our spiritual senses:

> *[I] do not cease to give thanks for you, making mention of you in my prayers: that the God of our Lord Jesus Christ, the Father of glory, may give to you the spirit of wisdom and revelation in the knowledge of Him,* ***the eyes of your understanding being enlightened***; *that you may know what is the hope of His calling, what are the riches of the glory of His inheritance in the saints, and what is the exceeding greatness of His power toward us who believe, according to the working of His mighty power which He worked in Christ when He raised Him from the dead and seated Him at His right hand in the heavenly places, far above all principality and power and might and dominion, and every name that is named, not only in this age but also in*

that which is to come. And He put all things under His feet, and gave Him to be head over all things to the church, which is His body, the fullness of Him who fills all in all (Ephesians 1:16-23, emphasis added).

The Apostle Paul prays this apostolic prayer for *"the eyes of your understanding"* to be enlightened. We all have a "knowing" released to us by the Holy Spirit. This "supernatural knowledge" could also be defined as the gift of discerning of spirits or the seer anointing. This anointing of the seer realm will often work in symphony with the unction of the Holy Spirit. When we exercise our spiritual senses, we can develop our ability to see and hear what God wants to show us at a specific time in a specific place. This is one aspect of chronological obedience.

When Paul says *"the eyes of your understanding,"* he is not referring to our natural eyes or eyesight. Paul is referring to the eye of the soul or spirit or our supernatural vision. The word translated "understanding" can mean deep thought, supernatural thought or mind, to have the mind of God, to have the mind of the Spirit of God, and/or to have or experience the mind of Christ. Paul desired for people to understand that we have a spiritual inheritance and spiritual nature that we can step into. We need to understand our true nature in Christ. We have the mind of Christ. When the eyes of our understanding are opened, we begin to appreciate and comprehend who we really are in Christ Jesus. We learn to see and hear God clearly.

When the eyes of our understanding are activated, we can begin to see and enter into the Kingdom of Heaven. When we begin to enter into the realms of heaven, we can begin to appropriate the power and authority that is our heavenly inheritance. Our spiritual senses allow us to be transformed into the likeness of Christ Jesus and activated into the seer anointing just like Jesus. Jesus was a seer. The Lord saw and heard what the Father was doing: *"The Son can do nothing of Himself, but what He sees the Father do; for whatever He does, the Son also does in like manner"* (John 5:19). Our spiritual senses enable us to step into the spiritual or heavenly dimensions where our supernatural inheritance is waiting for us. Your spiritual senses or the seer anointing are an element of your very being.

We are creatures created by God in His image with a spirit, soul, and body. We are created in God's image to "see." You are created to live and breathe in the seer anointing just like Jesus. Our five physical senses are the operation of our body, flesh, or carnal self. The eyes of our understanding or spiritual senses are the part of our spirit that can comprehend things that are present in the spiritual realms or dimensions in a similar fashion that our eyes, ears, nose, skin, and tongue perceive elements and phenomenon from the natural realm. Spiritual senses operate in the spiritual realm the way our five carnal senses detect elements in the natural realm. Our spiritual senses perceive elements and phenomenon from the spirit or heavenly dimensions.

Our spiritual senses enable us to enter into the spirit or heavenly places. They help us to enter into the fullness of the rest of the Lord. When the eyes of our understanding or spiritual senses are activated, we begin to experience life through our spirit and that part of our being becomes dominant in terms of perception. This can last for a few seconds or it can last for days as we learn how to *"walk in the spirit"* (Galatians 5:16; Romans 8:1, 4). This is also learning to be diligent to enter into the fullness of the rest of the Lord.

A verse in 1 Thessalonians can help you to understand your spiritual DNA. And this understanding can also help you to develop your ability to hear the Lord clearly. Let's look at this passage: *"Now may the God of peace Himself sanctify you completely; and may your whole spirit, soul, and body be preserved blameless at the coming of our Lord Jesus Christ"* (1 Thessalonians 5:23). In this scripture the Apostle Paul is sharing several important and elementary truths from the Kingdom of God. He is speaking about the wonderful operation of the Holy Spirit that can work for us to sanctify our lives as we submit to Him. In addition to this, Paul also outlines our spiritual makeup or composition. We are created by God *"in His own image"* (Genesis 1:27). God is a triune Being. This aspect of God's nature is commonly called the Trinity—God the Father, God the Son, and God the Holy Spirit. Since we are created by the Creator in His Image, we also have a triune nature.

Paul spells this part of our spiritual DNA out in the above scripture by saying, *"May your whole spirit, soul, and body be preserved blameless."* Your spirit, soul, and body comprise your nature. Since you are created in God's very image, we have three parts—a spirit, a soul, and a body. I want to look at these because it will help you to understand how the Creator of the heavens and earth can speak to you. Let's look at the soul and body first. In this passage the word for "body" comes from the Greek word *soma*. *Soma* literally means the body or flesh. But in this context, it also means a perfectly healthy body or a body that is in subjection to the Spirit of God. Your body is your flesh, and once you are born from above or born again, the Holy Spirit comes and indwells your flesh. We can choose to allow the Spirit of God, the Holy Spirit, to guide us and lead us. Just as He led Jesus, the Spirit of God can lead us by His Spirit through the ministry of the Holy Spirit (see Matthew 4:1; Luke 4:1; Romans 8:14; Galatians 5:18). God often speaks to you Spirit to spirit.

Your soul is another of the three parts of your spiritual nature. In the above passage, the word for "soul" comes from the Greek word *psuche*. *Psuche* literally means breath or spirit and is commonly translated *soul*. You have a soul which is made up of your mind, will, and emotions. *Psuche* is the root for the word *psychology*. As human beings, we are often led by our intellect and our minds. This is the most prevalent characteristic of our soul. Our personalities are derived from our soul. The science of psychology seeks to help people by dealing with emotional issues associated with the mind and soul. As we learn to rest in the Lord, we allow our minds to come into subjection to our recreated spirits. When this happens, we will be led more by our spirits than our minds, will, and emotions. Our spirits will become dominant in terms of perception, and at this point the Lord can speak to us more readily and clearly.

The Creator will speak to the creature Spirit to spirit, and we will begin to develop our ability to hear God and to be led by the Holy

Spirit in our daily lives. This is why learning to hear the voice of God is so important to entering into the rest of the Lord. For most people, our flesh and our souls (mind, will, and emotions) are the driving forces of our actions. Our bodies get hungry and require food and shelter. So, most our actions on a daily basis are geared to meet these physiological needs. Our minds and intellects also drive our actions, and the combination of these two aspects of our nature (soul and flesh) is the guiding force in most of our lives.

However, the Lord desires that we turn our natures inside out and allow our recreated spirits to guide and to lead us day by day, minute by minute, hour by hour. This comes by being diligent and developing our spirit's ability to recognize the Spirit of God when He speaks, nudges, or leads us. This is a learning curve and may take some time. However, when we submit to the Lord in this recreation of our spiritual nature, He is faithful to help us develop our spiritual senses as we exercise them by reason of use (see Hebrews 5:14). In this way, we learn to hear the Lord clearly. As we learn to hear God more clearly and learn to be led by His Spirit consistently, we are being diligent to enter into the rest of the Lord.

We will begin to understand that we can pass through the heavenly realms or dimensions to seek revelation, authority, and power from the very throne of God. God will begin to speak to us as a man does with a friend. In other words, we will begin to minister in the anointing or the mantle of Melchizedek. That mantle or anointing consists of operating in the seer anointing and learning to live, breathe, and walk in the anointing of the Holy Spirit twenty-four hours a day, seven days a week, 365 days a year. We will live in the realm of the seer anointing, and we will become seers or mature sons and daughters of God who will hear the Lord well at all times.

We will be transformed into Christlikeness, and then we will represent Christ in our sphere of influence and become a priest forever according to the order of Melchizedek. We will have the ability to recognize aspects from the spiritual realm; and as the Lord allows and gives us grace, we will actually demonstrate the ability to pass through the heavens and enter into the very presence of God and into the realms or dimensions of heaven just like Christ. Once we learn to enter into the Kingdom of Heaven, then we will understand how to manifest the Kingdom of God upon the earth. This is what Jesus did.

It is possible for each of us to mature and to "grow up" into the very nature and character of Jesus Christ. As we submit to this refining fire and ministry of the Holy Spirit, we will begin to see our very nature transformed. Our three-part or triune nature will begin to be turned inside out. Instead of being ruled and led by our soul and our flesh, we can be changed in a moment and in the twinkle of an eye. We will begin to see that we will be led by our "real self" or our spirit man (or woman).

We can develop our ability to be led by the Spirit of God. We see this in Romans 8:14: *"For as many as are led by the Spirit of God, these are sons of God."* As children of God, our spirits can become dominant for segments of time. Our spirit can become dominant for a few seconds. Our spirit can become dominate, in terms of perception, for a few minutes or even a few days. That is what I believe happened to me during the season that I experienced the visions and was allowed to enter into the heavenly realms that are documented in this book.

When this process begins to accelerate in our lives, we will begin to perceive attributes of the spiritual realm much more clearly than we did when we were driven by our carnal mind, intellect, soul, and flesh in terms of our perception. We will begin to perceive the spiritual realm in a much greater way; and the eyes of our spiritual understanding will be enlightened, opened, or anointed to see, hear, taste, touch, smell, and enter into the Kingdom of Heaven. This has been called the seer anointing.

Of course, Jesus was our role model for this. I have outlined this aspect of Christ's mission and ministry on the earth in great detail in the second book of my trilogy, *Dancing with Angels 2: The Role of the Holy Spirit and Open Heavens in Activating Your Angelic Encounters.* I cannot possibly share all of the material covered in that book, so I encourage you to get the book and read it. Read the book more than one time. Read the passages in the Bible that were written by seer prophets. Read Ezekiel, John's Book of Revelation, and the Book of Daniel. By doing these things, it will help you to activate your spiritual senses. Just prior to the Day of Atonement in 2012, I experienced an amazing season when the dynamics that I have just described manifested in my life. God helped to open my spiritual perception in a very unique and unusual way. In the next chapter let's look at some keys that can help you to be diligent to activate your spiritual senses that I learned from these supernatural experiences.

CHAPTER 26

Activating Your Spiritual Senses and 20/20 Spiritual Vision

The Lord began to speak to me just prior to the Day of Atonement about the true nature of our spiritual senses. We were hosting one of our Heaven Touching Earth Gatherings near Moravian Falls, North Carolina. Over the course of the four days of the School of the Seers, I began to have an unusual experience with my eyes. At first I began to see double. I prayed and asked the Lord for revelation about this phenomenon. The Lord just said, "It is Me, I want to show you something." Over the next four days, when the anointing of the Holy Spirit would manifest, I would see double. When this happened it seemed that the material of physical objects would begin to morph and transform in shape. They appeared to move like hot plastic or gently moving water. Objects looked like a mirage of water on a hot road. People, places, and things seemed to shimmer and flicker in and out of existence. This was most unusual! Furniture, automobiles, the sky, rock walls, buildings, and even people began to be transformed in this way in my vision.

Once the Lord told me that it was Him, I relaxed and began to "look" more closely each time this phenomenon began to happen. It seemed that when I would leave the meetings in the evenings and drive to our little cabin, this sign and wonder with my vision would increase. In fact, it became so intense after a day or two that I had to call Kathy once when I was driving so that she could pray for me.

This sensation and phenomenon with my vision continued to build in intensity. I prayed and asked the Lord what was happening with my vision, and He told me, "I am opening your spiritual eyes." This phenomenon with my vision was actually quite miraculous. In my heart, I said, "OK, Lord. If this is You, then I want to comprehend everything that You are trying to show me. Please allow the '*spirit of wisdom and revelation*' to come upon me" (Ephesians 1:17).

Shortly after that prayer, when I was seeing double, I began to look into the spiritual realm at the same time that I was seeing in the natural realm. I began to see angelic beings everywhere. I also began to see demonic beings everywhere. When these demons were aware that I could see them, they would scurry away in great fear and trembling. I saw demons all over one local restaurant and the people eating in there. I was seeing angelic and demonic beings in church buildings, an even in places like Wal-Mart. As I was looking at an especially ugly demonic being that was clinging to one man's back, I had an epiphany. I was experiencing in the natural exactly what I had seen on the Day of Atonement. On that day in 2011, Jesus had opened my spiritual eyes and allowed me to see all of the demons that were concealed within the gross darkness. The demons hidden by the darkness of the evil storm were now visible in the natural realm to me. This was an epiphany!

During this season I was seeing two dimensions at the same time. In fact, this phenomenon with my vision is still happening today. This continued during the entire time of School of the Seers. Because of that and through the help of the Holy Spirit, I was able to minister deliverance to many people in the ministry line. Many were healed and set free as the demonic parasites were rebuked and commanded to go to the feet of Jesus and into the pit. I was also able to pull demonic devices, yokes of darkness, and demonic weapons off of people's bodies. Each of these people was in turn healed in the natural, and others were delivered from emotional bondages. At night I would seek the Lord in prayer about this unusual anointing that was coming upon me. I began to wonder why God was allowing me to see into two dimensions at the same time. The Lord gave me revelation concerning this phenomenon. That is exactly what Jesus did. He saw into several dimensions at the same time. Jesus saw the heavenly dimensions, the earthly dimensions, and into the demonic realm simultaneously. This supernatural ability, to see into multiple dimensions at the same time, is one aspect of the mantle of Melchizedek. This is what Hebrews 5:14 is speaking about. We exercise our spiritual senses by using them, and the Lord was allowing me to exercise my spiritual senses in a wondrous new way!

This supernatural phenomenon is also what the Apostle Paul was teaching us about in Ephesians 1:16-23. You can actually have the eyes of your understanding or spirit enlightened to see into the spiritual dimensions or the heavenly realms that are all around you at this second. The language in this passage is actually speaking about having your spiritual vision illuminated or to be given or anointed with spiritual vision. When your spiritual vision is enlightened, you will see into the spiritual realms. I believe that is what I have been experiencing. I also believe that Jesus also saw into more than one dimension simultaneously. You can also see into more than one dimension simultaneously as you learn to exercise your spiritual senses. I should also mention that I have prayed Ephesians 1:16-23 over my life consistently for over a decade.

When you become diligent to enter into the fullness of the rest of the Lord, you are empowered by the Lord to minister as a royal priest according to the order of Melchizedek. Your spiritual senses will be exercised by reason of use and your ability to see into the spiritual dimensions will be increased and multiplied by the anointing of the Holy Spirit. This is an aspect of the gift of discerning of spirits (1 Corinthians 12:10).

In 2002 while I was in Tanzania, the Lord Jesus visited me and stood over me and spoke to me, teaching me about the seer anointing of old. (For more on this testimony please read Kevin's book *The Reality of Angelic Ministry Today: Dancing with Angels 1* or get *Unlocking the Mysteries of the Seer Anointing/The School of the Seers* available from our online Resource Center at www.kingofgloryministries.org/store). The phenomenon of seeing into more than one dimension simultaneously that I was experiencing was the manifestation of the seer anointing. I was benefiting from having exercised my spiritual senses over the last several years. I was seeing into several dimensions at once.

I like to call this 20/20 spiritual vision. This brings us back to the testimony about the prophet and the snowstorm. For years and in many places, I have heard the passage of scripture from 2 Chronicles 20:20 preached and taught. However, when I began to experience this phenomenon of seeing into more than one dimension at the same time, the Lord began to speak to me from this passage of scripture. The Holy Spirit revealed something to me that I had never seen or heard about 2 Chronicles 20:20. I believe that this revelation can help us to understand the importance of developing our spiritual senses. It can also inspire us to be diligent to hear the voice of the Lord clearly for ourselves as individuals. Again, remember that Jesus told me that it is very important for His people to learn to be diligent to enter into the rest of the Lord at this season. Hearing the Lord for yourself is one of the most important keys to entering into the fullness of God's rest. That is why you need 20/20 spiritual vision.

Therefore, let's look at 2 Chronicles 20:20 in context: *"Hear me, O Judah and you inhabitants of Jerusalem: Believe in the LORD your God, and you shall be established; believe His prophets, and you shall prosper."* In this passage of scripture, Jehoshaphat was seeking to hear from the Lord because a great and evil storm was approaching Judah. This dark and evil storm took the form of *"Ammonites, Moabites, and some of the Meunites"* (2 Chronicles 20:1, NLT). This assembly of armies greatly outnumbered the people of Judah, and in the natural realm it seemed that they had no hope. Prophetically these Ammonite and Moabite armies represent demonic forces. This is a perfect parallel to the dark and evil storm that I saw on the Day of Atonement in 2011 and again in 2012.

Jehoshaphat calls for a time of corporate fasting and prayer in the nation of Judah. Jehoshaphat is seeking to hear God so that the Lord can give him wisdom in this seemingly hopeless situation. Is it not interesting that as humans we often wait until it is totally hopeless

ACTIVATING YOUR SPIRITUAL SENSES AND 20/20 SPIRITUAL VISION

before we seek to consult God for His council? On the other hand, we are seeking to be diligent to enter into the rest of the Lord as we seek to hear from Him daily. In this passage the Spirit of the Lord comes upon one of the descendants of Zechariah, a Levite named Jahaziel, and he says, *"Listen, all you of Judah and you inhabitants of Jerusalem, and you, King Jehoshaphat! Thus says the LORD to you: 'Do not be afraid nor dismayed because of this great multitude, for the battle is not yours, but God's"* (2 Chronicles 20:15).

I believe that is exactly what the Lord God Almighty is saying about this dark and evil storm that is approaching in our time: *"Do not be afraid nor dismayed because of this great multitude, for the battle is not yours, but God's."* The key to Judah overcoming the demonic entities that were arrayed for war against them was their ability to hear God. We need to understand what God is doing. Then, like Jesus, we must do those things that we see our Father doing.

The Lord honored the nation's fasting and prayers and spoke to them through Jahaziel the Levite. Today, as we have learned, we no longer need a Levitical priest to mediate between God and man because we can hear God for ourselves. At times this calls for individual *prayer* with *fasting*, which are two keys to entering into the God's rest. This has always been God's plan: for the Creator to speak to the creature as a man speaks to a friend. In this passage of scripture, the Lord supernaturally annihilated the assembled enemies of Judah, and Jehoshaphat and the army of Judah found them all dead upon the battlefield when they arrived to make war.

As we continue to look at 2 Chronicles 20 in context, we see that God gave Jehoshaphat and the army of Judah a great victory and they seized so much spoil from the enemy that it actually took them three full days to carry it away! When the people took time to hear from the Lord and then obeyed God's voice and instructions, there was a great victory.

> *So when Judah came to a place overlooking the wilderness, they looked toward the multitude; and there were their dead bodies, fallen on the earth. No one had escaped. When Jehoshaphat and*

his people came to take away their spoil, they found among them an abundance of valuables on the dead bodies, and precious jewelry, which they stripped off for themselves, more than they could carry away; and they were three days gathering the spoil because there was so much (2 Chronicles 20:24-25).

Those scriptures are a prophetic promise of what God wants to do for His children today. God wants for us to hear His voice and to obey His instructions. Why? So that we can enter into the fullness of the rest of the Lord. We see how the fullness of the rest of the Lord is illustrated in Jehoshaphat's reign of Judah in verses 29-30: *"And the fear of God was on all the kingdoms of those countries when they heard that the L*ORD *had fought against the enemies of Israel. Then the realm of Jehoshaphat was quiet, for his God gave him rest all around."* These scriptures are perfect illustrations of what God wants to do in your life as you learn to be diligent to enter into the rest of the Lord. God wants to give you rest on every side! He wants for you to rule and reign in this life. He wants you to rule and reign in the midst of the dark and evil storm.

It will be the same in our day! The Lion of the tribe of Judah is raising up an end-time army of royal priests according to the order of Melchizedek who will hear God clearly. They will be diligent to enter into the rest of the Lord and allow the Lord to fight their battles for them. And like the people of Judah, these royal priests will declare and prophesy in the midst of the darkness and the evil storm: *"Do not be afraid nor dismayed because of this great multitude, for the battle is not yours, but God's."* The key to this kind of supernatural victory in Christ is being diligent to rest in the Lord. You must learn to hear God's voice for yourself as an individual. This brings us back to what the Lord showed me about 2 Chronicles 20:20: *"Hear me, O Judah and you inhabitants of Jerusalem: Believe in the L*ORD *your God, and you shall be established; believe His prophets, and you shall prosper."* First, God says, "Hear me!" In other words, before the prophetic promises of this scripture can operate or manifest in your life, you must hear God for yourself.

Believe in the Lord or Believe in His Prophets: You Choose

Next this passage says that we must "*believe in the* LORD *your God, and you shall be established.*" This is a very high and holy calling: to be established in the Lord. What this literally means is to be protected and supported by someone more powerful than you, like a parent or powerful Father. To be established by the Lord means to be rendered or transformed in your nature to be firm or faithful. It means to be endued with a supernatural trust or faith in God Almighty. It can also be defined as to learn to rest in God's power and to be permanently established, shielded, covered, or safeguarded. It can mean to be spiritually or morally true or certain in your place of safety and protection and to be granted the right or the grace to sit at the right hand of God. This is, of course, is exactly the way the scriptures have described your role as a royal priest according to the order of Melchizedek (see Psalm 110; Hebrews 4).

Once you learn to hear God, you can be established by Him. God will impart to you a supernatural assurance and faith to believe and to stand steadfast upon God and His Kingdom. You will be established by God, in Christ. You will learn to stand upon the Rock of Christ. You will learn to hear the Lord for yourself as these kinds of dark and evil storms approach. God will fight your battles for you and give you peace and rest on every side—just like Jehoshaphat.

On the other hand, 2 Chronicles 20:20 further teaches us to "*believe His prophets, and you shall prosper.*" This is the lesser and the inferior of the two options that God has given to you in 2 Chronicles 20; 20. The phrase *to prosper* here is the lesser of the two options. To prosper when we hear God's prophets means to push forward with hard work and contention. It means to move ahead by the sweat of your brow and strenuous labors. It means to work hard to make something happen. It is the opposite of resting in the Lord. To prosper can mean to break out or to go over a difficult obstacle or strong foe. A good analogy of this would be breaking out of a well-fortified and well-guarded position, such as Jericho. Jericho is, of course, another fine example of the Lord battling a seemingly unconquerable enemy through the power of His Spirit. To prosper, as used in this passage, can mean to push forward by your own strength and power or to come into a place of prosperity by your laborious work and strenuous efforts. Remember what God promised in Zechariah 4:6? *"'Not by might nor by power, but by My Spirit,' says the LORD of hosts."*

God wants us to learn to be diligent and to rest in Him so that we can be established by His Spirit. He wants for us to allow the Spirit of God, the *ruwach* of God, to work on our behalf. That is exactly what happened with Jehoshaphat and the people of Judah and Jerusalem. They sought to hear the voice of God. Then the Lord spoke to them and gave the wisdom and divine plans to overcome the dark and evil that was at their doorstep. Then it was not by their might (military strength), it was not by their strength (intellectual plans), but it was by the very Spirit of God (*ruwach* of God) that they plundered the evil and demonic storms of life. But the key was hearing God for themselves.

You see, when we hear God though His prophets, we can prosper. We can settle for the lesser or lower-grade promise of the two blessings from 2 Chronicles 20:20. It is great to listen to God's prophets because by hearing from God through them we can work and plow through; we can come into a place of prosperity by our own labors, work, and strenuous efforts (the sweat of our brow). But God has a better plan. We can hear God and be established. When we rest in the Lord God, He will speak to each of us clearly and will give us His divine plans for our lives; then we will walk in supernatural prosperity, power, and authority. This is a better way than hearing God in a second-handed nature through prophetic ministry or through prophetic individuals. We will be established in Christ and in His Kingdom as royal priests after the order of Melchizedek. These miraculous triumphs over the darkness and demonic storms will be sparked in our lives by the *ruwach* or Spirit of God as we wait and rest in His presence. Then we too will have rest and peace on all sides.

Once you learn to hear God clearly, you will start the process of allowing God to establish you by His Spirit. Then He will fight our battles for us. You need to be diligent to initiate this supernatural exchange in your life. This process takes time. I believe that understanding this message is essential for the Body of Christ at this hour. That is why the Lord Jesus told me to encourage His people to be "diligent to enter into the rest of the Lord."

Many people today are not diligent. In fact, there are a lot of lazy Christians in the church. Christians like this are, for the most part, living their lives in bondage and weakness. The god of this world has ensnared them, placing them into a place of powerlessness and complacency. Hosea 4:6 outlines the fruit of this kind of complacency and ignorance: "*My people are destroyed for lack of knowledge. Because you have rejected knowledge, I also will reject you from being priest for Me; Because you have forgotten the law of your God, I also will forget your children.*" People like this may not make it through the dark and evil storm. They may be like the Israelites who turned back to roam for forty years in the wilderness. They are not willing to be diligent to hear God for themselves, and therefore they become dependent on their spiritual leaders. When this happens, they reject God; and it is possible that He may also reject them as an individual, a community, a state, or even as a nation. Like the children of Israel, they will not enter into the rest of the Lord (see Psalm 95:11; Hebrews 3:11; 4:3). This is serious business to God.

Unbelieving people allow their pastors to feed them the milk of the word of God once a week, instead of feasting upon God's anointed word each and every day themselves (see 1 Corinthians 3:2). They allow the prophets to hear from God for them instead of developing their own individual ability to hear the voice of God daily. They allow the prophets to see what God is doing and base their actions on what other people see and hear. The man replaces the Messiah.

I have a wonderful friend, Pastor James Durham. He goes into the heavenly dimensions every day, and the Lord speaks to him and shows him amazing things. He sees and hears well from heaven. But I cannot see the way he sees. In fact, during the School of the Seers,

I put Pastor James's glasses on and my vision was very blurry! If we depend upon others for understanding about what God is doing and saying, our ears will become heavy and our vision dull. Jesus spoke about this kind of spiritual blindness when He quoted Isaiah 6:9-10: *"Go, and tell this people: 'Keep on hearing, but do not understand; Keep on seeing, but do not perceive.' Make the heart of this people dull, And their ears heavy, And shut their eyes; Lest they see with their eyes, And hear with their ears, And understand with their heart, And return and be healed."* Just like I could not see clearly with Pastor James glasses, you cannot see well through another man's prophetic word.

You see, just because James sees into the heavenly realms of dimensions every day, I cannot look into the heavenly realms through his glasses. If I use another man's glasses, everything that I see is blurry and unclear. I cannot see God clearly through another person's anointing. I cannot hear God clearly through another person's anointing. It is the same when we try to live our lives through the prophetic words of another man or woman. We will see very poorly. Our spiritual vision will be very blurry. We will see but we will not perceive. We need to see and hear what the Lord is saying from Heaven for ourselves each and every day as an individual. When we allow our lives and actions to be dictated to us through other people's prophecies, it is like looking through Pastor James' glasses. Our spiritual vision will be blurry and unclear. However, God desires for us to see well. He desires for us to turn to Him and to be healed or saved in the midst of the dark and evil storms.

This spiritual principle is also outlined in 1 Corinthians 13:8-9: *"Whether there are prophecies, they will fail; whether there are tongues, they will cease; whether there is knowledge, it will vanish away. For we know in part and we prophesy in part."* It is only by developing your spiritual senses and learning to discern and hear from God that you can hope to be established in Christ's Kingdom. When you are diligent to exercise your spiritual senses by reason of use, you will learn to discern between both good and evil. Again, I want to encourage you to learn to be diligent to exercise your spiritual senses and learn to hear and see what the God of the universe is

ACTIVATING YOUR SPIRITUAL SENSES AND 20/20 SPIRITUAL VISION

seeking to reveal to you. The Creator is seeking to have an intimate relationship with you, the creature. But you must learn to hear His voice. You must learn to develop your spiritual senses so that you can see what He is doing. In this way, you will be established in a greater level of the Lord's rest. You can enter into the fullness of the rest of the Lord. Then you will triumph over the dark and evil storms that appear on the horizon because you will be able to say, "This battle is not mine, but God's."

Learn to hear God for yourself! Learn to see what God is working and doing on your behalf. Then you will be established by God, and in this way you can become diligent to enter into the rest of the Lord. Be diligent to *"seek the LORD while He may be found"* (Isaiah 55:6). Learn to develop and exercise your spiritual senses until you have 20/20 spiritual vision!

Prayer of Impartation

At this moment I bless my God and the Father of my Lord Jesus Christ, who has blessed me with every spiritual blessing in the heavenly places in Christ. And I pray that the God of my Lord Jesus Christ, the Father of glory, may give unto me the spirit of wisdom and revelation in the knowledge of Him. Lord, I ask in the name of Jesus Christ of Nazareth that the eyes of my spirit might receive supernatural understanding and become enlightened.

I ask, Father, that I may know what is the hope of Your calling upon my life and comprehend what are the riches of the glory of the Lord's inheritance in me. Lord, reveal to me what is the exceeding greatness of Your power toward me, because I believe. Lord, release to me the revelatory understanding according to the working of Your mighty power which You worked in Christ Jesus as He rose from the dead and You seated Him at Your right hand in the heavenly places.

Father, you placed the Lord Jesus far above every principality and power and might and dominion and every name that is named, not only in this age but also in that which is to come. Lord, make known to me all of the fullness and unsearchable riches of Christ. Help me to see and comprehend what is the fellowship of the mystery, which from the beginning of the ages has been hidden in God who created all things through Jesus Christ

For this reason I bow my knees to the Father of our Lord Jesus Christ, from whom the whole family in heaven and earth is named. And I ask You, Lord, that You would grant unto me according to the riches of His glory, that I may be strengthened with might through Your Spirit in my soul and inner man. Lord, I pray that Christ may dwell in my heart through faith; that I will become rooted and grounded in the love of God.

Lord, I ask that I might comprehend with all the saints what is the width and length and depth and height—and to personally know and experience the love of Christ, which passes all knowledge, that I may be filled with all the fullness of God. And I thank You, Lord, who is able to do exceedingly abundantly above all that I can ask or think, according to the power of Your Spirit that works within me.

Lord, I thank You now that You are releasing to me the spirit of wisdom and revelation of Your Kingdom and the mighty effectual working of your power in my life, spirit, soul, and body. Thank you, Lord, that You are opening the eyes of my heart and helping me to see and discern the fullness of your Kingdom as it manifest in my life. And to You, Lord, be all the glory in the church by Christ Jesus to all generations, forever and ever. Amen.

CHAPTER 27

Conclusion: The Day of Atonement 2012

By now the evening sun was beginning to recede like a strong man who had run his race, and the evening shadows were ever so slowly moving across the swaying trees outside of my window. The Day of Atonement was now nearing an end. The winds seemed to swirl about my head in a supernatural way and the fragrance of roses and frankincense permeated the air in my little prayer room. As I opened my eyes, a bead of sweat trickled into my right eye causing it to burn.

It seemed that I could still hear the noises of millions of angelic beings as they moved about me in the heavenly realms. Once more it seemed that hooves pounded across the room of our little cabin here in the mountains. I closed my eyes and for a long time pondered in my heart everything that I had just relived. I had just lived once again the entire experience from the Day of Atonement of 2011. In my spirit I understood that this was significant. I pondered these things in my heart for a long time and continued to luxuriate in a wonderful supernatural vacuum of God's love and glory. I was resting in the presence and glory of God and asking Him for more revelation and understanding about what I had just experienced.

I could still see the words "The Rest of the Lord" etched into the sword of Christ in a supernatural manner. I could still see the manifest glory of God as it danced and pirouetted upon the sword of the Lord in my mind. I could still smell the perspiration and pungent odor of the Lord's mighty white stallion as it mingled with the smell of roses and frankincense that still filled the little prayer room. Suddenly I felt a familiar sensation, and it seemed that I was once more being catapulted up into the spirit and into the heavenly places. I once more was ascending into the heavenly realms, and I seemed to come to rest in the heavenly dimensions. Angelic worship and ethereal singing filled my ears as the glory of God again washed over my spirit, soul, and body.

Suddenly the Lord appeared in front of me once more and Jesus was surrounded by several angelic beings. Only this manifestation of Jesus was different. Jesus was adorned with beautiful priestly garments, and I immediately understood that the Lord was dressed in the robes and mantle of Melchizedek. This was the risen and victorious Christ. The Lord was appearing in the image of *the* royal Priest according to the order of Melchizedek. The power and authority that Jesus carried at that moment was amazing. Jesus was adorned in an immaculately beautiful priestly garment. I could hear bells tinkling as the Lord's priestly garments gently swayed in the supernatural breeze.

Suddenly the Lord stepped into my prayer room and the vision multiplied. In the Lord's right hand, Jesus held the same sword that I had seen on the Day of Atonement in 2011 and also earlier on this Day of Atonement in 2012. I was surprised that Jesus was actually standing in my prayer room. I was also astonished to see the Lord's magnificent sword glistening and reflecting the glory of God as the Lord stood there smiling at me. Perhaps I was somewhere between heaven and earth. Once again I saw etched upon the shaft of the Lord's sword were the words "The Rest of the Lord" dancing in the brilliant light of the glory realm.

In His left hand Christ held a beautifully embossed golden book that appeared to be a Bible. As I took my vision from the sword to look at the book, it began to burn brightly. Glorious blue and purple flames began to leap from the pages of the Bible in the Lord's left hand and shoot through the spiritual realm like arrows would shoot from the string of a powerful bow. Instantly I understood that the Lord was releasing revelatory knowledge and hidden mysteries from His Kingdom and His Word to His friends at this hour.

CONCLUSION: THE DAY OF ATONEMENT 2012

I watched as these arrows of wisdom and revelation were supernaturally released into all of the earth. Innumerable angelic beings seemed to accompany each blazing heavenly arrow as they were catapulted into all the nations of the earth. I glanced at Jesus to see Him smile broadly, and this also filled my heart with joy and the knowledge that the Lord is now raising up saints who will teach and preach His Word with delegated power and heavenly authority all over the earth. I also understood that these friends of God would be the ones who will choose to walk in intimacy, holiness, and communion with the Lord. They will be those who are diligent to enter into the fullness of the rest of the Lord. They will be overcomers who will walk in the mantle or anointing of a royal priesthood according to the order of Melchizedek.

As this understanding and revelation flowed through and into me, the power and glory of God enveloped me like a tidal wave and I understood the fact that this is exactly how God will release this end-time anointing upon the earth at this time. The glory of God will be poured out like a flood just as I had seen the glory of God pour out through the rip in the spiritual atmosphere on the Day of Atonement (Habakkuk 2:14; Isaiah 60:2). Nothing can stop the plans of God, and His Kingdom will come soon like a mighty spiritual tidal wave.

This understanding was wonderful and I praised the Lord in my heart, but my mind and body were enamored and immobilized by the glory and the proximity of Jesus robed as *the* royal Priest according to the order of Melchizedek. I looked again to see Jesus standing there beside me in my little prayer room. Christ smiled at me with pleasure and joy, and I believe that I returned His smile. As I did so there was another explosion of glory and power. Instantly the spiritual realm seemed to be rent open in the prayer room behind the Lord.

Suddenly behind the Lord Jesus Christ were two endlessly long lines of angelic beings with mantles draped over their arms. Jesus stood with the burning Word in His left hand and the sword of the Lord reflecting the glory of God in His right hand. There was an explosion of brilliant white light and glory, and it seemed as if seven stars were launched outward from the presence of the Lord. I understood that these stars were also going to the ends of the earth. For a moment I was blinded by the brilliance of this spiritual explosion and blinked my eyes repeatedly. When I was able to focus upon the Lord again, I noticed that there were thousands of angelic beings lined up in a V formation behind Jesus. I understood that these angels were all carrying the mantle of Melchizedek and weapons of spiritual warfare.

There were thousands upon thousands of these angelic beings nearby, and each one had a mantle or beautiful white robe draped over the right forearm. Instantly I understood that these angels were being released and assigned to place these mantles of Melchizedek upon those who choose to serve the Lord fully in holiness and purity at this hour (Zechariah 3). I understood that the eyes of the Lord *are* running to and from throughout the earth seeking friends of God so that He might show Himself strong on behalf of those whose hearts are loyal to Him (2 Chronicles 16:9). I also knew that the key to receiving these mantles of Melchizedek is to understand the rest of the Lord and to be being diligent to enter into the fullness of the rest of the Lord at this hour.

As this revelation was filling my spirit, Jesus stepped forward quickly and reached out with His right hand. I was truly astonished when the Lord seemed to freely offer me His sword (Matthew 10:8). It began to burn brightly with a blue flame. Without thinking I took the sword of the Lord from Christ's right hand. The words "The Rest of the Lord" were still inscribed into the metal of the shaft of the sword. I took a moment to maneuver the sword of the Lord with my wrist, and I was astonished at the ease with which the sword of the Lord maneuvered so effortlessly in my hand. The glory of God was still pirouetting upon the steel of the blade as I held the sword in my right hand.

It was as light as a feather but as sharp as a laser. I looked up to see the Lord broadly smiling at me. As He nodded His head, I understood that Jesus was actually giving me His sword. I understood that He was releasing and empowering me to give this mighty spiritual weapon to others too. I also realized that I had been empowered to use the sword of the Lord in my life and in the ministry. I was astonished at the goodness, generosity, and faithfulness of the Lord. I never dreamed that the Lord would give away His sword, especially to me. I added this weapon to the other sword that rests upon my waist. I was truly grateful and yet totally surprised at the generosity of the Lord. I looked into the beautiful eyes of Jesus and said, "Thank you, Lord."

As I was pondering this amazing supernatural gift, a fiery angel suddenly appeared at the right hand of the Lord with a burst of heavenly glory and power. As this angelic being appeared, there was a tangible transformation of the atmosphere in my little prayer room. This angelic being was about fourteen feet tall and consisted entirely of heavenly flames of fire. Instantly, the fire of God began to burn within my spirit and within my body. I began to get very hot! I thought this angel must be carrying the all-consuming fire of Almighty God (Hebrews 12:29). The reverential fear of the Lord fell upon me. I seemed to be lost in time and space and was under the fiery anointing of this angelic being as it stood there in the presence of Jesus burning and leaning over my prostrate body there in my little prayer room in Moravian Falls.

I realized that our God is a consuming fire. I also understood that the Lord is burning from His people all things that will keep us from walking in the fullness of His Kingdom and the fullness of His authority and power. That is if we allow this purging work of the Holy Spirit to set us free and cleanse us with God's healing fire. The scripture from Deuteronomy 9:3 flashed into my mind: *"Therefore understand today that the L*ORD *your God is He who goes over before you as a consuming fire. He will destroy them and bring them down before you; so you shall drive them out and destroy them quickly, as the L*ORD *has said to you."* Once more I understood that when we fully trust and rest in the Lord, God Almighty will fight our battles for us and He will give us rest on every side. That is another amazing aspect of the mantle of Melchizedek. It is a mantle or anointing of peace and holiness.

I understood that the Lord's consuming fire is a wonderful and healing supernatural aspect of Christ's Kingdom. However, too few of God's friends are willing to submit to this ministry of the Holy Spirit and receive God's all-consuming fire. However, that is what God will require of those who would seek to walk in the mantle and the anointing of Melchizedek at this hour. As Jesus and this flaming angelic being stood over me the intensity of the all-consuming fire of God ministered to me spirit, soul, and body. Soon the reverential fear of the Lord began to lift. And I knew that the Lord was releasing a wonderful healing into my life. I just wished that it did not hurt as bad whilst the fire was intense and somewhat painful. Suddenly I realized that I had seen this angelic being before.

I had seen this flaming angel in Jerusalem in November 2010. It was during that visit to the Holy Land that this angel had visited me in the Jerusalem Ramada Inn. That night I awoke to see this flaming angelic being standing in the room releasing this same all-consuming fire into the room where Kathy and I were staying. I believe that this was an angel of the Lord. At that time I had missed what the Lord was seeking to do. Since I was very tired, I actually fell asleep while the fiery angel of the Lord visited us there in Jerusalem, Israel. However, that was not the case during this visit. Perhaps I had not been ready or prepared to receive the all-consuming fire of God in 2010. Would you prepared if the all-consuming fire of God visited you today?

I lay there with Jesus standing with the Word burning brightly in His left hand and the thousands upon thousands of angelic beings standing in a victory formation behind the Lord. These angels all held the mantle of Melchizedek. The fiery angel of the Lord was still at the right hand of Jesus. I was astonished and wondered what I was supposed to do because I realized that there was a response required from me at that moment. I am also certain that God will soon require a response from you.

Suddenly the flaming angel took the Bible from the left hand of Jesus and the book was transfigured into a burning scroll. It was about the size of a roll of French bread. I was mesmerized by the

CONCLUSION: THE DAY OF ATONEMENT 2012

things that were unfolding in my little prayer room. This flaming angel of the Lord stood there holding in both of its hands the burning Word, which was now a burning scroll. The blue and purple flames coursing from the scroll were a perfect contrast to the brilliant colors of the fiery red and orange that was exploding from the countenance of the flaming angel of the Lord. Then Jesus looked deeply into my eyes and said, "This is the living word" (Hebrews 4:12). I turned my gaze upon the living, burning Word. I watched these beautiful purple and blue colors as they continued to boil and percolate up from the scroll. They were amazing to look upon, and I seemed to become lost in time as I pondered this magnificent display of Christ's Kingdom, glory, and power that was in unfolding right in front of me.

I knew in my carnal mind that this burning scroll represented the scripture from Hebrews 4:11-16:

> *Let us therefore be diligent to enter that rest, lest anyone fall according to the same example of disobedience. For the word of God is living and powerful, and sharper than any two-edged sword, piercing even to the division of soul and spirit, and of joints and marrow, and is a discerner of the thoughts and intents of the heart. And there is no creature hidden from His sight, but all things are naked and open to the eyes of Him to whom we must give account. Seeing then that we have a great High Priest who has passed through the heavens, Jesus the Son of God, let us hold fast our confession. For we do not have a High Priest who cannot sympathize with our weaknesses, but was in all points tempted as we are, yet without sin. Let us therefore come boldly to the throne of grace, that we may obtain mercy and find grace to help in time of need.*

The thought came into my mind: *Jesus is our forerunner. Jesus is the forerunner!*

Jesus said, "You must take and eat." Then Jesus smiled at me benevolently once more. At that instant the fiery angel (which I understood to be the angel of the Lord) took the flaming scroll in his flaming hands and held the scroll up for me to see clearly. Then the fiery angel said, "This is the revelation of the rest of the Lord." The fiery angel then bent down and placed the flaming scroll gently but quickly into my mouth. Instantly my lips the tongue began to burn, and as I ate the scroll it tasted sweet but soon turned sour in my stomach.

As this unfolded, I understood that it is the Word of God that is an all-consuming fire; and that as we are diligent to enter into the rest of the Lord, we can allow God's anointed and holy Word change us. The fire of God will pierce us spirit, soul, and body. And in this way we can be transformed by the cleansing and healing fire of God and be enabled to stand naked and prepared before the Lord. In fact, we will all be judged by God's Word when we stand before the judgment seat of Almighty God one day. It is only by the shed blood of Messiah that we are transformed and made holy and righteous in the presence of God. It is only the atoning blood of Jesus Christ that can prepare us, cleanse us, and make us fit to be kings and priests before the throne of God the Father. It is only the blood of Jesus that can prepare us to receive the anointing and mantle of Melchizedek (Revelation 1:4-6; 5:6-14).

Once we reach this place, we can come boldly to the very throne of grace and allow the High Priest of our confession, Jesus Christ the Royal Priest according to the order of Melchizedek, to intercede and pray for us as individuals. It is in this place that we cease from our own work and labors and enter into the fullness of the rest of the Lord. It is in this place that we allow the Lord to intercede and to pray for us. Then we just walk out those things that we see our Savior praying for us and interceding on our behalf at the right hand of the Father. This is entering into the fullness of the rest of the Lord. To walk in the mantle of Melchizedek is to discern and to understand the prayers that Jesus Christ offers up for us at the right hand of the Father.

My entire body continued to burn as I chewed the last bits of the scroll. At first my lips burned and then my esophagus and stomach caught fire. And at last my entire being was consumed by the fire of

God. Though the fiery scroll that was placed into my mouth was hot and bitter in my stomach, I was surprised that it tasted sweet and actually delicious in my mouth. The scroll tasted like fresh ripe juicy peaches in my mouth. However, in my stomach it felt like fresh hot onions or spicy jalapeño peppers.

The sensation was quite uncomfortable in my stomach. I was lost in my thoughts and was wondering what this all must mean. Then Jesus said, "It is time for my royal priesthood to arise. It is time for my people to learn to overcome the world. Tell my people that they must be diligent to enter into the rest of the Lord at this hour." I closed my eyes and allowed the all-consuming fire that was coursing through my entire being to minister to me from the inside out. I lay there tasting the remnants of the supernatural flavors of peaches and honey from the flaming scroll that Jesus had ordered the angel of the Lord to place into my mouth.

When I opened my eyes, the Lord was no longer standing at my side nor was the angel of fire in my prayer room. Only the lingering fragrance of honey and roses seemed to ride upon the gently circling winds that remained. The glory and power of God lingered here too. As I moved my right hand to my side, I felt the shaft of the sword of the Lord as it was sheathed at my side. This made me smile. I understood that Jesus has millions of mantles and millions of swords like this to give to His friends.

I understood that this message has multiple meanings with both spiritual and natural applications. I took the sword that had been given to me in my right hand and gazed at the words on the burning sword: "The Rest of the Lord." I understood that the rest of the Lord was the key to stepping into the mantle of Melchizedek. Once more I remembered what Jesus had told me: "Tell my people to be diligent to enter into the rest of the Lord at this hour."

Amen.

Prayer of Salvation

Perhaps you would like to be born again and receive Jesus as your Lord and Savior now. Just pray this prayer out loud:

Father God, I believe that Jesus Christ is the Savior or Messiah. I believe that Jesus is the only begotten Son of God and that He died upon the Cross to make payment for my sins. I believe that Jesus was buried in an unused grave, but that after three days He rose again to conquer death and sin. Lord, because I was born a human being, I was born a sinner. Lord, I ask you to forgive my sins now in the name of Jesus Christ of Nazareth. God, cover my sins with the atoning blood of Jesus and forgive me now. Amen.

Contact the Authors

Kevin and Kathy would love to hear your testimonies about how this book has impacted your walk with Christ. To submit testimonies contact them by e-mail.

King of Glory Ministries International
is available to teach the material covered in this book in much greater depth in our

The Sword of the Lord & The Rest of the Lord
~ School of the Supernatural ~

This school is coming soon in DVD and CD sets. For more information or to order additional resources visit our web page at:

www.kingofgloryministries.org
Email: info@kingofgloryministries.org
Phone: 336-921-2825 or 816-308-2786

Mailing Address:
King of Glory Ministries International
PO Box 903, Moravian Falls, NC 28654

Moravian Falls Miniature Art Gallery

Please visit our online art gallery to help support our ongoing humanitarian outreaches to build homes for at risk children and feed widows and orphans at:

www.MoravianFallsminiatureartgallery.com

A portion of the sales of all art purchased from this site will be used to help feed orphans in third world nations. Thanks for your support in this worthwhile cause.

Donate directly to our humanitarian works from Canada, America, or the UK.

You can also donate directly to our orphanage projects and other humanitarian works in the third world. If you are a citizen of Canada, America, or the UK, you can give directly through Hope for the Nations and your gift will be tax deductible in your home nation.

Look for the Hope for the Nations link on the King of Glory Ministries web page:

http://www.kingofgloryministries.org/donate.php

About the Authors

King of Glory Ministries International is all about the commission of Jesus Christ. The words of Isaiah 61 can be used to concisely summarize the call of our ministry.

> *The Spirit of the Lord GOD is upon Me, Because the LORD has anointed Me To preach good tidings to the poor; He has sent Me to heal the brokenhearted, To proclaim liberty to the captives, And the opening of the prison to those who are bound; To proclaim the acceptable year of the LORD, And the day of vengeance of our God; To comfort all who mourn, To console those who mourn in Zion, To give them beauty for ashes, The oil of joy for mourning, The garment of praise for the spirit of heaviness; That they may be called trees of righteousness, The planting of the LORD, that He may be glorified (Isaiah 61:1-3).*

We have sought to preach the gospel of the kingdom to the lost in many nations. As of this writing, we have visited thirty-three nations and five continents to proclaim the truth of Christ's total salvation and healing message, or the Gospel of the Kingdom that Jesus instructed His disciples to proclaim. (See Matthew 4:23; 9:35; 24:14). We have preached to hundreds of thousands of people and seen tens of thousands make the decision to receive Jesus Christ as Lord and Savior. We continue to minister in large crusade outreaches in Africa and other nations today as opportunity allows, and as the Spirit leads. Kevin and Kathy also minister in churches, King of Glory International Schools, and conference meetings in various nations.

The other critical calling of King of Glory Ministries International is to minister the love of the Father to widows and orphans. This humanitarian aspect of our call can be defined in the scriptures of James 1:27 and Psalm 68:5. James 1:27 tells us this: *"Pure and undefiled religion before God and the Father is this: to visit orphans and widows in their trouble, and to keep oneself unspotted from the world."* God has birthed in Kevin and Kathy a heart to minister in deed and not word alone. We also see this aspect of the Father's heart in Psalm 68:5: "*A father of the fatherless, a defender of widows, Is God in His holy habitation.*" Kevin and Kathy Basconi are ordinary people who love an extraordinary God. They co-founded King of Glory Ministries International (www.kingofgloryministries.org). They have a heart to share the gospel with the poor and the love of the Father to widows and orphans. They have visited more than thirty nations preaching the gospel and demonstrating the Kingdom of God in churches, conferences, and crusade meetings. The ministry is punctuated by many miracles, healings, and signs, and wonders that confirm the Word of God. They live in the mountains of North Carolina where they pursue a lifestyle of intimacy with Jesus. Kevin is an internationally published author and award-winning artist. He the author of several books, including the trilogy, *The Reality of Angelic Ministry Today*, books 1, 2, and 3. Kevin has been graced by God to see into the spiritual realm for over a decade and often sees and discerns angelic activity. Kevin is also called to equip the Body of Christ to operate in the seer anointing and to help people understand how to enter into the presence and glory of God.

Kevin is an ordained minister accredited with World Ministry Fellowship of Plano, Texas. King of Glory Ministries International is also connected to the apostolic leadership of Pastor Alan and Carol Koch of Christ Triumphant Church located In Lee's Summit, Missouri.

Dr. Paul L. Cox is co-director of Aslan's Place with his wife, Donna Cox. Aslan's Place is a ministry center dedicated to bringing freedom and wholeness to the wounded and captive. It also brings training and equipping to the body of Christ for spiritual warfare. Paul is a graduate of the California Graduate School of Theology where he earned his Doctorate of Ministry degree. As an ordained American Baptist pastor, Paul ministered at several churches as senior pastor.

www.aslansplace.com

Dancing With Angels 1

Dancing With Angels 1: How To Work With the Angels in Your Life is the first in a trilogy of books called The Reality of Angelic Ministry Today which are devoted to help people understand how to co-labor with God's angels and partnering with angelic ministry today.

Dancing With Angels 1 shares ten years worth of real-life, modern-day supernatural encounters and experiences. Author Kevin Basconi describes numerous heavenly places and various angelic beings and activities in the heavenly realms that are affecting your life on a daily basis. You will be amazed by these true events as you read this fast-paced, surprising testimonial.

$16.99

Dancing With Angels 2

In Dancing With Angels 2, Kevin will continue to build upon several scriptural principles associated with the angelic realm. I am going examine in great detail the importance of the Holy Spirit and His role in implementing or 'activating' angelic ministry. The Holy Spirit's ministry and role are extremely significant and of great consequence to our pursuit. I will seek to elaborate on the various ways you can work in symphony with the Holy Spirit in relationship to angelic ministry.

$16.99

Angels in the Realms of Heaven

In the first two books of this trilogy the majority of the angelic visitations or encounters that are depicted in the manuscripts occurred upon the earth or in the 'terrestrial realm'. In this third book I share a number of dramatic 'heavenly' angelic encounters. These kinds of heavenly angelic testimonies are inferred to throughout both of the preceding books of this trilogy.

$16.99

31 Word Decrees

2 for 1 Book Offer

This little book was birthed or "breathed into existence" by the Holy Spirit. Kevin Basconi has been speaking God's word over his life since he was saved, and delivered from a lifestyle of addiction and sin. In short order the Lord transformed Kevin's life and took him from poverty to prosperity, and from bondage to freedom, from sickness to health.

In 2011 the Lord began to speak to Kevin to write down word decrees the Holy Spirit spoke into his spirit that would be used by God's people to revolutionize their life, and circumstances too.

$12.99

Turbo School of Angelic Ministry

This intensive 3 Hour Training School is designed to help you understand basic principles about the anointing of the Holy Spirit, open heavens, & angelic ministry today.

School DVD Session Topics Include:

- Angels In The Canon of Scripture
- Jesus Our Role Model- Angelic Ministry In the Life of Christ
- Jesus and Open Heavens~The Holy Spirits Role
- In Open Heavens~How To Open The Heavens Over Your Life
- Angels And The Gift Of Discerning of Spirits~Angels That Serve

$29.99

Dancing with Angels – School of the Supernatural

The *Dancing with Angels School of the Supernatural* can revolutionize what you think about God's angels and help you to understand how to work with them in your life! This School of the Supernatural and teaching series is designed to help ordinary people understand how to step into their God ordained inheritance. We all have a spiritual inheritance and spiritual nature that we can step into and activate. The Lord will begin to accelerate this process in the coming season. Ordinary people will access the kingdom of heaven, and start to exercise their spiritual senses by reason of use. They will surely begin to experience the supernatural elements of God's kingdom

$75.00

The Seer Anointing

In this updated teaching on the seer anointing Kevin shares more revelation and insights with you about the anointing to see!
As the engrafted children of God we have received a supernatural inheritance that was released to us at the instant the Messiah, Jesus Christ, rose form the dead to release resurrection power to each of His people. We can learn to live our lives in this resurrection power.

2CD Set

$15.00

Dream God Dream's

This 2 Cd teaching series, *Dream God Dream's*, was birthed during a season of prayer, fasting and waiting upon the Lord. During this time Kevin experienced a powerful visitation of the presence of the Lord in a dream. Would you like to experience an activation of the gifting to dream God dreams? Many who have heard this message were immediately activated, or experienced a rebirth, or impartation to dream. God dreams are a prophetic gifting and ministry tool given to the Body of Christ directly from the realms of heaven. This teaching lays a firm biblical foundation to receive and believe the Lord for an impartation, and mantel to dream.

2CD Set

$15.00

This book was prepared for printing by

King of Glory Printing & Publishing

Our goal is to help unpublished authors facilitate printing of their manuscripts in a professional and economical way. If you have a manuscript you would like to have printed, contact us:

336-921-2825
or
816-308-2786

PO BOX 903
Moravian Falls, NC 28654

www.kingofgloryministries.org